LANGUAGE AND ORIG

Language and Origin: The Role of Language in European Asylum Procedures:
Linguistic and Legal Perspectives
Karin Zwaan, Maaike Verrips and Pieter Muysken (eds)
ISBN: 978-90-5850-586-6

Wolf Legal Publishers (WLP)
P.O. Box 31051
6503 CB Nijmegen
The Netherlands
www.wolfpublishers.nl

2010
© Authors/Centre for Migration Law
Layout: Hannie van de Put

Language and Origin: The Role of Language in European Asylum Procedures: Linguistic and Legal Perspectives

Karin Zwaan
Maaike Verrips
Pieter Muysken
(eds)

Table of contents

Part Three: Language and origin: Three case studies
Presentation

Part Four: Language in asylum procedures: A country survey
Presentation

Part Five: LADO as evidence
Presentation

Preface

This book would not have been possible without the support for an of the European Science Foundation, through its Standing Committee for the Humanities. We also acknowledge financial support from the Centre for Migration Law and the Centre for Language Studies of Radboud Universiteit Nijmegen. We are grateful to the Netherlands Institute for Advanced Studies (NIAS) in Wassenaar for hosting the workshop, and to Hannie van de Put for helping with the final editing.

List of Contributors

Eric Baltisberger studied political science at the university of Neuchâtel/Switzerland. After his master, he began working at the federal office for refugees (FOR), within the asylum procedure. He was member of the project group that studied the different methods and possibilities to realise LADO within the FOR. He is one of the founding members of the scientific unit LINGUA and was head of this unit from 1999 to 2010.

A.P.A. Broeders (MA, PhD) received an MA degree in English Language and Linguistics from the University of Nijmegen, where he subsequently taught Phonetics and Linguistics from 1972-1988. In 1988 he was asked to set up a forensic phonetics and linguistics facility at the Netherlands Forensic Institute, the Forensic Science Laboratory of the Dutch Ministry of Justice in Rijswijk (now The Hague), where he was subsequently appointed Head of the Department of Handwriting, Speech and Document Examination (1996-2001) and held the position of Chief Scientist (2002-2007). He is a founder member and former Executive Committee member of IAFPA (International Association for Forensic Phonetics and Acoustics) and from 1998 to 2002 was the (first) chair of the ENFSI Expert Working Group for Forensic Speech and Audio Analysis. In 2004 he was appointed to the chair of Criminalistics at the University of Leiden. In 2007 he was also appointed Professor of Criminalistics at the University of Maastricht, and Director of The Maastricht Forensic Institute. He is a member of the editorial boards of The International Journal of Speech, Language and the Law and Expertise en Recht. In addition to acting as court-appointed expert in hundreds of cases in the Netherlands, he has testified in Mauritius and for the International Criminal Tribunal for the Former Yugoslavia (ICTY) in The Hague.

Some recent English publications include: Broeders, A.P.A. (2009) Decision-making in the Forensic Arena, in H. Kaptein, H. Prakken & B. Verheij (red.) *Legal Evidence and Proof: Statistics, Stories and Logic*, Ashgate, p. 71-92. Broeders, A.P.A. (2008) Speaker Identification in the Forensic Arena, in F. Olsen, A. Lorz & D. Stein (red.) *Law and Language: Theory and Society*, Düsseldorf University Press, p. 56-85.

Tina Cambier-Langeveld obtained a degree in linguistics and phonetics at Leiden University (the Netherlands) in 1995. She then wrote a PhD thesis on durational lengthening effects in Dutch and English at the University of Amsterdam. She obtained her doctor's degree in 2000. In 1999 she entered the field of forensic phonetics when she joined the Netherlands Forensic Institute (NFI), where she was trained as an expert in forensic speech science. She was involved in various types of forensic casework within the field of speech science, such as speaker identification, transcription, the analysis of disputed utterances, voice line-ups and speaker profiling.

She is a member of the International Association for Forensic Phonetics and Acoustics (IAFPA) and she was chairperson of the IAFPA's Working Group on Language Identification, which was established to investigate standards and procedures involving LADO. Since 2005 she is employed by the Dutch Immigration and Naturalization

Service, where she is involved with language analysis as a means to check the claims of asylum seekers on their national and/or ethnic origin and language background. She supervises language analysis casework for a number of languages. She was appointed senior linguist in 2007.

Dirk Van Compernolle received the electrical engineering degree from the K.U. Leuven in 1979 and obtained a M.Sc. and Ph.D. from Stanford University in 1982 and 1985 respectively. His doctoral research was on speech signal processing for cochlear implants. From 1985 till 1987 he was at the IBM Watson Research Center where he performed research on robust speech recognition. In 1987 he joined the Electrical Engineering Department (ESAT) of the K.U. Leuven, Belgium, where he held various positions and where he has been professor since 1994 (mostly part-time). From 1994 till 1999 he was a Vice President at Lernout and Hauspie Speech Products in charge of the speech recognition and basic research divisions.

He is an active member of the international speech science community, especially for the Flemish/Dutch language community, where he has contributed as reviewer, editor and board member from many different organizations. Most notably he was the general chairman of INTERSPEECH 2007 in Antwerp.

His research interests include robust speech recognition, speech enhancement, microphone arrays, novel speech recognition paradigms.

Diana Eades (Research Fellow, University of New England, Australia) has been engaged in academic and applied sociolinguistic work in the legal process for more than 20 years. In addition to many journal articles and book chapters, she is the author of *Aboriginal English and the Law* (Queensland Law Society 1992), *Courtroom Talk and Neocolonial Control* (Mouton de Gruyter, 2008), and *Sociolinguistics and the Legal Process* (Multilingual Matters, 2010). She is the co-editor of *International Journal of Speech, Language and the Law,* and has variously been President, Vice-President and Secretary of the International Association of Forensic Linguists. She convened the Language and National Origin Group which authored the Guidelines discussed in this book.

Carolien van den Hazelkamp holds a master's degree in Dutch language and culture from the University of Utrecht. For her MA she specialized in language and language structure. She has been working as a staff member of the Taalstudio since 2004. In 2009 she completed a postgraduate course for expert witnesses in court at the center for legal postacademic education at the University of Leiden. She works on language analysis with special attention to cases from African countries. Her core responsibilities include the intake of cases, the selection of linguistic experts and the review of reports. In addition, she is involved with research activities in the field of LADO.

Priska Hubbuch holds a master in linguistics from the University of Fribourg, Switzerland. She has been working as a linguist for LINGUA within the FOM since 2002 and will be head of the unit starting from September 2010.

Katrijn Marijns' research investigates discourse practices in procedural settings. She is particularly interested in the discursive construction of evidence and identities across widely divergent contexts of legal inquiry. From 2000-2004 she did ethnographic work on communicative practices in asylum and migration context (Belgian asylum procedure). From 2006-2009 she examined issues of diversity and performance in the highest criminal court procedure (Belgian Assize Court). Her approach combines ethnography with sociolinguistics and discourse analysis to analyse the critical role language plays in legal-administrative procedures. Recent publications: *The asylum speaker: language in the Belgian asylum procedure*, St. Jerome 2006, *Multilingualism in legal settings*, Routledge 2011.

Tim McNamara is Professor in the School of Languages and Linguistics at The University of Melbourne, where he teaches and supervises graduate students in Applied Linguistics and is active in the Language Testing Research Centre (www.ltrc.unimelb.edu.au), which he helped to found in 1990. Prior to his career as a researcher, he taught English as a foreign/second language for 13 years in the UK and Australia, and became involved in teacher training through the Cambridge CELTA scheme. As an academic, Tim has held visiting positions at universities in Canada, the United States, Japan and the U.K., and most recently at the University of Vienna. His publications include *Measuring Second Language Performance* (Longman 1996), *Language Testing* (OUP 2000) and *Language Testing: The Social Dimension* (with Carsten Roever, Blackwell 2006), which won the Sage/ILTA Award in 2009. His main areas of research are in language testing, particular its social and political aspects, Rasch measurement in language testing, and language and identity.

Sylvia Moosmüller received her Ph.D. (dissertation title: *Soziale und psychosoziale Sprachvariation: eine quantitative und qualitative Untersuchung zum gegenwärtigen Wiener Deutsch*) in General and Applied Linguistics from the University of Vienna in 1984. She worked in various research projects dealing with phonetic and phonological variation in Standard Austrian German, speech synthesis, psycho- and sociolinguistics, and linguistic gender studies. She joined the Acoustics Research Institute with her work on a forensic phonetics project in 1992.

In 2007, she finished her Habilitationsschrift on the *Vowels in Standard Austrian German: an acoustic-phonetic and phonological analysis*. She has been a qualified Associate Professor in Applied Linguistics, Phonetics, and Phonology since 2008.

Sylvia Moosmüller lectures on acoustic phonetics, phonology, and sociolinguistics at the University of Vienna and at the University of Applied Sciences. Her research fields include phonetic and phonological variation in the varieties of Austrian German, acoustic phonetic description of vowels of selected insufficiently described languages, forensic phonetics, and sociolinguistics.

Sílvia Morgades Gil, PhD in Law (2007), Universitat Pompeu Fabra. Lecturer (*professora colaboradora*) in the Department of Law of Universitat Pompeu Fabra, in the area of Public International Law. She received the *Extraordinary Prize* for a Doctoral Thesis of the Department of Law, at Universitat Pompeu Fabra, in March 2009, for her essay on rights and guaranties of asylum seekers in the European legal space. Areas of interest: European Union Law, International Refugee and Asylum regime, Forced Migrations.

Her publications include book chapters and articles in scientific journals and the book: *Els drets humans com a motor de l'evolució del règim internacional de protecció dels refugiats* (Human rights as an engine of evolution for the international regime of refugee protection), Barcelona: Generalitat de Catalunya, 2008. Her more recent works include El derecho de asilo en la Unión Europea: realidades y perspectivas de regulación (The asylum law in the European Union: realities and regulation perspectives), in *Derecho, Inmigración y Empresa*, Barcelona: Itinera-Fundación Paulino Torras Doménech 2010, p. 161-201; and "The Externalisation of the Asylum Function in the European Union", in Ricard Zapata-Barrero (ed.) *Shaping the normative contours of the European Union: a Migration-Border framework*, Barcelona: Cidob Foundation edition, to be published in Autumn 2010.

Pieter Muysken (1950) is Academy Professor of Linguistics at Radboud University Nijmegen (Netherlands), having previously taught at Amsterdam and Leiden. He has carried out research and fieldwork in the Andes, Curacao, and the Netherlands. Recent books include (2000) *Bilingual Speech: A Typology of Code-mixing*; (2004) Adelaar with Muysken, *The Languages of the Andes*; (2008) *Functional Categories*; (2009-2010) Crevels and Muysken, *Lenguas de Bolivia I-IV*. His current research is concentrated in the Languages in Contact group in the Centre for Language Studies, Radboud University Nijmegen (www.ru.nl\linc).

Gregor Noll holds the Chair of International Law at the Faculty of Law, Lund University since 2006. His main fields of research are migration and refugee law, human rights law, the use of force and international humanitarian law. His most recent publication is Why Human Rights Fail to Protect Undocumented Migrants in a Special Issue on *The Laws of Undocumented Migration* of the *European Journal of Migration and Law* (Vol. 12, 2010) edited by him. Noll has authored a number of texts on evidentiary assessment and the asylum procedure.

Peter L Patrick is Professor of Sociolinguistics at the University of Essex, holds a PhD in Linguistics from Pennsylvania, and has taught at Georgetown University. His research focuses on language variation and change (especially Caribbean English Creoles) and linguistic human rights (including the role of language analysis in evaluating claims for asylum). His books include *Urban Jamaican Creole* (1999) and *Comparative Creole Syntax* (2007, w/J. Holm). As a forensic linguist, he has submitted testimony to US and UK criminal courts, and expert reports in the UK asylum process. He is a founding member of the Language and National Origin Group of linguists, co-author of the Guidelines for the use of language analysis in relation to questions of national origin in refugee cases (2004), member of the University of Essex Human Rights Centre, and as co-convenor of the Language & Asylum Research Group has been funded by the Economic and Social Research Council.

Claudia Pretto is Ph.D candidate in Constitutional and Comparative Law at Bari University, Faculty of Law. She is involved in Italian asylum and migration law studies, she works as legal consultant in migration/asylum law, she is member of the Italian Association on Migration Studies (ASGI). She is the editor of the section on legal migration and asylum law for the website of the Centre for information on migration issues

(Cinformi), at the Province of Trento, see www.cinformi.it/index.php/ utilita/ap-profondimenti_giuridici. Among her publications: *Double standards of protection: mutual 'influence' between 'new' and 'old' Europe?*; Changes in State Institutions and in the European Union, *Comparative European Public Law*, Issue No. 4, 2008; *EU citizens' expulsion in light of recent legislative provisions*, see www.devolutionclub.it; *Immigrant children' s integration and school legislation: compared European legal systems*, see www.cestim.it.

Vincent de Rooij holds an MA in Anthropology and a PhD in Linguistics (both at the University of Amsterdam). His PhD dissertation (1996) *Cohesion through contrast: Discourse structure in Shaba Swahili/French conversations, based on fieldwork carried out in Lubumbashi (DR Congo, ex-Zaïre) in 1991 and 1992*, shows how codeswitching is involved in creating cohesion in discourse.

From 1996 to 1999, De Rooij carried out a WOTRO post-doc research project titled Linguistic and cultural creolization on the Zairean Copperbelt. He is an assistant-professor at the Dept. of Sociology and Anthropology and a member of the Amsterdam Institute for Social Science Research (AISSR). In his teaching and research, his primary interest is on the construction of identities through language and on language ideologies.

The Haifa-based Professor **Judith Rosenhouse** won all her degrees with the Hebrew University of Jerusalem (BA cum laude, 1965, in Arabic and English Languages and Literatures; MA cum Laude, 1969, and PhD, 1974, in Arabic Language and Literature). The areas of her interest include dialectology, sociolinguistics, child language acquisition, phonetics, hearing impairment and rehabilitation, bilingualism and multilingualism, translation and more. She was employed at the Haifa University and later at the Technion - I.I.T. In the latter she served several terms as Head of the Department of General Studies (later renamed Dept. of Humanities and Arts). She has been book review editor for the Phonetician the bulletin of ISphS for more than ten years now. Since 2005 she has been a member of the board of directors of the Israel Alexander von Humboldt Club, being a recipient of several stipends from Alexander von Humboldt Foundation. She has specialized in Arabic dialectology and published several research books (e.g., *The Bedouin Arabic Dialects: General Characteristics and a Detailed Study of North Israel Bedouin Dialects*, 1984), bilingual and trilingual dictionaries (Literary Arabic, Colloquial Arabic and Hebrew), textbooks of Colloquial Arabic and edited books, as well as more than 150 articles in professional journals, encyclopaedias, handbooks, collections, Festschrifts etc. In addition she has published on Modern Hebrew. She won the New Israel Foundation Prize (1989) for her book *Medical Communication in Colloquial Arabic*, (in Hebrew) and the 2004 award of ISphS for services to the field of Phonetics. Since her retirement from the Technion and since then she has been pursuing her research and applied work with Swantech – Sound Waves Analysis and Technologies Ltd.

Blanche Tax is a Senior Policy Officer in UNHCR's Bureau for Europe in Brussels. She has worked as a protection officer with UNHCR in several field locations. Before joining the Brussels team in 2006, she was Head of a Field Office dealing with protection of and assistance to internally displaced persons in Sri Lanka. Previously, she was in charge of UNHCR's protection unit in Tbilisi (Georgia) and the refugee status determination unit in Bangkok (Thailand).

Before joining UNHCR in 2000, she worked with Amnesty International and the Dutch Council for Refugees on refugee protection in the Netherlands and she lectured Refugee and Immigration Law at Leiden University as a staff member of the Institute of Immigration Law.

She has degrees in law and history (international relations) from Utrecht University.

Dirk Vanheule, lic. iuris (Ghent U.), LL.M. (Toronto), dr. iuris (U. Antwerp) teaches and conducts research in constitutional, administrative and migration law at the Faculty of Law of the University of Antwerp and is chairperson of the Centre for Migration and Intercultural Studies there. He is also member of the Ghent Bar and practices in the areas of public law and migration law.

Jens Vedsted-Hansen is Professor of Law at the University of Aarhus in Denmark. His research interests include: Human Rights Law, Immigration and Refugee Law and Fundamental Rights in General Public Law.

His most recent publications include: European non-Refoulement Revisited, in P. Wahlgren (ed.), *Scandinavian Studies in Law*, Volume 55, Stockholm, p. 269-283; The absence of foreign law in Danish asylum decisions - quasi-judicial monologue with domestic policy focus?, in G.S. Goodwin-Gill & H. Lambert (eds), *The Limits of Transnational Law*, Cambridge: Cambridge University Press, p. 170-185.

Maaike Verrips obtained her Ph.D in linguistics at the University of Amsterdam in 1996, where she specialized in language acquisition, sociolinguistics and syntactic theory. She has directed De Taalstudio since she founded it in 2003. De Taalstudio aims to make knowledge of linguistic research accessible and available for practical purposes in a variety of domains. Language analysis is a major activity of De Taalstudio. Initially, most analyses were done by order of asylum seekers and their legal representatives in the Netherlands, who used them as second opinions in appeal procedures. Since 2008 De Taalstudio is offering services internationally, and recently signed a contract to provide systematic quality assurance and second opinions on LADO to the Norwegian Immigration Administration.

Karin Zwaan is the academic coordinator of the Centre for Migration Law, Radboud University Nijmegen, the Netherlands. She teaches Dutch migration law and refugee law at that university. She wrote her thesis on the safe third country exception (2003) and has published widely on refugee issues including books on UNHCR and the European Asylum Law (2005), the Qualification Directive (2006), the Procedures Directive (2007) and the use of language analysis in the Dutch asylum procedure (2008).

1.   Introduction

Pieter Muysken, Maaike Verrips and Karin Zwaan

1.   Objective of the Workshop

This book contains a series of papers presented at the *ESF Exploratory Workshop on Language and origin: the role of language in European asylum procedures*. This workshop took place over two days, at the Netherlands Institute for Advanced Studies in Wassenaar, April 22-23, 2010. The main objectives of the Workshop were stated in the original planning document:

> In recent years, language has been used as evidence in assessing asylum seekers' claims. Do they come from the country that they claim to originate from? Although this would seem quite simple, reliable assessments are hard to achieve. Many factors intervene: high variability, multilingualism, extended stays in refugee camps, lack of systematic knowledge about the languages, mixed ancestry. European countries have developed various techniques, but experts often disagree about these, and the validity of the results. This workshop brings together an interdisciplinary group of experts from different European countries to explore the different techniques and work towards improving them.

In line with ESF's policy for Exploratory Workshops, the meeting had a closed character and great care was taken to invite experts with various positions in refugee status determination and a variety of known viewpoints. Unfortunately, some language agencies still declined our invitation, expressing the fear that that their point of view was not welcomed. However, in spite of such difficulties, and in addition the eruption of the Eyjafjalla Volcano which closed the European Air space for almost a week – making it physically impossible for some of the participants to attend the meeting despite their extreme efforts - we think that the meeting was very successful in bringing together different points of view.

The decision to collect the papers into a book that makes the results of this meeting accessible to all who could not participate was supported unanimously. We are very thankful to all authors for their trouble to write up their contributions to this volume on such short notice. We are grateful to the participants in the original workshop for their input. Giorgio Banti, Enam El Wer, Melissa Moyer and Martin Skamla unfortunately were unable to contribute a written version of the paper they presented at the workshop.

2.   Scientific Content of the Event

Language Analysis (LADO) started life in the 1990s in various immigration departments, notably in Sweden and Switzerland, as a way of using language to determine the national and regional origin of asylum seekers. The first academic meeting took place in 2003. A group of concerned linguists produced a set of Guidelines in 2004 about proper use of LADO. In 2005, 2006, 2007 and 2008, small specialist workshops were held on the topic. These workshops were organized by LADO experts (De Taalstudio in 2005, 2006 and 2007, and LINGUA in 2008) and they were attended by language professionals mainly. The focus was on technical issues. Some differences between the practices of the various LADO-providers turned out to be rather contentious, for example the expert's profile and the format of expert reports. Some issues appeared to require input from the judicial domain.

This workshop brought together an interdisciplinary group of experts in a closed, constructive setting to exchange views, to learn to speak each other's language and to set priorities for future research and developments. As Pieter Muysken stressed in his introduction, the aim of the meeting was not to 'conclude' what is the best method for LADO, a contentious issue in the research community invited to the workshop.

In a general introduction to the workshop, the convenor Muysken presented the main research questions, both linguistic and judicial. A first set of questions concerns the very feasibility of using LADO as an instrument.

- Is it possible to determine the origin of asylum seekers on the basis of an analysis of characteristics of their speech?
- Which research methods and which techniques are available for these analyses, in practice (e.g. in immigration services and aliens police), and in linguistic science. Do recent advances in language recognition software provide a basis for reliable LADO-assessments?
- How can the validity and reliability of such analyses be determined?
- What is the validity and reliability of the analyses that are put forward at the moment?
- What are the advantages and disadvantages of various methods of data collection in the context of language analysis (an interview, a conversation with an interpreter, a recorded monologue, a dialogue, a translation of a list of words, etc...)?
- What are the requirements that experts who carry out such analyses should comply with?

Next, there is the question of the Guidelines for the Use of Language Analysis, published in 2004 and included in this volume as an appendix. The Guidelines have since been endorsed by several linguistics associations, but remain the subject of much debate.

- What has been the influence of these Guidelines on the use of language analysis in practice?
- Given insights and research since 2004, where will the Guidelines need to be adapted and refined?
- What other professional standards may be or have been proposed?

A third set of questions concerns the cultural and linguistic contexts within which LADO may or may not be applied:

2

- What contribution can native speakers make to valid and reliable language analysis? What are the respective roles for native speakers and specialised linguists in this process?
- How does an assessment of geographical and cultural knowledge affect the validity and reliability of language analysis?
- What is the effect of multilingualism on the way people speak and how this affect they way they are identified in asylum procedures?
- What can we learn from a more qualitative, ethnographic study of the interactions that the asylum seekers and officials engage in as part of the admission procedure?
- How does variation in the local languages, both geographic and social, affect unambiguous LADO assessments?

A final set of questions concerns the nature of the evidence involved in LADO, and the legal context for its use:
- The goal of LADO in the asylum procedure is to establish a person's main socialization - not the citizenship - absolutely or with a degree of probability. The result of LADO will be one element in the later decision about the asylum application. What degree of probability is required?
- Why is LADO mainly used as a 'falsifying' instrument? In the asylum procedure language analysis is used mainly when there are doubts with regard the nationality/origin of the asylum applicant. This turns LADO into a gate-keeping instrument.
- What is the role of the counter-expert, and who decides who is right, the expert or the contra-expert? The judge or the linguist?
- There is the need for harmonization within the Common European Asylum System, and so there is a need for European States to apply LADO in the same way, and using the same sources. Is there a need for a LADO European Support Office?
- What qualifications should a language analyst possess to make him/her a reliable source of information/proof (native speaker, native competence?) within the judicial process?
- What is the exact division of labor between the linguistic expert and the judicial expert?
- What is the nature of the evidence that comes from LADO?

Muysken also addressed the issue of the different stakeholders in LADO, with their respective potentially conflicting interests:
- the European governments who offer protection on the basis of International agreements like the UN Convention relating to the status of Refugees. Asylum requests are dealt with in accordance with (varying) national regulations. Complementary protection is offered on the basis of the European Convention on Human Rights. All this takes place under considerable political pressure to keep the costs of the selection, admission, and eviction procedures down and to ensure effective border control;
- European governments are potentially split between southern European countries who face massive influx on their borders, and northern countries that often serve as ultimate destinations for refugees;

- asylum seekers and their representatives, who seek admission and at least the benefit of the doubt;
- the language agencies, inside and outside government institutions, interested in contributing to cost-effective asylum procedures;
- the legal system, interested in compliance with legal standards;
- language professionals from the academic world, who welcome job opportunities and also need to guard the public image of their field of study;
- language professionals from outside the academic world, especially interpreters, who also welcome job opportunities and possibly extra income in LADO.

Obviously, these interests, and the ensuing agendas for action, often clash, and thus the field of LADO currently is the subject of hot debate. Given the remaining and even growing tensions between the wish of many European electorates to close borders, and the reality of a continuous influx of asylum seekers, this debate will continue. However, putting the issues on the table can help establish fair and efficient admission procedures.

3. This Volume

In this book, we only follow the exact format of the meeting very loosely. Rather, the papers of the meeting are presented in five parts:
1. Part One, The practice of LADO
2. Part Two: LADO and the study of language
3. Part Three: Language and origin: Three case studies
4. Part Four: Language in asylum procedures: A country survey
5. Part Five: LADO as evidence

Each part contains three to five chapters, and thus we hope to cover many of the issues raised above. Each part also starts with a brief Presentation summarizing these contributions.

4. Preliminary Conclusions and Directions for Research

The aim of Exploratory Workshops is to open up new directions in research. From the discussions during the workshop it has become fairly clear what those directions could be. Let us first summarise some of the overall conclusions.
1. LADO is unavoidable, in the sense that judgments about the origin of dialects appear to have played a role in refugee status determination since its earliest existence. If LADO does not acquire a regulated place in these determinations, it will not be possible to realise its full potential and the implicit role of such judgments will have undesirable legal consequences.
2. Even if the need for regulation will be recognized by the main stakeholders, the question still remains how. From the linguists' point of view, much can be gained with a degree of modesty of projected outcomes. Defining the limitations of LADO would be an improvement. For example, LADO may be validated for certain re-

gions but not for others, or validated to assess languages spoken from birth, but not languages spoken as second or third languages.

3. Currently, it is not yet clear to what extent LADO can produce results that conform to basic standards in linguistics while at the same time fulfilling the lawyers' needs for clear and reliable results. A major challenge lies in developing practices that fulfill both requirements.

There is an urgent need for further empirical research in this area, which preferably should be carried out in a European context. Several possibilities for new research were discussed at the workshop in the final session.

(a)   Language data bases for a specific region

One possibility would be to create a language data base for a specific country or region from which there has been, and can reasonably be expected to remain, a steady stream of asylum seekers. On the basis of such a database, the possibilities and limitations of LADO could be identified reliably.

(b)   Basic empirical research on issues linked to LADO

There is an urgent need for basic research on some general issues to inform LADO practice. Research questions that were identified include: to what extent can language be manipulated? How do people 'perceive' accents in various languages and how do they attribute regional identities to others? What are the typical structures in the refugee narratives, and what do these structures reveal?

(c)   Best practices research

Research questions in this domain include: What are the appropriate quality standards for interviews? What is the potential of language and speech technology for LADO, and what are its limits? What are the official and unofficial roles of interpreters? What is the best format for instructions to experts and for expert reports? Some of this research could take place in 'mock asylum contexts'.

(d)   Legal contextualization of LADO

A host of legal questions come to the fore, including: What is the legal basis for the roles of LADO agencies? How does LADO fit in with the EU Procedures Directive? What procedural safeguards should surround the use of LADO in refugee status determination? At what level should harmonization be achieved ?

5.   A New Era

It was generally felt that the meeting marked the start of a new era in the discussion of LADO. Over the two days, understanding of other approaches to the general issues increased, and discussions gained in depth. The beautiful and quiet surroundings, and excellent hospitality greatly contributed to the quality and intensity of the interactions and the constructive overall atmosphere during these days. Subsequent to the ESF workshop of April 2010, there have already been several new initiatives. During the workshop, the launch of the international Language and Asylum Research Group (LARG) was announced, a group that was subsequently established in June 2010. In the mean time LARG has been funded by the Economic and Social Research Council in the UK to organize a series of workshops on LADO in 2011 and 2012 with experts from a variety of backgrounds.

Also, a meeting on LADO, attended by users and practitioners was organized by several language agencies in Gothenburg (Sweden), and took place on November 22-23, 2010.

Part One: The Practice of LADO

Part One starts by laying out the two main current LADO procedures. *Eric Baltisberger and Priska Hubbuch* (LINGUA, Bern) introduce LADO with specialized linguists, while *Tina Cambier-Langeveld* (IND, Netherlands) argues for the validity of the practice of the Netherlands agency BLT to carry out LADO with linguists supervising native speakers. *Diana Eades* (Australia) introduces the background to the Guidelines for LADO from linguists. *Sylvia Moosmüller* (Austria) presents the resolution on Language and Origin that was adopted in 2009 by the IAFPA (International Association of Forensic Phonetics and Acoustics) and the background of that resolution.

LADO with Specialized Linguists – The Development of LINGUA's Working Method

Eric Baltisberger and Priska Hubbuch

Introduction

LINGUA was founded in May 1997 as a specialized unit within the Swiss Federal Office for Migration (FOM; known up until 2004 as the Federal Office for Refugees, FOR). Its task is to carry out analyses of origin for people seeking asylum and other foreigners. These analyses of origin become necessary when asylum seekers or foreign nationals (in the LINGUA context usually referred to as 'subjects') cannot produce any valid identification documents and, in addition to this, there are doubts about the subjects' claims concerning their region of origin. The aim of LINGUA is to carry out a verification of the subjects' statements about their origin in a manner that will stand up to scrutiny before a court of law and which is relevant to the asylum procedure, or expresses relevant presumptions of origin for subjects that are to be repatriated. It is for this purpose that the subjects' speech as well as their cultural knowledge of the regions concerned are analysed and evaluated. In order to carry out the analyses, LINGUA works with external analysts (called 'experts' in the LINGUA context). Most of them are academically trained linguists who analyse a conversation carried out with the subject and produce a report consisting of an evaluation of the subject's cultural knowledge as well as of a linguistic analysis of his/her speech. It is important to note that a LINGUA report never aims to determine a subject's nationality but always refers to the country and/or region or, at least, the (linguistic) community which have had the biggest influence on the subject's process of socialization.

The present paper is going to focus on the different processes and experiences in the history of LINGUA that have led to the decision to make the academic training in linguistics one of the main requirements for LINGUA experts.

Preliminary Projects

In the mid 1990s the Federal Office for Refugees was confronted with an increasing number of asylum seekers who did not present any identity documents. Also, after the hearings on the asylum motives, case officers in charge of taking asylum decisions expressed serious doubts concerning the claims about the country of origin of some of these people. The case officers' doubts were mostly based on inconsistencies in asylum seekers' accounts and/or lack of knowledge regarding the claimed countries of origin. Doubts were especially present when it came to constellations where a country found itself in a war or another precarious situation that threatened the whole or parts of the population while the situation in the neighbouring countries was calmer and more stable, at least as far as potential asylum motives were concerned. Whereas people coming from conflict areas would be more likely to get asylum status or receive temporary protection, there was a high probability that asylum demands from those coming from the neighbouring countries would be turned down and that these people would not be allowed to stay in Switzerland. The country constellations considered to be problematic at the time were Afghanistan/Pakistan, Kosovo/Albania, Liberia and Sierra Leone/ other Anglophone West African countries, Palestine/other Arabic-speaking countries, as well as Sri Lanka/Southern India.

Questionnaires were thus established in order to evaluate the country knowledge of asylum seekers whose accounts regarding their claimed country of origin had not been convincing so far. They helped to confirm certain doubts, but the limits of this kind of verification became rapidly clear: within a very short time the questions were known to most of the newly arriving asylum seekers who consequently learnt the correct replies and thus prepared themselves for their asylum hearings. Another disadvantage of the questionnaires was that they were very general and the questions were not always adapted to the subjects' individual backgrounds.

Subsequently, the FOR initiated several projects regarding some of the aforementioned country-constellations. The aim of all those projects was the same: to obtain information in order to confirm or disconfirm the claimed country of origin. They were, however, different in their approach and structure: For the Afghanistan/Pakistan project the FOR hired a specialist of Afghan origin who was familiar with the region in question and who also had a fair knowledge about the linguistic particularities of the Pashto language. He conducted interviews with asylum seekers claiming to come from Afghanistan but who were suspected to come from Pakistan. During these interviews, both, the specialist and the asylum seeker, were in the same room although separated by a folding screen in order to protect the specialist's anonymity and integrity. For the Kosovo/Albania project, the specialists hired by the FOR were native speakers familiar with Kosovo and Albania. They conducted their interviews by video conference and focussed mostly on the geographical and regional knowledge of the asylum seekers. On the basis of the interviews conducted the specialists, in both these projects, wrote short reports which constituted the result of their investigations.

For the third project, which included several of the above mentioned country constellations, the experiences made by the Swedish authorities in charge of asylum demands served as a model. An interview with an asylum seeker conducted by a case officer – if necessary with the support of an interpreter – was recorded. The recording was then sent to either one of the analysts working for the Swedish authorities or to one of the specialists that were hired for the project in Switzerland.

The three projects showed that it was indeed possible to confirm the suspicion expressed by case officers, namely that some asylum seekers made false claims concerning their country of origin, quite certainly in order to heighten their chances of receiving a better status in Switzerland. As a consequence, in Mai 1997 the FOR board decided to create the LINGUA unit with the aim to further develop methods as those mentioned above and to provide well-founded analyses of origin that could be used in the asylum procedure and would be acknowledged by the appeal authority.

The Creation of LINGUA

The two staff members in charge of the development of the new LINGUA unit had both been involved in the above-mentioned projects and were thus familiar with the different approaches and their respective advantages and disadvantages. They decided to discontinue face-to-face interviews, or interviews were interviewer and asylum seeker were in the same room, after an incident with a subject who, angry about the questions he was asked, had torn down the folding screen and threatened the specialist. Video conferences were abandoned equally, at least for the initial phase. The technology was unwieldy and too expensive; furthermore the Kosovo/Albania project did not reveal any advantages in the specialist being able to see the subject during the interview. As for the interviews between case officer and subject, these were discarded too: due to the lack of experience of case officers the topics discussed during such interviews were often inadequate for an analysis and the fact that an interpreter had to be called in for most interviews clearly was a disadvantage. The method that was finally chosen – and which is still in use today – was to organize interviews by telephone, conducted by an expert (as the specialists came to be called) without any intermediary. With this method, it was also possible to schedule several interviews in a row between an expert and subjects located in different registration centres at the Swiss border. This method, in which the person conducting the interview is the same who also writes the analysis, has come to be known as 'direct analysis'.[1]

At first, the analyses were based solely on the notes that the experts took during the interview with the subjects. It soon became clear, however, that handwritten notes were not sufficient and that a more a solid basis for the analyses was needed. It was thus decided to record the interviews. After some rather adventurous first recordings that were obtained by placing a microphone on the telephone's loudspeaker, the quality of recordings was improved by using tape recorders that were directly plugged into the telephone line. Some years later the acquisition of telephones with built-in CD writers allowed LINGUA to further enhance the quality of the recordings.

The different FOM projects realized before the creation of LINGUA also had an impact on LINGUA reports: while the reports of the Swedish partner unit focussed mainly on the subject's language, LINGUA always tried to combine linguistic aspects on the one hand with aspects of country knowledge on the other. This combination corresponded to what was needed by the FOM and was thought to yield the most complete and precise results.

The Legal Context

The basic precept of using analyses of origin in the area of asylum is not literally laid down in Swiss asylum law. Article 32.2.b. of this law states that any deception concerning the identity of a subject can be determined through a dactyloscopic test or 'other

---

1   For more information on direct analysis and LINGUA interviews in general, see L. Meyer, Sprachanalysen zur Herkunftsbestimmung im Asyl- und Ausländerbereich, Kriminalistik 11/2006, p. 708-712.

means of proof'. LINGUA reports are recognized as being amongst the latter.[2] On October 20th 1998, the Swiss Asylum Appeal Commission (ARK; now Federal Administrative Court) pronounced itself for the first time on the value of LINGUA analyses within the Swiss asylum procedure: Since the name of the expert and the report itself are not published, the appeal court stated that the reports produced by LINGUA cannot be regarded as formal expertises within the realms of Swiss law. However, since the minimal demands regarding the guarantee of reliability, objectivity and neutrality were upheld, LINGUA analyses were regarded as having a heightened degree of proof.[3] Using LINGUA analyses to verify the origin of asylum seekers is, as a consequence, legally confirmed and is now an integral part of the Swiss asylum procedure.

The Initial Phase

The requirements for experts hired by LINGUA in the beginning were closely linked to the country and language constellations to be analysed, to the technical possibilities and to the state of research in the domain of such analyses which, at the time, was scarce. The major constellation during that time was Kosovo/Albania, and most of the requests for analyses that were sent to LINGUA concerned speakers of Albanian who claimed to come from Kosovo but were suspected by the case officers to actually come from Albania. It should be remembered that during that time Switzerland was faced with an extraordinarily high number of people who fled from the situation in Kosovo. Switzerland was one of their main destinations, assumingly because of the relatively large Kosovar Diaspora that was already present in the country.

In order to carry out the analyses LINGUA at first engaged experts with an intimate knowledge of the region in question and a native or near native proficiency in Albanian. At that time, no conscious decision was taken for or against collaboration with either native speakers or linguists. The great majority of the cases could be treated by evaluating the subjects' country knowledge coupled with some observations on their language. Very often, these observations referred to lexical differences between the varieties of Albanian spoken in Albania and Kosovo which were at least partly due to the fact that Albania had been isolated for many years. In addition, the experts had to fulfil some personal requirements such as neutrality, trustworthiness and independence from the country of origin's government as well as from any kind of politically involved group in the respective country.

For technical reasons experts had to come to the LINGUA offices to conduct their interviews and also mostly wrote their reports there. It was thus logical to focus on pos-

---

2 Article of law: http://www.admin.ch/ch/e/rs/142_31/a32.html; Message regarding the Federal decision concerning urgent measures in the field of asylum and foreign nationals on 13.05.1998 (with the following link to the Federal Archives, in French: http://www.amtsdruckschriften.bar.admin.ch/loadDocQuery.do?context=results&documentIndex=2&dsUID=4f9fdc:129e9b 25b2c:-6cc0#detailView (insert 10109469 into the search field), p. 2835.

3 Text of the ARK decision 1998/34 on 20.10.1998 http://www.ark-cra.ch/emark/1998/ 9834280PUB.htm.

sible experts residing in Switzerland (or sometimes also in adjacent parts of the neighbouring countries). However, linguists with an expertise in the relevant languages were hardly to be found in such a confined geographical area. As a consequence, most experts hired during that time were native speakers without linguistic training. LINGUA tested their aptitude by submitting to them recordings that had already been analysed by other experts and by thoroughly discussing with them the results of their analyses. Only those who successfully completed the testing phase were engaged and their subsequent work was under the supervision of the LINGUA staff. The experts' analyses were cross-checked regularly by other native speakers and – if possible – submitted to academic linguists who evaluated the reports.

The Need for Linguists

The need to re-evaluate the requirements for experts became obvious when LINGUA started to be confronted with people from Kosovo claiming to come from the border regions with Macedonia or Montenegro. Also, the more LINGUA dealt with other regions such as the Maghreb, the Middle East, and West Africa, the more it became clear that in order to treat such cases adequately a proper training in linguistics was indispensable. It was not only the increasingly diverse and complex linguistic areas that made it necessary to rethink the requirements for experts, but also the more complex biographical backgrounds of the subjects: most of the subjects did no longer claim to have always lived in the same country or even the same region, but there was a growing number of people claiming to have lived in several linguistic areas before coming to Switzerland. Many of them belonged to ethnic groups which are present in several countries or claimed to have lived in border regions. There were many multilingual subjects and others who claimed to be monolingual although their language proficiency was so limited that it was obvious that the language they spoke could not be their native tongue. Others again claimed to speak small local languages which could not be identified.

In 1999, LINGUA officially informed the FOR board that it was no longer enough to hire native speakers without any linguistic training to carry out analyses for LINGUA. In order to treat complex cases in a satisfactory manner it was necessary to find people who did not only speak the languages concerned and were familiar with the regions in question, they also had to be able to deal with questions of dialectology, language interference, multilingualism, sociolinguistics, language acquisition or language identification, just to name a few. However, to find academically trained linguists who agreed to work with a governmental unit, in a domain as sensitive and emotionally charged as the asylum domain, was (and still is) not an easy task. Moreover, as mentioned above, linguists with an expertise in languages relevant for LINGUA were only rarely to be found in Switzerland. This was especially true when it came to African languages.

To guarantee an accurate treatment of the cases submitted to LINGUA, the unit was thus forced to start looking for possible experts abroad. The collaboration with these experts however was complicated and time consuming: to fly in experts for just a couple of interviews was not possible for many reasons. Consequently, requests for LINGUA analyses were collected over a period of time before the experts came to

Switzerland for one or two weeks in order to conduct the necessary interviews and write the reports. Needless to say that with this working method it could take quite some time until a case got treated which is one of the reasons why LINGUA's decision to work with academically trained linguists was met with some scepticism within the FOR.

These concerns were certainly not unfounded, but the cooperation with academically trained linguists clearly improved the quality of LINGUA reports. While at the beginning the linguistic part of a report often consisted merely of some phonological and lexical observations that supported the usually much more elaborate country knowledge evaluation, many other linguistic features were now taken into account to do justice to the often quite complex biographical backgrounds of the subjects. In some cases, the sociolinguistic situation in a given region had to be looked at, in others special attention had to be paid to morphology, syntax or tonology, depending on the constellation to be treated and on the (claimed) individual background of a subject. The linguistic argumentation became more developed and scientific. Linguistic processes and features were described, and not merely listed, which made it easier for the LINGUA staff and case officers alike to understand how experts came to their conclusions. At the same time, the scientific and well developed argumentation also heightened the credibility of the analyses before the appeal court.

The continuous enhancement of the standards in the linguistic section also meant that several of the native speaker experts, who were still working for LINGUA, saw themselves confronted with requirements that they could not fulfil anymore. Since its beginnings, LINGUA had a set of minimal criteria to guarantee certain quality standards for its reports. The criteria were of a quantitative nature and simply stated the minimal number of features (in the linguistic section) and points (in the country knowledge section) that had to be evaluated, whereby all the features and points quoted had to be pertinent to the case in question. Most of the linguist experts exceeded these minimal criteria by far, not only quantitatively: they took into account many aspects that were potentially influencing a speaker's linguistic behaviour and presented exhaustive argumentations that explained the sometimes complex linguistic features and personal backgrounds. Consequently, a report merely fulfilling the minimal standards was soon considered to be insufficient by LINGUA. With some few native speaker experts it was possible to reach the new standard with the support of the LINGUA staff, others resigned, some of them stayed with LINGUA but abandoned their analytical tasks and henceforth conducted interviews for those linguist experts who, for various reasons, were not in a position to do so themselves.

An additional consequence of the collaboration with academically trained linguists was that it helped LINGUA and LADO in general to achieve a wider acceptance within the academic world. Some experts discussed their work with LINGUA with their peers or presented aspects of their work at conferences. All this led to a growing interest of scientists in LADO which, in turn, helped to further develop this up to then not very well known domain.

Technical Aspects

The arrival of new technologies finally enabled LINGUA to implement its reflexions on the requirements for the engagement of experts made over the past years. After the introduction of conference calls it was no longer necessary for an expert to be physically present at the LINGUA offices in order to conduct an interview. The 'availability factor' which up to then was an important requirement for LINGUA experts thus became expendable - at least as far as geographical availability was concerned. However, recordings were still sent to the experts by postal service which was problematic since on the one hand the treatment of cases was considerably delayed and on the other hand there were security concerns depending on where an expert was residing. The latter problem could often be solved by sending recordings via diplomatic bag to the Swiss representations of the countries concerned which, however, did not speed up the process.

When LINGUA started working with digital recordings in 2004, this opened up the possibility to transmit interview recordings over the internet. However, it was necessary to secure the transmission in order to minimise the risk of interception by a third party. Once a solution to this problem was found, recordings could be sent immediately after the interview to the experts. Exceptions had still to be made for experts living in countries where there was a risk that non-authorized persons including governmental authorities would get access to the recordings. In these cases, the diplomatic bag remained a viable option to send recordings to the experts. In some cases, however, even this was not possible and LINGUA either had to give up the collaboration or – like before – collect enough cases so that the expert could come to Switzerland from time to time and treat them on site.

Still, on the whole, the technical developments considerably simplified working on distance and enabled LINGUA to consistently search for and work with linguists from all over the world.

The Cooperation between LINGUA and Linguists

From its creation in 1997, the LINGUA unit has itself evolved and today consists of a small team composed of academically trained linguists and administrative personnel. Each linguist is responsible for certain linguistic and geographical regions and it is in his/her responsibility to find appropriate experts, make them aware of the specific task at hand and cooperate with them in their work. The LINGUA linguists can be considered as a link between the FOM on the one hand and the expert on the other hand or, in other words, as a link between administration and academia. As part of the FOM they are familiar with the needs of the office, as academically trained linguists they are aware of the possibilities and limitations of linguistic analyses.

If a potential expert is found, a first contact is established and the potential expert is interested in working with LINGUA, it is the linguists' responsibility to initiate the testing process and to supervise it. All experts are tested before they are put under contract and start treating cases for LINGUA. Essentially, the testing process is still the same as it has been at the beginning of LINGUA: potential experts are thus still asked to analyse interview recordings that have previously been analysed by other experts and to write reports. Unlike in the beginning, however, the more developed argumentation in the reports nowadays allows the supervising linguists to not only compare the results of the analyses but to focus on the manner of how the results are achieved. Much importance and attention is thus given to the argumentation, the weighting of the different points and the explanations of the linguistic phenomena observed in a subject's language. In addition, the supervising LINGUA linguists and the potential experts discuss in detail the subjects' claims and their implication on the analysing process.

Whenever possible, the discussions on the test cases are held face-to-face with the potential expert. Given the sensitive nature of the task, LINGUA usually insists on a personal meeting before a contract is signed. Apart from the discussions on the test cases, these meetings also offer an opportunity to talk more generally about the work of LINGUA experts, to inform the potential experts about the FOM and its various tasks and to give additional explanation on the expert's role within the FOM as well as on the impact of linguistic analysis in the in the different stages of the asylum procedure. LINGUA also needs to take the necessary precautions in order to avoid engaging experts who could abuse their role to the advantage or disadvantage of certain groups of asylum seekers. Therefore, potential experts are often presented to people working at the COI (country of origin information) unit at the FOM. They discuss with the potential experts specific (e.g. political) aspects of the countries of their expertise to minimise the risk that a potential expert's subjective views would later influence his/her work.

Although a personal encounter is certainly never enough to fully assess a person and his/her qualities and qualifications, the meetings at least provide an occasion for LINGUA to get an impression of a potential expert. While such encounters are obviously much easier to organize with people who live in Switzerland, LINGUA still adheres to the necessity of personal meetings with all potential experts. If necessary, LINGUA linguists travel abroad to meet them, either in their country of residence or on linguistic conferences where these potential experts are present. If the personal meeting as well as the collaboration on the test cases proves to be satisfactory for the expert as well as for LINGUA, the expert is put under contract.

In their collaboration with the experts, the main task of the supervising linguists is to ensure that LINGUA reports are non-ambiguous, that they do not contain any inconsistencies or unfounded statements, that they are relevant for the case at hand and that they are comprehensible also for non-linguists. In order to do this, LINGUA linguists scrutinize the argumentation of every report, and discuss with the experts the points that seem to be unclear or likely to raise questions by a case officer or the appeal court.

Experience has shown that discussions on the reports are usually more productive when held with linguist experts than with native speaker experts at least when it comes to the linguistic part of LINGUA reports. One reason for this is that linguists are used to describing linguistic processes and dispose of a vocabulary that allows them to do so accurately. The argumentation in the reports is thus more developed, transparent and, since it is written in a standardised language, more comprehensible. Also, the argumentation is supported by research data, which sometimes consists of data gathered by the linguist experts themselves during their field trips. Since LINGUA is often confronted with languages on which there is only little data available, if any, this point is certainly of special importance. Due to their training, linguist experts are also more aware of the different factors that can influence a person's linguistic behaviour which means that they usually have a more complete grasp of a given speaker's situation. Last but not least, linguists have learned to have an objective perspective on language and are less prone to folk linguistic beliefs. Still, given the importance a LINGUA analysis can have for people in the asylum domain, the reports of all experts under contract are regularly cross-checked.

On the other hand, experience also has shown that not every qualified linguist is by definition a qualified expert. One of the reasons for this might be that many linguists are not used to work in a forensic context. Depending on how one defines the term of 'forensic linguistics', linguistic analyses within the asylum procedure can be considered as belonging to this field. It is in the nature of such analyses that they take a stance in regard to a specific question and it seems to be exactly this point that some linguists have difficulties to come to terms with. While a thorough scientific description of a subject's language is certainly very helpful, what ultimately counts for the case officer and for the appeal court is the conclusion that is reached based on this description. One of the main tasks of the LINGUA linguists is therefore also to support the experts by bringing in the forensic perspective.

Finally, LINGUA's cooperation with linguists is not restricted to those who are working as experts. The FOM offers the possibility to apply for funds for research projects in order to improve the quality of work of the different units within the FOM. These research projects are usually carried out in collaboration with external researchers. With this funding, in 2006 LINGUA was able to hire a team of external researchers who had a closer look at LINGUA interviews that serve as basis for the analyses. One of the outcomes of this research was a training concept that is now used to instruct LINGUA interviewers. In 2009 another research project was initiated with the aim to re-evaluate the minimal criteria for LINGUA reports. At the time of writing it is not yet clear what impact this new research project will have. First results are expected by the end of 2010.

The Cooperation between LINGUA and Native Speakers

On the basis of the experiences made since its creation, LINGUA generally holds the view that a linguistic analysis should be carried out by a linguist. There are some exceptions to this rule, i.e. native speakers who are not linguists but who, thanks to further education and support of the LINGUA linguists, are able to analyse recordings adequately and write reports that suffice the requirements. In most cases, however, the time investment in order to reach the required linguistic level and to achieve a well developed argumentation in the linguistic part of the reports is too big for both, the native speaker experts as well as the LINGUA linguists. Still, the past years also clearly revealed that native speakers' intuitions and observations can be very valuable. One of the main questions for LINGUA today is therefore how these qualities can be used in LINGUA's daily work.

At present, LINGUA employs native speakers mainly as interviewers. Although the majority of the cases are still treated by direct analysis where the expert conduct their own interviews with the subjects, there are also experts who, e.g. due to the time difference between Switzerland and the country they live in, are not able to conduct an interview with a subject. LINGUA thus put together a pool of native speakers who conduct interviews but do not analyse them (in this context, LINGUA speaks of 'indirect analyses', i.e. the analyses is not written by the same person who conducts the interview). All interviewers (including the linguist experts who conduct interviews) receive a specific training based on the research project on LINGUA interviews mentioned above. The interviewers are free to communicate to the LINGUA staff their impressions and observations following an interview but they are not obliged to do so. If given, these impressions can sometimes have an impact on the further proceedings in a case. Should the impressions and observations of an interviewer drastically contradict the result of an expert's analysis, this will quite certainly entail a more thorough discussion of the analysis in question. Very often, such contradictions are also a reason for the supervising linguist to ask another expert for a second analysis.

The native speakers working with LINGUA sometimes also function as informants for linguist experts – especially for those who are not themselves native speakers of the language in question. A future task will certainly be to further develop this collaboration and to find a way for the contribution of native speakers to be acknowledged and used within the domain of linguistic analysis in the asylum procedure.

Conclusion

The history of LINGUA is a long and certainly not yet concluded process of learning by doing. Many decisions were and still are highly dependent on the given circumstances; at the same time LINGUA aims to suffice scientific requirements. There is no claim that the method chosen by LINGUA is perfect or must be valid for all units involved in such analyses. Rather, it seems to be the best possible solution in the given (Swiss) context at the present time. LINGUA will undoubtedly continue to evolve, particularly in view of the valuable input of experts and the highly stimulating discussions with scientists from different disciplines who thus contribute to the development of a domain that until only some years ago was virtually inexistent in the academic discussion. These inputs and discussions are essential regarding the further development of quality standards in this highly sensitive and complex domain and, along with it, the correct and respectful treatment of people seeking asylum.

References

Corcoran, C. (2004) A critical examination of the use of language analysis Interviews in asylum proceedings: a case study of a West African seeking asylum in the Netherlands, *The International Journal of Speech, Language and the Law*, Vol. 11, (2), p. 220-221.

Eades, D., H. Fraser, J. Siegel, T. McNamara, T. and B. Baker (2003) Linguistic identification in the determination of nationality: A preliminary report, *Language Policy*, 2(2), p. 179-199.

Eades, D. and J. Arends (2004) Using language analysis in the determination of national origin of asy-lum seekers: an introduction, *The International Journal of Speech, Language and the Law*, formerly *Forensic Linguistics*, Vol. 11, (2), p. 179-199.

Eades, D. (2009) Testing the claims of Asylum Seekers: the role of language analysis, *Language Assessment Quarterly* (6), p. 30-40.

Fraser, H. (2009) The role of 'educated native speakers' in providing language analysis for the determination of the origin of asylum seekers, *International Journal of Speech Language and the Law*, 16(1), p. 113-138.

Language and National Origin Group (2004) Guidelines for the use of language analysis in relation to questions of national origin in refugee cases. *International Journal of Speech, Language and the Law*, Vol. 11(2), p. 261-266.

Maryns, K. (2004) Identifying the asylum seeker: reflections on the pitfalls of language analysis in the deter-mination of national origin. *The International Journal of Speech, Language and the Law*, Vol. 11(2), p. 240-260.

Meyer, L. (2006) Sprachanalysen zur Herkunftsbestimmung im Asyl- und Ausländerbe-reich. *Kriminalistik* 11, p. 708-712.

Singler, J.V. (2004) The 'linguistic' asylum interview and the linguist's evaluation of it, with special reference to applicants for Liberian political asylum in Switzerland. *The International Journal of Speech, Language and the Law*, Vol. 11(2), p. 220-240.

Workshops and conferences

7th Biennial Conference on Forensic Linguistics/Language and the Law/ IAFL (Interna-tional Association for Forensic Linguists) in Cardiff/Wales, 1-4 July 2005 (http://depts.washington.edu/iafl/index.htm)

Workshop 'Language Analysis in Refugee Status Determination', 16th Sociolinguistics Symposium, Limerick/Ireland, 6.-8.7.2006 (http://www.ul.ie/ss16/WS06.html)

Second European IAFL Conference on Forensic Linguistics/Language and the Law in Barcelona/Spain, 14.-16.9.2006 (http://www.iula.upf.edu/agenda/iafl_bcn_06/)

4 days of Swiss Linguistics, Basel/Switzerland, 20.-21.11.2006

Workshop on Language Analysis in the determination of national origin of refugees in Amsterdam/the Netherlands, 21 June 2007.

Workshop on linguistic analyses within the asylum procedure in Lausanne/Switzerland, 23.-24.07.2008 (http://www.bfm.admin.ch/content/bfm/en/home/themen/mi-gration_analysen/sprachanalysen/workshop_2008.html).

The Validity of Language Analysis in the Netherlands

Tina Cambier-Langeveld

1. Introduction

In recent years, two schools of thought have developed about the application of 'Language Analysis for the Determination of the Origin of asylum seekers' (LADO). One school advocates the use of a trained native speaker working under the supervision of a linguist. This is the method adopted by the Dutch Immigration and Naturalization Service (INS), and by a number of Swedish companies. The other school is in favour of using a linguist specialized in the language in question; in the Netherlands, this method is generally used in counter analyses requested in asylum cases. It is also used by LINGUA, part of the Swiss Federal Office for Migration (Baltisberger and Hubbuch 2010, this volume) and the German Bundesamt für Migration und Flüchtlinge (BAMF). This paper aims to give some insight into the merits of each of the competing methods as they are performed in the Netherlands.[1]

In the LADO procedure as applied by the Dutch INS,[2] linguists work together on each case with a freelance trained native speaker of the language(s) involved. The linguist is referred to as 'the supervising linguist' (or simply 'linguist') and the trained native speaker is referred to as 'the analyst'. I will start out by giving a working definition of the 'native speaker' whose expertise is needed in the practice of LADO (par. 2). I will then describe in detail the role of the 'supervising linguist' (par. 3).

I will also present the results of a study examining the validity of language analyses performed in the Dutch context (par. 4). These are cases in which the true identity of the applicants became known after the analyses had been done. The data consist of 124 cases in which analyses for the government were done, and 8 cases (a subset of these 124 cases) in which a counter analysis was submitted to the INS.

Finally (par. 5), I will lay out my criticisms of the 'Guidelines for the Use of Language Analysis in Relation to Questions of National Origin in Refugee Cases' (2004; henceforth referred to as the 'Guidelines').

---

1   As is set out in Baltisberger and Hubbuch (2010, this volume), LINGUA uses linguists specialized in the language as experts (i.e. analysts), but also employs supervising linguists, who test and instruct these linguists. The criticism that is expressed below with regard to the 'Guidelines' and to non-forensic linguists performing LADO therefore does not apply to LINGUA. The description of the method with the trained native speaker and supervising linguist as given below is also specific to the Dutch context.

2   In Dutch: Immigratie- en naturalisatiedienst (IND).

2. The Native Speaker: A Working Definition

The forensic context of LADO implies that we may be dealing with less than fully cooperative speakers, who may be hiding knowledge of a language, presenting a second language as their first language, or adding speech features that do not belong in their natural speech variety. The task involved in LADO therefore differs from linguistic analysis *pur sang*: it is not just about analysing language, but also about judging language (authenticity, grammaticality/acceptability, level of competence, etc.). I have argued in Cambier-Langeveld (2010) that both linguistic expertise and native speaker competence should be involved in LADO, in such a way that the analysis benefits from both the analytical capabilities and theoretical knowledge of the linguist and the experience that the attentive native speaker has with the language (varieties) involved.

I realize that using the term 'native speaker' is begging the question of its definition. In the practice of LADO, a native speaker can be defined as a speaker who has first-hand, extensive and continuous experience with the language area and with other speakers of the language and the relevant varieties, starting from an early age. This definition puts particular focus on the native speaker's lifelong experience with a language in spontaneous settings. It includes what Davies (2004:438) calls a 'native speaker by birth (that is by early childhood exposure)' and a 'native speaker by virtue of being a native user'.

Our definition excludes speakers who have mastered a language either at a later stage in their lives or only through formal schooling. These are referred to by Davies (*ibid.*) as a 'native speaker (or native speaker-like) by being an exceptional learner', a 'native speaker through education in the target language medium' and a 'native speaker through long residence in the adopted country'. I exclude the latter three for present purposes, because it is precisely the ability to judge language that is particularly difficult to acquire for one who acquires his language skills at a later age or solely through formal education in the language: 'The adult non-native speaker can acquire the communicative competence of the native speaker; (…) what is more difficult for the non-native speaker is to gain the speed and the certainty of knowledge relevant to judgments of grammaticality' (Davies 2004:437).

Discussing the reality of the concept of the native speaker who has acquired the language at an early age (i.e., necessarily in the prepuberty years), Davies (2004:433) states: 'A native speaker is also expected to "know" another native speaker, in part because of an intuitive feel, like for like, but also in part because of a characteristic systematic set of indicators, linguistic, pragmatic and paralinguistic, as well as an assumption of shared cultural knowledge'. This matches the concept of the native speaker that I have referred to elsewhere as the native speaker needed in LADO (Cambier-Langeveld 2007; Cambier-Langeveld and Samson 2007, 2008). Of course, it is not quite as simple as this quote suggests: the expectation that native speakers can recognize other native speakers is not always fulfilled (see the literature overview in Fraser 2009), and therefore we cannot rely on such native intuitions without proper evaluation. This is why native speakers must be tested, trained and supervised by a linguist with relevant expertise (details below).

Another related issue is the question what the analyst should be a native speaker of. Experience shows that small so-called tribal languages[3] are rarely encountered in the context of LADO. Identification of such a language can generally be achieved by a linguist, by using a questionnaire including a word list and consulting the literature. In the context of LADO, the more common task is to distinguish between related varieties within cross border languages. An analyst cannot be a native speaker of all varieties within a language. Usually then, the analyst is a native speaker of at least one variety within a particular language (preferably the variety commonly claimed by applicants), and he is familiar with varieties other than – but closely related to – his own. Another common scenario is that the analyst is a native speaker of the suspected language variety rather than the claimed one, when the claimed variety is spoken only by a very small minority group. Again, no *a priori* assumptions can be made here, and predefined limitations would not do justice to the effect that individual backgrounds, training and experience have on a person's ability to analyze language varieties other than his own. A crucial point here is that the analyst's knowledge of the relevant varieties is tested, developed and determined by the supervising linguist. It is the supervising linguist who determines the capabilities and limitations of each individual analyst, which may vary widely and do not follow national or political borders.

3.   The Role of the Supervising Linguist

The Office for Country Information and Language Analysis (In Dutch: *Bureau Land en Taal*, henceforth BLT) of the Dutch INS currently employs four academically trained linguists as 'supervising linguists'. The role of the supervising linguist within BLT's language analysis procedure has been the subject of various misrepresentations and misperceptions. For example, Corcoran (2004:200) refers to BLT as a 'small administrative office' that 'coordinates contracts' with native analysts, while Eades and Arends (2004:190) claim that the only direct involvement of the linguists in the carrying of LADO and the drawing up of analysis reports is 'to approve these reports by initialling them.' Such claims show a lack of acquaintance with the facts, yet claims to the same effect have been made by critics and in the media ever since.

In addition, critics of BLT's method tend to evaluate the expertise of the analyst and the supervising linguist separately, while the strength of the method lies in them working *in tandem* on each case. Finally, the value of individual testing and training by the supervising linguist tends to be overlooked or ignored by the critics.

It has been pointed out by the reviewers that the term 'linguist' covers very different specializations, such as phonetics and phonology, theoretical syntax, applied linguistics and language acquisition, expertise of a specific language, etcetera. The supervising linguists of BLT need to have a thorough linguistic background at an academic level (MA

---

3   'Tribal language' is a convenient short-hand term used within the INS to refer to a language with a relatively small number of speakers, spoken in a limited geographical area, generally only as L1, with most of its speakers also having a competence in a language of wider communication (lingua franca).

or PhD) covering all aspects of linguistics, which is why the general term 'linguist' is appropriate here. Specific expertise is acquired on the job, as described below.

The tasks of the supervising linguists will be described in some detail below.

a)   Recruitment

Language analysis is not offered as a research tool for any language and all regions. The first task of the linguist is to decide whether language analysis has anything useful to offer for a particular area or a particular language. Asylum policies may make distinctions that do or do not match linguistic distinctions. It is up to the linguist to investigate whether the language situation in a given area is such that it offers the possibility to answer relevant questions in an asylum case. Of course, linguistic boundaries are not absolute, and the match does not have to be 100 per cent for language analysis to be useful in at least a large subset of cases.

If it seems possible and useful to offer LADO for a particular language area, the linguist will try to locate candidate analysts. This is not done through publicized selection procedures, but rather through informal channels. In practice, either a candidate contacts BLT on his own initiative, or one of BLT's linguists approaches the candidate. On the basis of this first contact (usually by mail, e-mail or telephone) the linguist decides whether or not a candidate will be invited for an intake.

b)   Intake

At least two linguists are involved in the first stage of the selection procedure. The candidate will be invited for an extensive talk at the INS offices. First, he will be asked to give an account of his life history and his language skills. This will enable the linguists to decide whether he qualifies as a native speaker of a language (or languages). The linguists will also note whether the candidate is able to communicate effectively in a common language (in practice: English or Dutch).

The candidate will then receive concrete information about LADO. The tasks of a language analyst will be outlined and explained, and it will be explained that a language analyst will get further training, and that he will be under continuous scrutiny in the performance of his tasks.

A 'country of origin specialist' from within BLT will be involved in the intake to check whether the candidate analyst has up-to-date knowledge of his country and his region of origin. Questions will be asked on his current contacts and sources.

During the intake talk, the linguists will gain a first impression of the candidate's mental capacities, his level of education and his professional attitude. Already at this stage, some candidate analysts have been rejected. Others may decide for themselves that this work is not for them.

c)   Testing

During the second part of the selection procedure, a candidate analyst will be tested on his ability to differentiate between the relevant language varieties and on their ability to supply verifiable, linguistically relevant information on their language.

First, the candidate will be questioned by a linguist on (socio)linguistic aspects of his language. Then he is asked to listen to, and discuss, several speech samples. The linguist will thus be able to decide whether or not the candidate is a competent and reliable language consultant. Linguists who have consulted native speakers as a part of linguistic fieldwork will confirm that as a linguist, one can tell good consultants from less useful ones by actually discussing their language with them.[4]

As to the speech samples, the candidate analyst will have to draw the correct conclusions in a number of test cases. He must also be able to cite relevant and verifiable linguistic distinctions. It is important that a candidate thus shows his ability to volunteer relevant information as evidence for his conclusions. Some native speakers demonstrate an ability to identify regional varieties correctly, while being unable to apply the analytical approach required from a language analyst. Their ability tends to crumble under the pressure of having to underpin their conclusions with clear, explicit and tenable linguistic evidence. Such native speakers cannot work as language analysts. Some native speakers who have had some prior training in linguistics turn out to be unable to recognize and identify regional varieties correctly. Such native speakers cannot work as language analysts either.

Some native speakers may show themselves to be either overconfident or overcautious; these may be able to work as language analysts, while each needing different kinds of coaching by the supervising linguist.

In order to verify the linguistic information provided by the candidate analyst, the linguist may have at his disposal published sources on the language, information provided by other analysts and by other language analysis bureaus, as well as recordings from a number of different speakers.

Typically, while analyzing one language variety, a good language consultant will cite contrasting examples from related language varieties, illustrating differences in pronunciation, lexicon and grammar (morphology, syntax). It should be possible to confirm these examples by consulting published sources and/or by listening to recordings of these other varieties. A reliable language analyst will also be consistent in his analyses and in the features that they cite as relevant.

d)   Supervision

Once the candidate has shown potential, he will start on his first 'real' language analyses. His work will be continuously supervised by a linguist. In practice this means that the analyst will listen to a recording, record relevant facts in writing and formulate a result. He will then have a face-to-face discussion of the case findings with the linguist at the INS offices.

The most important element of the linguist's supervision is checking whether the cited evidence supports the result, and seeing that the result is formulated clearly and explicitly. A definitive language analysis report will then be drawn up and signed by both the analyst and the linguist. The linguist thus functions as a sort of gatekeeper who

---

4   Cf. Dixon (2010, 1:316): 'One strikes up a relationship with each of a small coterie of intelligent, reliable, interested, and willing language consultants. The consultants will get on "the same wavelength" as the linguist, understanding what the linguist is trying to do (…).'

ensures that the final report can withstand the pressures of a legal procedure that may involve the request of a second opinion by an independent expert.

Supervision may also entail the carrying out of cross-checks, that is, analyses by another analyst or other analysts of the same case. Analysts are informed that such checks are carried out on randomly selected cases, and they are often given feedback afterwards. Such cross-checks are meant to safeguard the quality and objectivity of the analyses and they enable the linguist to further evaluate analysts' abilities and competence.

This continuous supervision and random cross-checking means that analysts, having passed the tests of the selection procedure, will not have leeway in subsequent cases to draw conclusions as they please. Each case is evaluated individually.

Minor elements of the linguist's supervision are ensuring that the reports are written in correct Dutch[5] and checking that the speech samples quoted by the analyst are correctly and consistently transcribed and faithfully represent the samples as heard on the recording.

e) Training

The discussing of language analysis cases may bring to light certain gaps in the analyst's factual or methodological knowledge. The linguist will then provide training to fill these gaps. For instance, the linguist may point out and explain additional useful linguistic distinctions, known to the linguist from other sources, of which the new analyst may not be aware. The linguist may also present the analyst with recordings that are helpful as teaching or training materials, in order to widen the analyst's familiarity with other language varieties than his own native variety.

Almost all analysts need training in the transcribing of speech samples. All analysts working for BLT are literate, but it is often the case that they are not used to transcribing their native language. Also, an analyst may have difficulties with transcribing dialect variants if he is educated in the standardized, literary form of his native language. The linguist may then provide instructions and training.

The analyst will further be instructed by the linguist on potential pitfalls awaiting a lay person, such as those mentioned in the 'Guidelines' and those relevant to forensic analyses. This training is continuous. Both the analyst and the supervising linguist will steadily widen their acquaintance with the language and the language varieties involved as their experience and their sources expand.

f) Assessment

On the basis of his ongoing supervision, the linguist will establish the boundaries of each analyst's expertise and competence. It is thus the supervising linguist who determines which language varieties and/or which language area can be covered by each in-

---

5   All reports issued by BLT are written in Dutch. Reports issued by outside agencies will be added to files in their original language, accompanied by a Dutch translation if not written in Dutch or English.

dividual analyst. In order to gain a more precise insight, the linguist may present 'impossible' cases to the analyst, e.g. border cases; the analyst will then be expected to report to the linguist accordingly.

The expertise of some native speakers covers a large geographical area, while others can only perform analyses for the area in and around their home town. The former is common among native speakers with a varied family background or internal migrants; the latter is particularly common among native speakers who were born and raised in a large urban centre (typically a country's capital city).

On the basis of his assessment of an analyst's abilities, the supervising linguist will determine which analyst can be put on a particular case and whether a second analysis by another analyst is in order. Of course, a language analyst who is uncertain of a case may himself suggest a cross check.

g)   Data Gathering

In order to verify the validity and correctness of linguistic information supplied by the analyst, the linguist will check the existing literature on a language. The linguist will also compare and bring together linguistic information on a particular language area from different angles and from various sources, such as general information from *Ethnologue* and similar sources, country reports, information from other native speakers, information gained directly from experts working in the field, and information provided by counter experts. Finally, the recordings of language analysis interviews, especially of those who are genuine, are an invaluable source of information.

All this information generally provides a consistent picture of the language situation and the relevant linguistic features in a certain area. Each new language analyst is tested and trained accordingly.

h)   Working with Native Speakers

Having each worked extensively with many native speakers for many years, the linguists of BLT have hands-on experience with all sorts of them. Working in fixed pairs allows for an efficient build-up of knowledge and expertise and it also allows linguists to get the best possible idea of an analyst's abilities.

Through discussing language analysis cases, each of the linguists working for BLT has had literally hundreds of hours of direct, face-to-face contact with native speakers of various foreign languages. It may be noted here that few linguists working in academic positions can claim the same. The intensity of contacts with individual analysts ensures that there is very little if any opportunity for analysts to make inflated claims about their competence and ability. Such claims will not survive contacts that may run up to six or more hours a week for months on end.

Apart from passing the tests, analysts are required by the Dutch INS to sign a code of conduct and to obtain a certificate of good conduct (police records check). Any breach of the rules laid down in the code or failure to obtain the certificate will result in termination of an analyst's work for BLT. In addition, analysts working for BLT are not allowed to work as interpreters for the Dutch INS. This is to ensure that analysts are not confronted with recordings of conversations in which they themselves acted as interpreters.

4   Validity of Language Analyses in the Netherlands

In a study by Eades *et al.* (2003), a selection of cases was examined from the Australian Refugee Review Tribunal (RRT), involving language analyses performed by overseas agencies using native speakers as analysts. According to Fraser (2009:115), this examination revealed that the language analyses involved were 'sometimes of shockingly low quality'. It is important to note that whether the conclusions of the reports were actually correct or not has never been determined. It may thus well be the case that they were all perfectly correct. It may also be the case that they were all completely wrong.

This is a well-known problem in forensic science: the accuracy of a research instrument cannot be assessed from actual casework, since the correct outcome of cases is not known. Repeated testing, or testing agreement across several experts, is a measure for consistency and reliability, but not for validity and accuracy. If and when a scientific study is undertaken, it is difficult to replicate forensic conditions.

However, as it happens, a political decision in the Netherlands has resulted in the correct outcome (i.e., the real origin of asylum seekers) becoming known in a number of asylum cases in which LADO had been carried out.

In 2007, the Dutch Parliament granted amnesty to a well-defined group of asylum seekers whose application had originally been turned down. Part of that group was offered the opportunity to inform the INS of their real identity, and they would receive legal status under their real identity even if it were different from the identity they had claimed earlier. As a result, a number of individuals presented the INS with documentary evidence of their true identity and origin. In this set of real cases, the correct outcome has thus become available after the forensic analyses have been done. This offers the unique opportunity to compare the outcome of a number of analyses, carried out in the real forensic context, to the truth, i.e. the correct outcome.

The kind and number of documents underpinning the established identity varies, from birth certificates to passports, school diploma's, driver's licences and more. All cases in which the identity was established afterwards and in which a language analysis had been done, were checked by an experienced decision maker, to see if there was really a basis for assuming the now known (established) identity to be beyond reasonable doubt. This resulted in 124 cases in which the true identity, based on documentary evidence, could be compared to the results of the analyses already performed.

The overall results are presented below. 'Established fact' is derived from the established identity (based on documents) in relation to what was claimed at the time the analyses were done.[6] In Table 1, the overall results of the analyses performed for the Dutch government are given. The government reports were issued by trained native speakers working under the supervision of a linguist.

---

6   Possibilities to re-use the recordings from these cases for a proficiency test for other agencies are being examined. Details on these cases can therefore not be published at this time.

Table 1 - *Results from the government analyses (carried out by trained native speakers supervised by linguists) in 124 cases*

Established fact		Outcome of government analyses	
claimed origin false	110×	claimed origin refuted	109×
		not possible to say	1×
claimed country of origin true, ethnicity false	3×	claimed country of origin confirmed, ethnicity refuted	3×
claimed origin true	11×	claimed origin confirmed	7×
		claimed origin refuted	**4×**
Total	124×		124×

Results not in line with the established identity are printed in bold face.

In Table 2, the results of all counter expert reports available in this set are presented (this subset of eight cases is discussed in detail in Cambier-Langeveld, 2010). These counter expert reports were drawn up by counter experts working on their own.

Table 2 - *Results from counter experts (specialized linguists working on their own) in 8 cases.*

Established fact		Outcome of counter analysis	
claimed origin false	8×	claimed origin not supported	1×
		impossible to determine	2×
		claimed origin very plausible	**1×**
		claimed origin very likely	**1×**
		claimed origin likely	**1×**
		claimed origin 'possible and defendable'	**1×**
		claimed origin confirmed ('there can be hardly any doubt')	**1×**
Total	8×		8×

Results not in line with the established identity are printed in bold face.

4.1 Discussion of Results

Table 1 shows that there are four problematic cases, in which the outcome of the language analysis by the government does not match the established identity. Examination of these four cases, however, reveals that it involves a specific subset: in all four cases, the established identity was assumed to imply an origin from Sierra Leone, yet in all four cases, *the sole basis for the established identity was a birth certificate*. Since LADO is not

TINA CAMBIER-LANGEVELD

suited to determine the place of birth, but rather aims to establish the most likely area of socialization, there could be a valid explanation for the apparent mismatch.

To investigate these cases further, analyses have been ordered from other LADO agencies, using the same recordings (without providing any information on the background of these cases, of course). The analyses returned so far confirm that *the applicants involved could indeed not be traced to the speech community of Sierra Leone.* Two of them can more likely be traced to the speech community of Nigeria, and one of them can more likely be traced to the speech community of Guinea. The results of these four language analyses can thus not be regarded as (necessarily) incorrect, since birth certificates mean nothing in terms of language background, and the results with respect to language background are confirmed by independent analyses.

The same does not apply to the cases that are problematic in Table 2. First of all, the results of the five problematic analyses run counter to the conclusions made by the government analyses, which had already refuted the claimed origin in these same cases. Second, the established identity and implied origin were often based on more convincing documents. For example, in the case where the counter expert states that there can be 'hardly any doubt' that the claimed origin is correct, the actual country of origin (different from the claimed one) was supported by an abundance of documents: passport, legalized birth certificate, marriage licence, identity card, etc. It must be noted, however, that the conclusion of this counter expert was also based on an additional recording which had been made without INS supervision. For more detailed discussion, the reader is referred to Cambier-Langeveld (2010).

It must be noted that these 124 cases are relatively old (mostly < 2003). Most of the analyses were done before the 'Guidelines' were published, and before a commercial company stepped in as intermediary between asylum seekers' representatives on the one hand and counter experts on the other. It is worthwhile however to point out that the kinds of problems encountered in the eight counter expert reports involved (see Cambier-Langeveld 2010) may in the present time be found in reports made by counter experts who have explicitly been selected in accordance with the 'Guidelines'. Similar observations were made with respect to counter expert reports by Norrbom (2010). Note also that the counter experts involved in these eight cases include signatories of the 'Guidelines'.

Please note that the observations above, and the overall impression of LADO reports by linguists which may appear from them, may be influenced negatively by the fact that in the Dutch context, these linguists are retained by legal representatives for the asylum seekers. This means that they are retained to raise questions about the validity of the initial INS report, and may have received certain instructions or information that could lead to a bias. Filling the position of counter expert in asylum cases may also be attractive to certain linguists who have a negative bias toward asylum policies in general and who may see it as their calling to protect the asylum seeker. In other words: the distinction between an objective and impartial counter expert on the one hand, and a witness for the defence on the other may be blurred in some cases.

5.   What is Wrong with the 'Guidelines'

The 'Guidelines' prescribe that LADO must be done by qualified linguists with recognized and up-to-date expertise both in linguistics and in the language in question. However, there is no scientific study which supports the notion that such specialized linguists perform better than (carefully selected and supervised) native speakers when it comes to the determination of speaker origin. The 'Guidelines' suggest that governments should always give specialized linguists precedence over native speaker analysts, while the data presented here suggest that the opposite may be true under certain conditions, e.g. as conditions are in the Netherlands.

In a recent study by Wilson (2009), a direct comparison of native speakers and trained linguists in their ability to recognize Ghanaian English was made. While the conditions of her study may not allow for the results to speak directly to the present debate, the results of this study do lead Wilson to make the following comment concerning the 'Guidelines':

> …due to the history of LADO there are strong reasons why these guidelines were created and are being supported. Nevertheless, perhaps thorough, direct training methods and natural skill or talent for such analysis should be given emphasis over academic qualifications and how many papers one has published. (Wilson 2009:24)

The 'Guidelines' can be seen as supporting only the 'trained linguist = the analyst' methodology, thereby singling out one possible approach to LADO as if it were the only existing, acceptable option. The authors of the 'Guidelines' do not seem to have considered the possibility of having the linguist in the role of supervising linguist, as described above. Furthermore, they do not recognize the relevance of the expertise of native speakers, nor do they mention the forensic nature of LADO. These are the main reasons why the *Working Group on Language Identification* of the IAFPA proposed a Resolution to be placed on the IAFPA's website, which explicitly accepts two existing approaches (see Moosmüller 2010, this volume).

The final version of the IAFPA Resolution also points out that 'individual competences and experience affect the quality of the analyses, regardless of the method. Specific training and testing is therefore recommended.' This statement was recently corroborated in a study by Masthoff et al. (2010). In a dialect identification task, 15 German experts on forensic analysis of speech were asked to assign 20 different speakers of German to 14 specified dialectal areas, using any method they deemed fit. Methods employed included acoustic analysis, consultation of databases, consultation of the literature and perceptual analysis. The results showed that the performance predominantly depends on the individual (innate or trained) skills of the expert, rather than on the methodology or the procedures followed. The logical consequence is that such skills need to be established individually, through a process of testing, before one can rely on them.

6. Conclusion

The data presented show that trained native speakers working under the supervision of a linguist may yield good results in LADO. The data also reveal that specialized linguists, some of whom are signatories of the 'Guidelines', have given demonstrably incorrect conclusions. In all, this shows that the idea of a strictly analytical approach (performed by a linguist, without the judgment of a native speaker) being a more scientific and therefore superior method is untenable. Instead, the quality of the analyses depends more on individual skills, which can be tested and further developed, e.g. by supervising linguists.

BLT has developed an effective working method that not only combines linguistic expertise with the language competence of a native speaker, but also allows for testing, training, and developing expertise. I have described this method in detail. We believe this method ensures correct results to the best of our ability given the current state of scientific knowledge.

References

Baltisberger, E. & P. Hubbuch (2010) LADO with specialized linguists - the development of LINGUA's working method (this volume)

Cambier-Langeveld, T. (2007) *Hot issues in the field of "Language Analysis"*, IAFPA 16th Annual Conference, Plymouth, UK, 22-25 July 2007.

Cambier-Langeveld, T. (2010) The role of linguists and native speakers in language analysis for the determination of speaker origin, *International Journal of Speech, Language and the Law*, 17(1), p. 67-93.

Cambier-Langeveld, T. & A.-M. Samson (2007) *Language analysis: how to include both linguistic expertise and native competence, and why*, Workshop on Language Analysis in the determination of national origin of refugees, Amsterdam, the Netherlands, 21 June 2007.

Cambier-Langeveld, T. & A.M. Samson (2008) *Language analysis by the Dutch Immigration and Naturalization Service (IND)*, Presentation at Amsterdam Centre for Language and Communication, Faculty of Humanities, University of Amsterdam, the Netherlands, 8 February 2008.

Corcoran, C. (2004) A critical examination of the use of language analysis interviews in asylum proceedings: a case study of a West African seeking asylum in the Netherlands, *International Journal of Speech, Language and the Law*, 11(2), p. 200-221.

Davies, A. (2004) The native speaker in applied linguistics, n A. Davies & C. Elder (eds), *The Handbook of Applied Linguistics*, New York: Blackwell, p. 431-450.

Dixon, R.M.W. (2010) *Basic Linguistic Theory*. Vols 1-2, Oxford: Oxford University Press.

Eades, D. & Arends, J. (2004). Using language analysis in the determination of national origin of asylum seekers: an introduction, *International Journal of Speech, Language and the Law*, 11(2), p. 179-199.

Eades, D., H. Fraser, J. Siegel, T. McNamara & B. Baker (2003) Linguistic identification in the determination of nationality: A preliminary report, *Language Policy*, 2(2), p. 179-199.

Fraser, H. (2009) The role of 'educated native speakers' in providing language analysis for the determination of the origin of asylum seekers, *International Journal of Speech, Language and the Law* 16(1), p. 113-138.

Language and National Origin Group (2004) Guidelines for the use of language analysis in relation to questions of national origin in refugee cases, *International Journal of Speech, Language and the Law*, 11(2), p. 261-266.

Masthoff, K., Y.H. Boubaker & O. Köster (2010) *The tell-tale dialect: Analysis of dialectal variation of German native speakers in telephone conversations*, IAFPA 19th Annual Conference, Trier, Germany, 18-21 July 2010.

Moosmüller, S. (2010) IAFPA Position on Language Analysis in asylum procedures (this volume)

Norrbom, T. (2010) *Issues in counter reports directed at language analysis reports*, Gothenburg Workshop on Language Analysis, Gothenburg, Sweden, 22 November 2010.

Wilson, K. (2009) *Language analysis for the determination of origin: native speakers vs. trained linguists*, MSc dissertation, University of York.

Guidelines from Linguists for LADO

Diana Eades

1.   Introduction

In June 2004, a group of 19 linguists from 6 countries released a 2000 word document entitled Guidelines for the Use of Language Analysis in Relation to Questions of National Origin in Refugee Cases (hereafter "the Guidelines"). This paper aims to explain the origin and motivation, development, authorship and content of these Guidelines, as well as their scholarly and judicial status.

2.   Origin and Motivation

The idea for the Guidelines arose during discussion in a colloquium session convened by the now late Dr Jacques Arends from Universiteit Amsterdam at the August 2003 conference of the international Society for Pidgin and Creole Linguistics (SPCL), held in Honolulu, USA. In this colloquium, titled '"Language analysis" in assessing asylum applications of speakers of pidgins/creoles', linguists from a number of countries discussed and exemplified concerns about linguistic inadequacies in the use of language analysis in the determination of the origin of asylum seekers (referred to as LADO). Many of the linguists' specific concerns and experiences related to speakers of pidgin and creole languages in West Africa – hence the session in the pidgin and creole conference. Papers were presented by Jacques Arends (focused on West African asylum seekers in the Netherlands), Chris Corcoran (a case study of a Sierra Leonean asylum seeker in the Netherlands), and John Singler (based on his work with Liberian asylum seekers in Switzerland). I was invited to be discussant at this session, because I was at that time working at the University of Hawai'i, where the conference was being held, and because of my relevant work with four other Australian colleagues. This Australian work had involved examining decisions of 58 Australian appeals in the Refugee Review Tribunal in cases in which LADO reports had been used. Many of these published Tribunal decisions included excerpts from the LADO reports, with some decisions quoting the full report. Our resulting report, presented to the Australian government, was titled 'Linguistic identification in the determination of nationality: A preliminary report'. This report – later published in the international journal *Language Policy* (Eades et al 2003) – concluded (p. 179) that the 'language analysis' being used in Australian asylum seeker cases at that time appeared 'to be based on "folk views" about the relationship between language and nationality and ethnicity, rather than sound linguistic principles'. (Note that the Australian cases did not involve pidgin or creole languages. For reasons of geography and politics, most LADO cases in Australia at that time involved asylum seekers claiming to be from Afghanistan, and the main language variety involved was Hazargi Dari.)

The SPCL conference colloquium decided to produce guidelines about the ways in which linguistic analysis can shed light on questions of speakers' origins, and about limits to the ways in which it can be used. The aim was to bring relevant linguistic issues to the awareness of governments, legal professionals and refugee advocates. There was also concern that some people with some linguistics background/training might be making naïve analyses, without a consideration of the sociolinguistic complexities involved in linking speech patterns to ways of talking. So it was also hoped that the Guidelines would provide some specific guidance to linguists asked to do LADO reports, who may not have considered these issues carefully.

3. Development and Authorship

To develop the Guidelines, a group of about 20 linguists engaged in lengthy email deliberations over a 10-month period (in 2003/2004), primarily about how best to explain relevant linguistic issues to non-linguists. This email discussion group had no organisational affiliation or basis. Despite later complaints that the email group had been an IAFL (International Association of Forensic Linguists) activity, there was no connection. In fact, only 2 of the 19 signatories were IAFL members or came to IAFL conferences at that time. Nor was there any affiliation with SPCL, although I believe that 5 of the signatories were members of this organisation.

The resulting Guidelines document was authored by 19 signatories from 6 countries, whose collective name is Language and National Origin Group (hereafter LNOG). The names and affiliations of all signatories is provided at the end of the Guidelines. About half the members of LNOG already had direct LADO experience, either in producing reports for immigration departments, or in responding to such reports as experts providing counter-analysis. The other members had academic expertise relevant to the linguistic issues involved. The group includes people who at that time were full professors of linguistics from universities in Australia, Belgium, Sweden, the United Kingdom and the United States. It also includes scholars whose work on language analysis in relation to asylum seekers has been published in several leading international refereed linguistics and anthropology journals (see Blommaert 2009, Corcoran 2004, Eades 2005, 2009, 2010, Eades and Arends 2004, Eades et al 2003, Fraser 2009, Jacquemet 2005, 2009, Maryns 2004, Singler 2004).

4. Content

The Guidelines document comprises 7 general guidelines and 4 specific ones. The former address the general limitations of linguistic expertise, for example explaining that linguists should not be asked to make determinations about national origin, nationality or citizenship (Guidelines #1 and #2). Rather, linguistic analysis can sometimes be used to draw reasonable conclusions about the country of socialisation of a speaker – that is where the speaker has learned, implicitly and/or explicitly, how to be a member of a local society, or of local societies. And there is no necessary connection between a person's region of socialisation on the one hand and the political or bureaucratic categories of national origin, nationality or citizenship, on the other hand. However, sometimes the indications about a person's region of socialisation which are revealed in the linguistic analysis of that person's speech may assist immigration departments in their determination of the political or bureaucratic dimensions. Another issue addressed by the general guidelines concerns the qualifications and expertise required to carry out LADO. Guideline #3 states that "language analysis must be done by qualified linguists", and Guideline #7 explains that "the expertise of native speakers is not the same as the expertise of linguists".

The remaining 3 general guidelines address what can be expected of linguists in providing an expert opinion about LADO, namely

- linguists having the right and responsibility to qualify the certainty of their assessments, but not in quantitative terms (Guideline #4),
- the need for linguists to determine what kind of data is required to perform the analysis, and to refuse to do such analysis where the data is insufficiently useful or reliable, e.g. where the recording is of poor audio quality or insufficient duration (Guideline #5), and
- the need for linguists to provide specific evidence of professional training an expertise, with the right to require that this information remain confidential (Guideline #6).

The full Guidelines appear as an annex to this book and there is discussion of them in Eades (2005, 2009, 2010). The more specific guidelines (#8-#11) provide basic linguistic guidance on four topics:

#8) the relationships between linguistic borders and national borders
#9) language mixing
#10) where the language of the interview is not the speaker's first language
#11) where the dialect of the interviewer or interpreter is different from the dialect of the interviewee.

Much of what is contained in the Guidelines is at the level of introductory linguistics.

5.   Professional Endorsements

The Guidelines have been widely circulated to governments, lawyers, refugee advocacy groups, and linguistic organizations. They have been endorsed by a number of professional linguistic organizations, including Algemene Vereniging voor Taalwetenschaap (Netherlands Society for General Linguistics), the American Association for Applied Linguistics, the Applied Linguistics Association of Australia, the Association Internationale de Dialectologie Arabe, the Australian Linguistics Society, the British Association of Applied Linguistics, the International Association of Forensic Linguists, the Linguistics Association of Great Britain, De Nederlandse Vereniging voor Toegepaste Taalwetenschaap (Netherlands Association of Applied Linguistics) and the Society of Pidgin and Creole Linguistics. They have also appeared in several publications which deal with refugee issues, including the Journaal Vreemdelingenrecht (Journal for Aliens'

Law) in the Netherlands, and Asylmagazin (Asylum Magazine) in Germany, as well as two important linguistics journals: Applied Linguistics (Vol 26 No 4, 2005), International Journal of Speech, Language and the Law (Vol 11 No 2, 2004).

6. Criticisms

Criticism of the guidelines has come from two sources that I am aware of: a handful of scholars, some of whom are employed to do LADO, and one ruling of a lower court in the Netherlands.

Cambier-Langeveld (2010) has criticised the Guidelines' insistence (in Guidelines #3 and #7) that native speakers without linguistic training are not qualified to do LADO. She argues that there is a failure to 'recognise that both types of expertise (trained linguists and native speakers) are relevant and should be included in LADO' (p. 71). She is also concerned about the failure of the Guidelines 'to recognise that academic linguists, specialized in the language varieties involved, are not *by definition* capable of making accurate judgments about the regional origin of speakers either...' (p. 71). Recent discussions at several conferences and workshops have also highlighted the contested nature of the claim in Guideline #3 that 'language analysis must be done by qualified linguists'. This aspect of the Guidelines was uncontroversial among the 19 signatories, so members of the Language and National Origin group which authored the Guidelines have been somewhat surprised by the strength of the objection from LADO practitioners with linguistic training to this position. The current argument related to this point appears to revolve around the expertise needed to make the judgment about whether the language spoken by the applicant is consistent with the claims being made about the applicant's origin. On the one hand, the Guidelines argue that such a judgment cannot be made by anyone without relevant linguistic training, regardless of whether or not they are a native speaker of the relevant language variety (see also Eades 2009, Fraser 2009). On the other hand, Cambier-Langeveld (2010: 85) and others (not yet published) argue that this judgment can be made by 'a trained native speaker ... under the tight supervision of a linguist' (who is unlikely to know the language variety in question).

The only judicial criticism of the Guidelines that I am aware of has come from a recent (November 2009) ruling from the civil court in the Hague that the Guidelines are 'not independent since it appears that the director of De Taalstudio (dr. M. Verrips) is part of the Language and National Origin Group'. I cannot agree with the Hague civil court ruling, and I think it is important to point out that:

- the Language and National Origin Group who authored the statement comprised 19 scholars, and this group included linguists who had performed language analysis on behalf of immigration departments; and
- it is common for scholars to use their expertise in two different applied ways: sometimes in providing expertise to governments or courts on a specific matter or case, and at other times to produce guidelines, handbooks, or reports which outline research findings generally. Just because a scholar is engaged in both such applications of scholarly work is no indication of lack of independence.

7.   Judicial Attention

The Guidelines were referred to in a 20 September 2007 judgment of the Council of State of the Netherlands (the highest appeal court for government decisions, including asylum applications) in a case in which the Dutch immigration authority had objected that the contra-expert had not worked under supervision comparable with that carried out by the government's experts. In dismissing this objection, the judgment referred to the fact that the contra-expert had been selected according to the Guidelines and had worked in accordance with them. As such, the Council ruled, "[these] data [including the qualifications of the contra-expert listed in the contra-expertise] can be verified and do not provide any basis for the opinion that the author of the contra-expertise is not independent. [. . .] The contra-expertise must therefore be regarded as an expert counter-opinion [. . .]" (Maaike Verrips, pers. comm., 7 July 2008). This Council of State judgment did not find any problem with the independence of the Language and National Origin Group who authored the Guidelines.

In Australia, linguists' concerns about LADO have been referred to by decision-makers at the level of tribunals and appeal courts, both directly (e.g., RRT, 2004; Federal Magistrates Court of Australia, 2003) and indirectly (e.g., Federal Court of Australia, 2005). It is worth mentioning here that the use of LADO has been greatly reduced in Australia in the past three or four years. While this may be partly related to the awareness raised by linguists about the problems involved in LADO work, political and demographic factors have undoubtedly played the major role.

8.   Conclusion

In looking at the current situation regarding the Guidelines, I think it is fair to say that:
-    most of the basic information in the Guidelines about investigation of the relationship between the speech of asylum speakers and their claimed origins is at an introductory level of linguistics and remains uncontroversial among linguists
-    the surprisingly controversial area is the role of native speakers without linguistic training in making judgments about the claimed origins of asylum seekers
-    many linguistic issues involved in LADO are in need of research and clarification – e.g. to what extent can origin be verified on the basis of analysis of a person's second (or third etc) language? how can LADO work in increasingly frequent cases of individual and societal multilingualism intersecting with deterritorialised language practices, which as Jacquemet (2005: 273) points out, present a problem for our "taken-for granted, common-sensical knowledge of what is a 'language' (see also Jacquemet 2009, Blommaert 2009).

I hope that the basic work begun in the Guidelines can be developed, while at the same time carefully designed research projects can shed more light on some of these central and complex questions about the relationship between language and origin. The newly established Language and Asylum Research Group was set up to facilitate and support such research and further discussion.

References

Blommaert, Jan (2009) Language, asylum, and the national order, *Current Anthropology*, 50(4), p. 415-425.

Cambier-Langeveld, Tina (2010) The role of linguists and native speakers in language analysis for the determination of speaker origin, *International Journal of Speech, Language and the Law*, 17(1), p. 67-94.

Corcoran, Chris (2004) A critical examination of the use of language analysis interviews in asylum proceedings: a case study of a West African seeking asylum in the Netherlands, *International Journal of Speech, Language and the Law*, 11(2), p. 200-221.

Eades, Diana (2005) Applied linguistics and language analysis in asylum seeker cases, *Applied Linguistics*, 26(4), p. 503-526.

Eades, Diana (2009) Testing the claims of asylum seekers: The role of language analysis, *Language Assessment Quarterly*, 6(1), p. 30-40.

Eades, Diana (2010) Language analysis and asylum cases, in: Malcolm Coulthard & Alison Johnson (eds), *The Routledge Handbook of Forensic Linguistics*, London: Routledge, p. 411-422.

Eades, Diana & Jacques Arends (2004) Using language analysis in the determination of national origin of asylum seekers: An introduction, *International Journal of Speech, Language and the Law*, 11(2), p. 179-199.

Eades, Diana, Helen Fraser, Jeff Siegel, Tim McNamara & Brett Baker (2003) Linguistic identification in the determination of nationality: A preliminary report, *Language Policy*, 2(2), p. 179-199.

Fraser, Helen (2009) The role of 'educated native speakers' in providing language analysis for the determination of the origin of asylum seekers, *International Journal of Speech Language and the Law*, 16(1), p. 113-138.

Jacquemet, Marco (2005) Transidiomatic practices: Language and power in the age of globalization, *Language and Communication*, 25, p. 257-277.

Jacquemet, Marco (2009) Transcribing refugees: The entextualization of asylum seekers' hearings in a transidiomatic environment, *Text and Talk*, 29(5), p. 525-546.

Language and National Origin Group (2004) Guidelines for the use of language analysis in relation to questions of national origin in refugee cases, *International Journal of Speech, Language and the Law*, 11(2), p. 261-266.

Maryns, Katrijn (2004) Identifying the asylum speaker: reflections on the pitfalls of language analysis in the determination of national origin, *International Journal of Speech Language and the Law*, 11(2), p. 240-60.

Maryns, K. (2006) *The Asylum Speaker: Language in the Belgian Asylum Procedure*, Manchester, UK: St Jerome Press.

Refugee Review Tribunal, Australia (RRT) (2004) *N04/48762, Decision and reasons for decision*, retrieved 19th March 2008 from http://www.austlii.edu.au/au/cases/cth/rrt/2004/701.html.

Federal Court of Australia (FCA) (2005) *M17/2004 v Minister for IMIA* [2005] FCA 86, retrieved 17 Sept 2005 from http://www.austlii.edu.au/au/cases/cth/federal_ct/2005/86.html.

Federal Magistrates Court of Australia (FMCA), *WAIO v Minister for Immigration 2003, FMCA 114*, retrieved 5 September 2005 from http://www.austlii.edu.au/au/cases/cth/FMCA/2003/114.html.

Singler, John V. (2004) The 'linguistic' asylum interview and the linguist's evaluation of it, with special reference to applicants for Liberian political asylum in Switzerland. *International Journal of Speech, Language and the Law*, 11(2), p. 222-239.

IAFPA Position on Language Analysis in Asylum Procedures

*Sylvia Moosmüller**

IAFPA

The International Association for Forensic Phonetics and Acoustics (IAFPA) currently encompasses approximately 100 members. Its aims are to foster research and provide a forum for the interchange of ideas and information on practice, development and research in forensic phonetics and acoustics and to set down and enforce standards of professional conduct and procedure for those involved in forensic phonetic and acoustic casework (see http://www.iafpa.net/const.htm).

Preliminary Considerations

Language Analysis in asylum procedures constitutes a relatively new field in forensic linguistics and phonetics. Cambier-Langeveld (2010) estimates that language analysis has been utilized in asylum procedures for well over ten years now. As Cambier-Langeveld (2010) points out, the analyses to be performed in the context of asylum applications encompass two tasks:
a) to determine the region where the person was socialized (classification task),
b) to examine the applicant's declaration regarding his or her claimed origin (verification task).

In a usual asylum application procedure, the main interest of the administration lies in an answer to the question whether or not the claimed origin of the applicant corresponds with the actual origin of the applicant. Therefore, language analysis in the context of asylum procedures focuses primarily on task b) (see also discussion of Case 7 in Cambier-Langeveld 2010: 80f). Language analysis performed in the context of repatriation, on the other hand, may focus primarily on task a).

Though similar, these two tasks have to be kept apart, both from a terminological and from an analytical point of view. From a terminological point of view, task b) should be rather termed 'Language analysis for the examination of claimed origin (LAECO)', whereas task a) might well be termed LADO (Language analysis for the determination of origin), an acronym that is widely used in the literature. Analytically, it

* I am grateful to Angelika Braun and Tina Cambier-Langeveld for their helpful comments. The resolution printed in this text reflects IAFPA's official view and is also published on IAFPA's website. Since I fully back the resolution, it was my intention to write the text in the spirit of this resolution; however, it has to be considered that the wording is mine.

makes a difference whether one has to determine the region where a person was socialized or whether one has to establish if a person is competent in a variety or in varieties spoken in a specified region. This difference might also entail methodological consequences.

Short Historical Outline

In 2004, the Language and National Origin Group published 'Guidelines for the use of language analysis in relation to questions of national origin in refugee cases' in a special issue on 'Language analysis and determination of nationality' in the International Journal of Speech, Language and the Law, guest edited by Diana Eades and Jacques Arends. The introductory part states that 'such analysis usually involves consideration of a recording of the asylum seeker's speech in order to judge their country of origin' (p. 261); i.e., the focus of the Language and National Origin Group seems to be on task a), not on task b).

Although the 'Guidelines' are meant to 'assist governments to assess the general validity of language analysis...' (p.261), especially general guideline 3 which reads that 'language analysis must be done by qualified linguists' (p. 262) caused a dispute over scientific approach.[1]

In 2006, at the Annual General Meeting of IAFPA in Gothenburg, Tina Cambier-Langeveld presented the field to the members present. IAFPA members felt that this field has points of contact with forensic phonetics because

- IAFPA has members involved in language analysis in asylum procedures,
- this sort of analysis includes phonetic analysis,
- speaker profiling and working on forensic speech materials in foreign languages may include task a),
- language analysis in asylum procedures is a potentially forensic topic.

Tina Cambier-Langeveld was assigned to prepare a statement to be discussed at the next conference.

In 2007, at the Annual IAFPA meeting in Plymouth, a representative of De Taalstudio (The Netherlands) and some members of IAFPA discussed whether there is reason to state that in addition to linguistic expertise (as stressed in the 'Guidelines'), it should also be compulsory to consult a native speaker of the language or variety under investigation. This discussion brought no unanimity, since views on this lacked empirical evidence. On the other hand, it became apparent that there was no empirical basis for excluding the approach in which a native speaker works under the supervision of a linguist either. The Language and National Origin Group does not explicitly mention this possibility and therefore shows no signs of having investigated its merits. This is why the following interim resolution was worded and accepted by the membership:

---

1 Further drawbacks of the 'Guidelines' published in 2004 are discussed in Eriksson (2008) and Cambier-Langeveld (2010). For a justification of the 'Guidelines' see Fraser (2009) and Eades (2009, this volume).

'In cases involving the analysis of language and speech for the determination of national identity IAFPA recognises the contribution to be made by:
1. Linguists and educated native speakers with the latter working under the guidance and supervision of the former;
2. Linguists with in-depth research knowledge of the language(s) in question.

The conclusion expressed should in all cases reflect not only the strengths and weaknesses of the material analysed but also of the personnel involved.'

In order to finalize the Resolution, members present at the Annual General Meeting felt they needed more information on the topic, which is why a working group was installed. The working group consisted of four members of IAFPA:
- Tina Cambier-Langeveld (Chair)
- Anders Eriksson
- Sylvia Moosmüller
- Linda Shockey

The Working Group was established to investigate standards and procedures in cases involving the analysis of language and speech in asylum applications. The WG decided to invite interested parties (practitioners, academics, critics; IAFPA members and non-IAFPA members) to become a consultant for the WG. The list consisted of 17 members (companies and private persons) from 10 different countries, including all companies/organizations working for governments.

The WG decided to run a survey in which questions were asked on current practice, methodology, the expertise involved, the reports, quality control and research. All institutions who are actively practicing language analysis in asylum procedures (from the Netherlands, Switzerland, Sweden, Belgium, and Germany) took part in the survey.

On 2-3 April 2008, a meeting was held in Leiden (the Netherlands), where the members of the WG exchanged views and ideas with a number of practitioners from the Netherlands, Sweden and Switzerland. At this meeting, a preliminary set of 'minimal requirements' was collected for the linguist + native speaker approach and for the linguist without native speaker approach.

In 2008, at the AGM meeting in Lausanne, the WG presented a revised version of the interim position. At that time, however, part of the membership felt they had insufficient background information to vote on it. Therefore, the WG was appointed for another year and took this opportunity to inform the members.

In 2009, at the AGM meeting in Cambridge, the revised version of the interim position was put to vote. Of the 30 members present, 20 voted in favor, 0 against, and 6 abstained. The resolution was put on the IAFPA website. In addition to the earlier point addressed, the WG felt it was important to stress that it involves a form of forensic analysis, and thus requires special skills and competence. It reads as follows:

'In cases involving the analysis of language and speech for the determination of national identity IAFPA recognizes the contribution to be made by:

1. Linguists and trained[2] native speakers with the latter working under the guidance and supervision of the former;
2. Linguists with in-depth research knowledge of the language(s) in question.

It is not a valid assumption that a native speaker, linguist or specialized linguist is by definition also a qualified analyst, capable of performing the type of analysis referred to here. Language analysis is a form of forensic analysis that requires additional skills and competence. Individual competences and experience affect the quality of the analyses, regardless of the method. Specific training and testing is therefore recommended.

The conclusion expressed should in all cases reflect not only the strengths and weaknesses of the material analysed but also of the personnel involved.'

Since the task of the working group to finalize the interim resolution set up at the AGM in Plymouth was now fulfilled, the working group was dissolved.

Conclusion

Up to date, there is no scientific reason to prefer one approach over the other. The literature overview given by Fraser (2009) bears only on assignment abilities by native speakers without special training and supervision by a linguist. The fact that native speakers vary in their ability to recognize accents can only serve to confirm that testing of individual competences is necessary. Fraser provides no evidence that suggests that linguists are better judges of speaker origin than native speakers. Moreover, this overview bears only on task a), whose requirements are different from task b). Therefore, the question whether one approach gains advantage over the other cannot be answered with conventional linguistic tools, whose main purpose lies not in the forensic application.

References

Cambier-Langeveld, Tina (2010) The role of linguists and native speakers in language analysis for the determination of a speaker's origin, *International Journal of Speech, Language and the Law* 17 (1), p. 67-93.

Eades, D. (2009) Testing the Claims of Asylum Seekers: The Role of Language Analysis, *Language Assessment Quarterly* 6, p. 30-40.

Eades, D. (2010) Guidelines from linguists for LADO, in Karin Zwaan, Pieter Muysken and Maaike Verrips (eds), *Language and origin: The role of language in European asylum procedures: Linguistic and legal perspectives*, Nijmegen: WLP 2010.

---

2 'Educated native speaker' has been changed into 'trained native speaker', firstly because 'educated', referring to the level of previous education, is a term that is hard to handle, especially for the geographic areas concerned, and secondly because 'trained' implies a more crucial characteristic of the native speaker, which is the specific training by the supervising linguist for the task at hand.

Eriksson, A. (2008) *Guidelines, what guidelines?*, IAFPA 17th Annual Conference, Lausanne, Switzerland, 20-23 July 2008.

Fraser, H. (2009) The role of 'educated native speakers' in providing language analysis for the determination of the origin of asylum seekers, *International Journal of Speech, Language and the Law* 16(1), p. 113-138.

Language and National Origin Group (2004) Guidelines for the use of language analysis in relation to questions of national origin in refugee cases, *International Journal of Speech, Language and the Law*, 11(2), p. 261-266.

Part Two: LADO and the Study of Language

Part Two starts with a paper by *Ton Broeders*, who brings the perspective of forensic science to bear on the issues, stressing that a state-of-the-art logical formulation of conclusions requires that the forensic expert compares the likelihood of the evidence on the basis of Hypothesis A with the likelihood of the evidence given hypothesis B. The paper by *Tim McNamara, Maaike Verrips and Carolien van den Hazelkamp* stresses the similarities between LADO and other types of language testing and proposes a research agenda for LADO based on decades of language testing research. *Peter Patrick* then introduces the reader to the study of Language Variation and its implications for LADO. Similarly, *Pieter Muysken* introduces the reader to the field of Multilingualism. *Dirk Van Compernolle* presents recently delveloped speech recognition technology, and considers its potential for LADO. Van Compernolle concludes that, though it is possible in principle to establish the dialectal origin of speakers with speech recognition software, a great many technical conditions have to be fulfilled, which makes the technique less useful at present for LADO.

Decision Making in LADO – A View from the Forensic Arena

A.P.A. Broeders

Introduction

The use of language analysis to determine the national origin of asylum seekers (LADO) may be viewed as a legitimate forensic application of linguistics. In recent years, forensic scientists generally have become increasingly aware of the logical problems involved in answering the questions they have traditionally been asked to address. The advent of DNA analysis and the interpretation model associated with it has been particularly instrumental in this. Unlike experts working in traditional fields like fingerprint examination, DNA experts typically refuse to address the hypothesis of common origin of source and reference material. Rather than making source attribution statements, they will not directly pronounce upon the question of the origin of the trace material but will phrase their conclusions in terms of the relative probability of the evidence obtained given two mutually exclusive hypotheses. It is suggested that a similar interpretative model may be used in language analysis undertaken as part of the procedure to deal with requests for political asylum. The analyst should seek to determine the probability of the linguistic evidence under two competing hypotheses of origin rather than pronounce directly upon the probability of the claimed origin given the linguistic evidence.

Language Analysis in Asylum Procedures

Language analysis is used in various European countries as part of the decision making process in granting requests for political asylum. In the Netherlands, asylum seekers who are unable to convince the authorities of their claimed nationality by means of official documents such as passports or other forms of evidence that are deemed sufficiently reliable are given the opportunity to support their claimed origin by linguistic evidence obtained from an interview with the asylum applicant conducted in the language (variant) the applicant claims to be a native speaker of.[1] While there is considerable controversy over the way in which linguistic evidence may be elicited, examined and weighed in this context and over the role of native speakers as experts in the assessment of the linguistic evidence, there seems to be consensus among linguists over the way the conclusions to which the findings of the linguistic examination lead, should

---

1 Cambier-Langeveld (2010). For a critical appraisal of LADO see Fraser (2009) and Detailleur (2010).

51

be reported. This is somewhat surprising in view of recent developments in the interpretation of forensic evidence, and the role of the expert as opposed to the decision
maker in the forensic arena.

The Linguist's Degree of Certainty

In 2004 a group of linguists published a set of 'Guidelines for the use of language analysis in relation to questions of national origin in refugee cases'.[2] Section 4 of these guidelines, headed 'Linguists' degree of certainty', addresses the question of what the linguist
may or may not conclude on the basis of his examination. It contains the following passage: 'Linguists should have the right and responsibility to qualify the certainty of their
assessments, even about the country of socialization. It should be noted that it is rarely
possible to be 100 per cent certain of conclusions based on linguistic evidence alone (as
opposed to fingerprint or DNA evidence), so linguistic evidence should always be used
in conjunction with other (non-linguistic) evidence. Further, linguists should not be
asked to, and should not be willing to, express their certainty in quantitative terms (e.g.
'95 per cent certain that person X was socialized in country Y'), but rather in qualitative terms, such as 'based on the linguistic evidence, it is possible, likely, highly likely,
highly unlikely that person X was socialized in country Y'. This is because this kind of
language analysis does not lend itself to quantitative statistics such as are often found in
some others kinds of scientific evidence.'[3]

While there is no doubt about the well-intentioned nature of these words in this
passage, it would appear to be based on mistaken notions of the way in which the
weight of fingerprint and DNA evidence or even expert evidence in general may be
determined. A brief discussion of the state of play in the forensic arena may therefore be
in order here to inform subsequent discussion of these issues with respect to LADO.

Individualization versus Classification

Within the forensic sciences, several criminalistic processes may be distinguished. Two
of these are individualization and classification.[4] The purpose of individualization is to
determine the unique source of a trace, that of classification to determine whether a
particular trace can be assigned to a group of similar objects. Both dactyloscopy (fingerprint examination) and DNA-typing are processes aimed at individualization. In dactyloscopy, the purpose of the exercise is to find (the finger of) the individual that left the

---

2   Language and National Origin Group (2004).
3   Language and National Origin Group (2004: 262-263).
4   Other processes, following Inman & Rudin (2002), are: identification ('What substance is this?'),
     quantification ('What is the concentration/weight of the substance?'), association ('Is the sub-
     stance/trace crime-related?') and reconstruction (The construction of a time line: 'What criminal
     events took place in what order, at what time and where?').

finger trace at the crime scene; the purpose of DNA-analysis is to find the single individual who is the donor of the cell material left at the crime scene.[5]

Language analysis undertaken for the determination of national origin (LADO) clearly differs from both fingerprint and DNA-analysis in that it is not a form of individualization but essentially a classification process: the purpose of the exercise is to determine whether the speaker belongs to a group of speakers, more specifically – usually – the group of speakers in which he was socialized and learnt to speak his first language. Examples of classification processes in forensic science are the (sub)classification of fibres into man-made fibres and natural fibres, the (sub)classification of blood into human versus animal blood, the (sub)classification of firearms in terms of make and calibre, of paint in terms of colour and composition, or of shoes in terms of make, size, model, sole pattern etc. it is therefore the process of forensic classification rather than that of individualization that is relevant to a discussion of decision making in LADO.

Categorical Conclusions

Although fingerprint evidence continues to be presented as categorical (and infallible), there is no logical basis for this practice.[6] It has its basis in the so-called 'positivity doctrine', according to which fingerprint experts or dactyloscopists will report only categorical yes/no-decisions. However, fingerprint experts differ from almost all other forensic science practitioners in this self-imposed obligation to report absolute identifications and eliminations only.[7] Qualified conclusions, such as 'possible' or 'probable', are not allowed under penalty of decertification by the International Association for Identification (IAI), whose membership comprises, in the main, North American fingerprint experts.

The essence of the individualization problem lies in the fact that it is an essentially inductive process. Logically speaking, we can only arrive at a conclusion of common origin of a finger mark and a reference fingerprint if we can exclude all other sources, and that is impossible. The population from which a finger mark originates is typically indefinite in size and frequently largely unavailable for examination. The best we can do, therefore, is to draw a sample from the potential population and study the distribution of the relevant characteristics. The larger the sample, the more insight we will gain about the distribution of these features and about the probability of finding potential sources who could leave traces that correspond to those of the crime scene. But we will never be able to say, on the basis of a sample only, that we have eliminated all possible sources. This means that, logically, there is no basis for absolute identifications or individualizations.

---

5   These are the questions that are addressed at source level. They answer the question: Who left the trace material? A second question that needs to be addressed, at activity level, is: How (and when) was the trace material deposited?

6   On fingerprint evidence see Cole (2001). On the lack of logical basis for his practice see Broeders (2009).

7   In addition to 'inconclusive', if the standard required for identification is not met.

Probabilistic Conclusions

While we cannot avoid induction in inferring identity of source, elimination (or exclusion) of a potential source may sometimes be arrived at through a deductive process. If, for example, the DNA profile of the suspect does not match that of the crime scene sample (and no mistakes have been made at any stage in the examination process), it may be concluded that the crime scene sample does not originate from the suspect and the suspect may be eliminated as the donor of the cell material. However, if the suspect's profile *does* match, the conclusion reported is not that he *is* the donor of the cell material collected at the crime scene but that he *may* be the donor. The weight of this evidence depends on the frequency of the profile of interest in the relevant population. As there are empirical data about the distribution of DNA markers in the population, it is possible to calculate (or, strictly estimate) the expected frequency of occurrence of the profile of interest in the population. It is this 'estimated frequency' of the profile that the DNA expert will report, in addition to the finding that the suspect may be the donor. So, if for example the suspect matches the profile obtained from the crime scene sample and the frequency of the sample in the population is estimated at less than 1 in 100,000, it is this statistic that the DNA expert will report.

The Prior Probability

It is important to realize that whether the DNA actually originates from the suspect cannot be determined in the absence of an estimate of the so-called *prior probability* of the suspect being the donor. This prior probability basically amounts to a − frequently largely subjective − estimate of the probability of the suspect being the donor made on the basis of the non-DNA evidence. So, in addition to the evidence, in this case the DNA match, in order to assess the probability of the suspect being the donor, we need to have additional information about the case, such as the number of individuals other than the suspect who need to be considered as potential donors, or, in more general terms, the weight of the other, non-DNA evidence. If, on the basis of other, non-DNA information about the case, there is reason to believe that another 5,000 men need to be considered as possible donors, the probability of the suspect being the donor of the crime scene material is greater than if only 50 other men need to be considered. In the former case, with a prior probability of 1 to 5,000, the probability of the subject being the donor would be (1 to 5,000) x 100,000 = 100,000 to 5,000, or 100 to 5 (= 100/105) = 95.2%. In the latter case, with a prior probability of 1 to 50, it would be (1 to 50) x 100,000 = 100,000 to 50, or 10,000 to 5 (= 2,000/2,001) = 99.95%. If, on the other hand, only one more person qualified as a potential donor, so the prior probability would be 1 to 1 or fifty-fifty, the probability of the suspect being the donor would be (1 to 1) x 100,000 = 100,000 to 1 (= 100,000/100,101) = a staggering 99.999%.

The example illustrates two points. We cannot make statements of the probability of the hypothesis of common origin of a trace on the basis of the trace evidence only. We can logically only make statements about the converse, i.e., the probability of the evidence given a particular hypothesis: if the suspect is the donor we would expect the trace to have the same DNA profile. But we cannot transpose the conditional and say:

if the suspect has the same profile as the trace, he must be the donor. We can address that probability only if we can make an estimate of the prior probability of the hypothesis of common origin. In a more formal notation: we can determine the probability (P) of the evidence (E), given a particular hypothesis (H), i.e., P(E|H), but we cannot calculate P(H|E), the probability of the hypothesis given the evidence, *unless* we can bring additional information to bear on the issue, in the form of the prior probability of the hypothesis. The suggestion in the Guidelines that it is 'possible to be 100 per cent certain of conclusions based on […] fingerprint or DNA evidence' alone is therefore clearly erroneous. It ignores the inductive character of the process of inference of identity of source. We cannot logically make probability statements of the origin of traces unless we take all possible sources into consideration any more than we can conclude that all swans are white unless we have been able to check all swans for colour.

Application to Other Types of Evidence

The same reasoning may be applied to other types of forensic identification or classification evidence, as well as to cause-effect arguments. As a concrete example, the fact that a suspect wears size-13 shoes merely enables us to say that, if he left a shoeprint at the crime scene, it was a size-13.[8] But if we subsequently find a size-13 shoeprint on the crime scene, the shoe size information alone gives us no basis to say that it was the suspect who left it rather than one of the other shoe-size-13 wearers in the area (or beyond). The mere fact that the suspect wears size-13 shoes does not make him more suspect than anybody else with this size shoes. By the same token, the mere fact that we find numerous similarities between the handwriting of the writer of an anonymous letter and the reference material produced by a suspect should not, *on the basis of these similarities alone*, lead us to draw conclusions about the degree of probability that the suspect did in fact write the letter. If we do this, we are guilty of making a fundamental logical error which, in the judicial context, has come to be referred to as the prosecutor's fallacy, a term which – probably wrongly – suggests that prosecutors are particularly prone to this fallacy.[9] In fact, it is an example of a more general type of error that is often made in the context of probability statements or inverse reasoning, and it has come to be known as the 'fallacy of the transposed conditional'. Applied to a cause-effect argument: while it is correct to say that the street will be wet if it has been raining, the converse is clearly not true. The single observation that the street is wet does not allow us to infer that it must have been raining, or even that it has probably been raining. Alternative explanations are possible: the street may have got wet when the police used water cannon to break up a demonstration, or it is wet because somebody has just been washing his or her car. So we can make a statement about the probability of a particular finding (e.g., a wet street) under a particular hypothesis ('it has been raining') but not about the probability of this same hypothesis merely on the basis of the finding that the street is wet. It is our estimate of the prior probability of rain in say, the UK versus Du-

---

8   Assuming, of course, that the suspect was not – deliberately or accidentally – wearing a different size shoe.

9   Thompson & Schumann (1987).

bai, that leads us to arrive at different conclusions, given the same evidence, as to the cause of that state of affairs.

The Weight of Evidence – The Likelihood Ratio

In the above example of the shoe print, the crime scene trace was left by a size 13 shoe. Suppose this size shoe is worn by one person in 40. We can now determine the weight of this evidence by calculating the ratio of the probability of finding a size 13 trace if the suspect left it and the probability of finding it if a random member of the population left it. If the suspect was wearing his usual size shoes, the probability of finding a size 13 shoeprint would be 100%, or 1. If a random member of the population left it, the probability of finding this trace would be 1 in 40. The ratio of 1 to 1/40 = 40. This figure, which is referred to as the likelihood ratio, constitutes the weight of the shoe size evidence. Similarly, for DNA evidence, the likelihood ratio of a match on a profile with an estimated frequency of less than, say 100,000, would be 1 to 1/100,000 = 100,000. The likelihood ratio (LR) is a measure of the degree to which the particular item of evidence under consideration reduces the uncertainty about the hypothesis of common origin. In the shoe sole example the LR of 40, reduces the group of potential suspects by a factor 40, leaving one potential suspect on average for every 40 potential suspects to be considered before the shoeprint evidence was available. It is defined as the ratio of the probability of finding the evidence under one hypothesis and the probability of finding the same evidence under a rival, alternative hypothesis.[10] Because it explicitly addresses the probability of the evidence under two competing hypotheses, it is a powerful antidote to what is sometimes referred to as tunnel vision, the tendency to look for evidence that will confirm a particular hypothesis of interest, without taking

---

10 An introduction to his type of approach may be found in Robertson & Vignaux (1995). In the medical context, the term diagnostic value is used to express the same notion. The diagnostic value of a test (result) is arrived at by dividing the relative number of correct (positive or negative) test results by the relative number of false (positive or negative) test results. In more technical language, by dividing the sensitivity of the test by (1 − the specificity), where the sensitivity is the percentage of correct positives the test produces and the specificity the percentage of correct negatives. If the sensitivity of the test is 90% and the specificity is 95%, the diagnostic value of a positive test result would be 90/(100-95) = 18 and the probability of the patient being infected would be 18 times greater now that the test result is known than it was estimated to be before the test result was known. To determine the actual probability of infection for a given individual (technically, the positive predictive value), we would need to combine the weight of the evidence (i.e., the diagnostic value of a positive test result, in this case 18), with the prior probability of infection for this individual. If the individual belongs to a so-called high-risk group for HIV, the prior probability of infection will be higher and therefore the actual probability of infection will also be higher than for a person who tests positive but does not belong to a high-risk group. For an interesting treatment of the notions of diagnostic value and likelihood ratio see Gigerenzer (2002). On sensitivity and specificity see http://www.rapid-diagnostics.org/accuracy.htm.

account of alternative explanations for the evidence, as frequently occurs in so-called suspect-driven investigations.[11]

Discrete versus Continuous Variables

In general, we can say that the weight of evidence is related to the *similarity* of the trace with the reference material on the one hand and the *frequency* of occurrence of that degree of similarity in the relevant population on the other. In the above examples involving DNA and shoe sizes, the variables of interest are discrete or categorical and the similarity could be said to be either complete or entirely absent: the DNA-markers and the shoe sizes are the same or they are different. If they are different, the suspect's shoe or body can be eliminated as the source of the trace. However, in many cases, the correspondence between trace and source will not be perfect. Many variables are not discrete (like blood type or shoe size) but continuous. Examples are quantitative variables such as length, weight or shape. For these variables, there will always be a difference between trace and reference materials because in both cases we are dealing with samples that will at best only approximate the 'true' population value for the feature of interest. Traces originating from a single source will typically show a relatively small degree of *within-source* variation, while samples of reference material originating from different sources will typically show a relatively larger degree of *between-source* variation. As a result, in these cases the numerator of the likelihood ratio will not be 100% or 1, but say 80%: a degree of similarity as great as that found between trace material and reference material will be found in 80% of cases if both originate from the same source and in say only 20% of cases if trace material and reference material originate from different sources. The likelihood ratio would then be 80/20 = 4. If, however, the degree of similarity found would be expected in only 20% of cases under the hypothesis of common origin and in 40% of cases under the hypothesis of different origin, the likelihood ratio would be 20/40 = ½, and the evidence would actually weaken the common source hypothesis rather than strengthen it. In the first instance, the likelihood ratio would exceed 1 and the evidence would (weakly) support the hypothesis of common origin; in the second instance, the likelihood ratio would be less than 1 and the evidence would – again weakly – support the alternative hypothesis, that the trace did not originate from the same source as the reference material.

By way of illustration: in automatic speaker identification, we might calculate a distance measure between a questioned speech sample and a reference sample from the suspect, and determine the probability of finding this degree of distance or less between various speech samples from the suspect versus the probability of finding this degree of distance or less between various samples from different members of the speech community. The ratio of these probabilities, say 80% versus 5%, would produce the likelihood ratio, in this case 80/5 = 16. We would then be able to say that a distance measure as small as or smaller than the one found is 16 times more likely if the material

---

11 In a suspect-driven investigation the police tend to focus on collecting evidence that will confirm the suspect's involvement in the crime. In a crime-driven investigation, the investigators base the direction of the investigation on the clues provided by the crime rather than by the suspect.

originated from the suspect than if it originated from a random speaker in the population. If, on the other hand, we found a degree of distance between the questioned speech sample that was found in less than 10% of cases for samples originating the same speaker but in more than 60% of cases involving a comparison of samples from different speakers, the likelihood ratio would be 10/60 = 1/6, and the finding would be 6 times more likely for samples from different speakers than for samples from a single speaker.

Language Analysis

In language analysis for the determination of nationality, we might expect to face similar data. First of all, language varieties are difficult to define, as they tend to overlap to a greater or lesser extent. Apart from the case of so-called shibboleths, there are probably not too many categorical 'killer criteria' that may be used to categorically differentiate one language variety from another. Typically, there will be various subtle qualitative as well as quantitative differences, especially in areas where the social structure is not conducive to the emergence of a regional or national standard language variety. The presence of language continuums may render both categorical elimination and inclusion fraught with difficulty, aside from the logical problems associated with inclusion statements discussed above.[12] Under these circumstances, a more fruitful approach would be to focus on the probability of the findings of the language analysis given the claimed (nationality and) language versus the probability of these same findings given the rival hypothesis of a different language background. In fact, the alternative hypothesis may be fitted to the circumstances of the case. If there are indications to suggest that a particular claimant may pretend to be a native speaker of a language variety other than the variety of socialization, the best approach might be to assess the probability of the findings of the analysis under the following two hypotheses: H1 – the claimant is a native speaker of X, versus H2 – the claimant is a native speaker of Y but pretends to be a native speaker of X.[13]

---

12 According to Detailleur (2010: 14-15), the Netherlands Immigration and Naturalization Service (IND) uses a reporting format comprising three categorical conclusions (the speaker definitely may be retraced to the language community in country X; the speaker definitely may not be retraced to the language community in country X; the speaker may be retraced to the language community in country X and in country Y); one mixed statement (the speaker definitely may not be retraced to the language community in country X but probably to that in Y; one probability statement (the speaker probably may not be retraced to the language community in country X) and a non-conclusive 'no judgment', with X standing for the claimed country of origin. Note that in all these cases the conclusion refers to the (probability of the) hypothesis not to the probability of the evidence given a pair of rival hypotheses.

13 '… we may be dealing with less than fully cooperative speakers, who may be hiding knowledge of a language, faking knowledge of a language, presenting a second language as their first language, or adding speech features that do not belong in their natural speech variety. They may even have practised speaking a language variety other than their own. As a result, it cannot be taken for granted that the speech sample is complete and fully representative, nor that all the speech features encountered are authentic', Cambier-Langeveld 2010: 73.

The Use of a Logical Conclusion Format

In response to the logical objections raised to the use of traditional probability scales in forensic identification and classification, a number of proposals have been made in recent years for the introduction of logically correct verbal probability scales.[14] The Netherlands Forensic Institute (NFI) in The Hague has recently introduced a reporting format that seeks to avoid these problems. Used primarily in the various forensic identification disciplines, this format is as follows:

> The findings of the comparative examination are
> equally likely/
> more likely/
> much more likely/
> very much more likely
> under the prosecution hypothesis Hp that the suspect is the source of trace material as/than under the defence hypothesis Hd that a random member of the population is the source of the trace material.

In those, exceptional cases where the forensic scientist arrives at a subjective conviction that the trace material originates from a particular source (as in physical fits of torn paper, or qualitatively superior shoeprints or tool marks), he or she would still be expressing his or her subjective conviction, but emphasizing that this is precisely that – a subjective conviction, not a scientific fact. A similar principle might be applied in LADO. Note, that, other than in the reporting of DNA typing results, the conclusion format does not have a quantitative character. The absence of quantitative empirical data makes this impossible. The verbal phrases used instead of course clearly have a probabilistic basis but the probabilities are informed by the analyst's experience and may be seen as internalized frequency estimates.

Applied to the realm of LADO decision making, the conclusion format might look as follows:

> The findings of the language analysis are
> equally likely/
> more likely/
> much more likely/
> very much more likely
> under the claimant's hypothesis Hc that claimant is a speaker of language variety X, spoken in A as/than under the alternative hypothesis Ha that claimant is a speaker of language variety Y spoken in B.

In order to arrive at a probability statement of the hypothesis of origin, the decision maker would subsequently combine the weight of the evidence expressed in the conclusion of the linguistic analysis with the (prior) probability of the hypothesis of origin based on the rest of the evidence. The role of the language analyst would thus be com-

---

14 See for example Broeders 2007.

parable to that of the forensic expert in a legal decision. It is the tier of fact, the judge or the jury, who addresses the ultimate issue. It is not the expert.

References

Broeders, A.P.A. (2006) Of Earprints, Fingerprints, Scent Dogs, Cot Deaths and Cognitive Contamination: A Brief Look at the Present State of Play in the Forensic Arena, *Forensic Science International* 159(2-3), p. 148-157.

Broeders, A.P.A. (2007) Principles of Forensic Identification Science, in T. Newburn, T. Williamson & A. Wright (eds.), *Handbook of Criminal Investigation*, Willan Publishing, p. 303-337.

Broeders, A.P.A. (2009) Decision-making in the Forensic Arena, in H. Kaptein, H. Prakken & B. Verheij (eds), *Legal Evidence and Proof: Statistics, Stories and Logic*, Ashgate, p. 71-92.

Cambier-Langeveld, T. (2010) The role of linguists and native speakers in language analysis for the determination of speaker origin, *International Journal of Speech, Language and the Law* 17(1), p. 67-93.

Cole, S.A. (2001) *Suspect Identities: A History of Fingerprinting and Criminal Identification*, Cambridge MA: Harvard University Press.

Detailleur, J.N. (2010) *Shibboleth aan de poort: de theorie van de taalanalyse als middel herkomstbepaling in de Nederlandse asielprocedure versus de praktijk van een Soedanese Arabischsprekende asielzoeker met vermeende Nuba-achtergrond*, doctoral thesis, Dept. of Middle East Studies, University of Leiden, The Netherlands.

Fraser, H. (2009) The role of 'educated native speakers' in providing language analysis for the determination of the origin of asylum seekers, *International Journal of Speech, Language and the Law* 16(1), p. 113-138.

Gigerenzer, G. (2002) *Calculated Risks: How to Know when Numbers Deceive You*, NewYork, NY: Simon & Schuster.

Inman, K. & R. Rudin (2002)The Origin of Evidence, *Forensic Science International* 126, p. 11-16.

Language and National Origin Group (2004) Guidelines for the use of language analysis in relation to questions of national origin in refugee cases, *International Journal of Speech, Language and the Law* 11(2), p. 261-266.

Robertson, B. & G.A. Vignaux (1995) *Investigating Evidence: Evaluating Forensic Science in the Courtroom*, Chichester: John Wiley & Sons.

Thompson, W.C. & E.L. Schumann (1987) Interpretation of Statistical Evidence in Criminal Trials: The Prosecutor's Fallacy and the Defence Attorney's Fallacy, *Law and Human Behavior* 11, p. 167-187.

LADO, Validity and Language Testing

Tim McNamara, Maaike Verrips and Carolien van den Hazelkamp

Introduction

This paper considers the practical issue of language analysis in the determination of the origin of asylum seekers in the light of theories of validity from the field of language testing and assessment. It argues that it is useful to conceptualize language analysis as a form of language assessment, and suggests an agenda for research on aspects of the validity of the procedure.

LADO and Language Testing

Language tests are mostly used to establish proficiency in a language, usually in educational or gate-keeping contexts. Testing typically involves measurement of degree of knowledge, so that comparison of test candidates in terms of 'more' and 'less' knowledge is normal in this process. Language testing has a strong basis in the theory and technical analytic methods provided by psychometrics (Bachman 1990, 2004; McNamara & Roever 2006). As the name suggests, psychometrics as a field is mainly cognitive in focus, and often assumes a context of learning. The construct on which the assessment is based is some conceptualization of knowledge of and practical competence in a language.

It may seem at first sight surprising to relate the practice of language analysis to language testing. Language analysis is sociolinguistic rather than psycholinguistic in focus: is the individual a member of a given speech community? What has been his/her language socialization? The aim of the analysis is to determine whether the individual has knowledge of one or more specific varieties that are associated with a claim to protection, on the basis that there is a link between such knowledge and the socialization of the individual. Often, determining what a person does not know is as important as determining what they do know.

However, despite this important difference, both language testing and language analysis are constrained by the same principles. Both procedures involve:
- observing and interpreting *evidence* from a language user's performance
- in order to reach *conclusions* about what they know (or don't),
- and to make *decisions* based on these conclusions.

For example, in English-speaking countries such as the US, the UK, Canada and Australia, language tests such as IELTS and TOEFL-iBT are used to decide whether international students are ready to be admitted to universities in those countries.[1] Evidence is sought from student performance on tasks which simulate the communicative demands of the target situation (such as comprehending the input of lectures), and inferences are drawn from this performance about the student's readiness to undertake such tasks in the real situation. A decision to admit or not is then based on this inference. Similarly, language analysis is used to help decide whether the asylum seeker's application can be supported. Evidence of the applicant's language knowledge is sought, usually from an interview, and inferences are made as to his/her place(s) of primary socialization. These inferences are then relevant to the final decision about granting or denying asylum. In fact, this chain of evidence → inference → decision is common to assessment in many other areas of life. Police deciding whether to charge a person with a crime base their decision on their interpretation of evidence leading to inferences about the person's likely involvement in a criminal act. Doctors make medical decisions based on evidence which is interpreted in order to make inferences about a person's state of health. In all such assessment processes, it is necessary to distinguish between the evidence elicited through the procedure, and the interpretation of the significance of that evidence. In each case we move from the known (evidence) to the unknown (interpretation about what is unseen). These interpretations we can call *claims*, and they are used as the basis for the decisions. Now in all the cases we have considered, these claims may *in fact* be unwarranted or erroneous. The police reach conclusions which may subsequently, on further examination, be shown to be unreasonable. This happens in appeals procedures and court hearings. We regularly seek second opinions from doctors, especially in serious cases of disease, and the second opinion does not always confirm the first. Similarly with the inferences drawn from language tests, or from language analysis; they may not be fair and reasonable. The systematic interrogation of interpretations yielded by assessments is known as *validation*. Without validation, language tests – and language analysis - are like a police force without a court system.

Given the need to validate assessments, including those from language analysis, what is there to guide us in the conduct of validation? This has been the question addressed by validity theory over the last 50 years and more. The still classic treatment of the subject is that of the American educational theorist Samuel Messick. Messick (1989: 13) defines validity as follows:

> Validity is an integrated evaluative judgement of the degree to which empirical evidence and theoretical rationales support the adequacy and appropriateness of inferences and actions based on test scores or other modes of assessment.

The reference to *inferences* should be clear from the preceding discussion: all assessments involve inferences from evidence – in the case of language analysis, not from 'test scores', but from 'other modes of assessment'. Once inferences have been made, *actions* will follow – in the case of asylum seekers, the granting or denial of some form of pro-

---

1 These tests have other uses as well in Anglophone and non-Anglophone countries, for example in determining immigration status and in employment, although the tests were not primarily designed for these purposes.

tection, depending on the inference. How *adequate* (reasonable) are such inferences (and, accordingly, how appropriate are the *actions* which follow from them)? The *reasoning* ('theoretical rationales') forming the basis for interpreting the evidence must be examined. In addition, *empirical evidence* must be sought and *competing explanations* considered.

Kane: Steps in Validation

Because of the generality and broad scope of Messick's discussion of validity, subsequent validity theorists have tried to make the process of validation more orderly. Foremost among these is Michael Kane (e.g. Kane 2001), who defines a series of challenges to the meaningfulness and fairness of assessments arising at each step of the assessment process. How these might be applied in the context of language analysis is set out in Figure 1 below.

Issues arise in the process by which the evidence is gathered, in the methods of analysis used, the generalizability of the conclusions reached, the interpretation of the data and the use of the report in decision making. Let us consider each of these in turn. This overview is based on information gathered during seven years of casework by two of the authors, as well as on the (very limited) information available from public sources, mainly the presentations at http://www.ejpd.admin.ch/content/dam/data/migration/laenderinformationen/sprachanalysen/program-e.pdf.

Step 1: Eliciting the Language Sample for Analysis

There is considerable variation at present among the various agencies carrying out language analysis as to how the speech sample for the analysis is elicited. The variables involved are summarized in Table 1. For each dimension of variation – speech genre, topic, participants, channel, code and length – there are a number of possibilities.

The *speech genre* is usually an interview, but it is sometimes a monologue, and evidence from more equal interactions, for example a conversation with a speaker of the same variety who is not a government representative, is sometimes used in appeals. Within each genre, there is the possibility of further variation. Interviews vary in terms of whether they are structured or not, how conversational they are, and the extent to which they contain 'quiz' elements. Given that the situation by definition is formal and highly consequential, it is likely to elicit a formal register in sociolinguistic terms, and this will have implications for validity.

The *topics* dealt with also vary, for example the extent to which they include or exclude knowledge of the country and culture of the claimed region of origin.

The *participants* in the interaction, other than the asylum seeker, represent another dimension of variation. In many jurisdictions, the interview is conducted by the case officer, usually with the help of an interpreter. In other cases the interview is conducted either by the person responsible for carrying out the language analysis, who may be either a native speaker or a non-native speaker, and with or without formal academic training in linguistic analysis, or by a trained or untrained interviewer, typically a native speaker of the asylum seeker's L1 or a variety close to it.

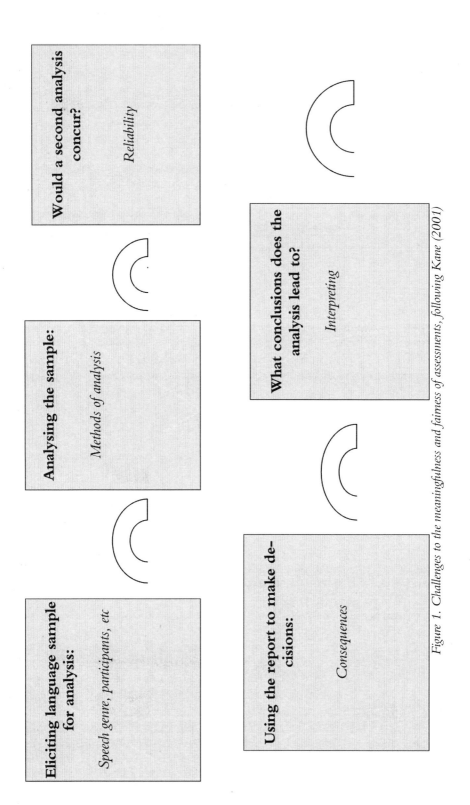

Figure 1. Challenges to the meaningfulness and fairness of assessments, following Kane (2001)

Eliciting language sample for analysis:

Speech genre, participants, etc

Analysing the sample:

Methods of analysis

Would a second analysis concur?

Reliability

What conclusions does the analysis lead to?

Interpreting

Using the report to make de-cisions:

Consequences

Channel is another important variable. Increasingly, interviews other than with case officers are carried out via telephone, for logistical reasons, and to preserve the anonymity of the interviewer and asylum seeker involved.

The *code* used in the interaction varies from the asylum seeker's L1, to a variety closely associated with it, to an L2, often a lingua franca.

The *length* of the interview, and the resulting amount of usable data, varies considerably, often as a function of variation in the participants. When an interpreter is involved, a considerable amount of the time is taken up in translation back and forth.

From the point of view of the validity of assessments, any one of these variables, and combinations of variables, may affect the chances of a certain outcome. In order to validate the process, research needs to be carried out into the potential impact of any of the variables, either alone or in combination. We will return to the question of a research agenda later in the paper.

Speech genre	Interview	Structure	(structured)	(unstructured)
	Monologue			
	Dialogue			

Topics	(+ knowledge of country)		(- knowledge of country)	

Other participants	No other participant (monologue)			
	Case officer			
	Interpreter			
	Person responsible for analysis	Native speaker status	(+ NS)	(-NS)
		Training in linguistics	(+ formal academic training)	(- formal academic training)
	Interviewer, non-analyst	Training	(+ training as an interviewer)	(- training as an interviewer)

Channel	Face to face
	Telephone
	Combination (e.g. case officer, + interpreter on telephone

Code	Asylum seeker's first language
	Asylum seeker's second language (lingua franca)
	Variety related to asylum seeker's first language
	Combination (e.g. lingua franca + asylum seeker's first language)

Length	Brief (5 minutes)
	Moderate (up to 30 minutes of usable language from asylum seeker)
	Full (up to one hour of usable language from asylum seeker)

Table 1. Variables in the elicitation procedure

It has been assumed so far that the asylum seeker will be cooperative in providing a speech sample. In certain cases, for example where an asylum claim has failed and it is desirable to use language analysis to determine origin in order to facilitate repatriation, the cooperation of the interviewee cannot of course be assumed. It is not clear what can be done in such a situation. The flip side of this is a kind of false cooperativeness, where a person making a false claim for asylum imitates speech features associated with a region or an ethnicity likely to form the basis for a successful asylum claim. This issue of 'authenticity' will be discussed further below.

Step 2: Analysing the Sample

The main issue here is the process of analysis. There are two aspects here, although they are related:
1) the features of speech that should be attended to, and how to deal with uncertainty of indeterminacy in the data (conflicting evidence, sufficiency of evidence, and so on), and
2) the qualifications of the analyst.

On the first issue, any aspect of language may be relevant and if deemed so could be investigated systematically: lexis, morphosyntax, phonetics and phonology, suprasegmentals, pragmatics. On the second issue, as the procedure will require analysis of linguistic features below the level of awareness, the contentious question of the credentials of the analyst arises. The Guidelines for the use of language analysis are clear about this: 'Judgements about the relationship between language and regional identity should be made only by qualified linguists with recognized and up-to-date expertise, both in linguistics and in the language in question, including how this language differs from neighbouring language varieties'. There is also a contrary view that what is required is a 'native speaker ear', under the supervision of a linguist, however this is defined. Clearly, this variability in approach and practice is another area demanding validation research (see also Cambier-Langeveld, this volume; Baltisberger and Hubbuch, this volume).

Step 3: Would a Second Analysis be Similar?

A fundamental question in language assessment is whether the judgement that is reached is an artefact of the particular assessment situation – who the judge was, what the task was, what the conditions of performance were, etc. – or whether the *same* judgement about a person would be reached with different tasks, a different judge, and under different conditions. Of particular interest is the impact of the judge in judgements, on which there is a vast literature in the field of language assessment. Studies have been carried out on this topic for over 150 years, since a study in the middle of the 19th century demonstrated that a person's chances of being admitted to Oxford and Cambridge, which involved an essay examination, depended approximately 50% on the quality of the essay written, and 50% on who happened to be the examiner (Linacre, 1989). Increasingly sophisticated methods of determining the impact of the judge on assessment outcomes have been developed. As performance-based assessments of language proficiency have become increasingly necessary as languages move from the subject of academic study to practical necessities for participation in contemporary business, education, travel and recreation, judge-mediated assessments of speaking (in particular) have become more important, and methods have been developed to ensure their quality. The most advanced of these methods, using complex statistical techniques, can model the probabilities of a given outcome under varying conditions, so that it is now possible to estimate precisely the likely impact of a judge with given characteristics on a person's chances of a successful outcome in a given assessment context (McNamara 1996; Bond & Fox 2007). The normal means of establishing the impact of judges is to have repeated assessments of the same set of candidates, to see how much variability in the scores is associated with the assessment occasion, specifically in this case the judge, and to what extent the scores are stable across judges. We observe consistency *within* judges – whether they give the same scores to a set of speaking performances after some time has elapsed, and they no longer remember the candidates or the scores – and consistency *across* judges, each considering the same set of cases. In the case of language analysis the same issue of judge consistency in principle arises. For intra-judge variability, ideally, the judges should be unaware that they are judging the same set of cases again. This might be possible when a judge handles many cases from a given region, and is likely to have forgotten particular cases after a suitable lapse of time. For inter-judge consistency, getting judgements from more than a single judge on a given set of cases would require the existence of several experts on a given region, which might in some cases be unachievable.

Step 4: What Conclusions Does the Analysis Lead To?

The fourth step is the most complex, using the analysis as the basis for a conclusion about the state of knowledge of the applicant and its implications for the socialization of that person. What is required here is a theory of the relationship of the evidence and the conclusion reached: this is known as the assessment *construct*. Messick (1989) suggests that an important threat to the validity of interpretations is what he calls *construct under-representation*. In other words, the complexity of the relationship between the evidence and what we would like to infer from it is not fully taken into account. In language analysis, this is a major problem. The sociolinguistic construct underlying the procedure is in fact often poorly specified. This may be because the necessary up-to-date sociolinguistic fieldwork is made impossible by war, political instability, inaccessibility to researchers, and so on. The need for up-to-date sociolinguistic information is made more urgent by the rapid changes in the sociolinguistics of many areas, for example in urban vernaculars in African cities. Or it may be dauntingly complex: there is considerable inter-individual variation within members of a single speech community, often related to age, education, and other factors. Moreover, language analysis is necessarily retrospective: it is not about the variety that a person speaks now, but the variety that they spoke when they were in the region of origin. Thus the influence of succeeding events, including the often tortuous journey from the place of socialization to the place where asylum is sought, and the period of time already spent in the country where the language analysis is being carried out, can cloud the picture. All of these things must be taken into account in representations of the construct. (For a brief discussion of various practices, see Verrips, in press).

A further but rather different aspect of construct underrepresentation is what is sometimes referred to as the issue of 'authenticity', that is, that the characteristics of speech from a certain region are such that they cannot simply be learned and convincingly imitated for the purposes of deception by someone not actually from the region concerned. Articulating the difference between an authentic and an inauthentic performance is a further challenge for research.

Step 5: Using the Report to Make Decisions

The final step involves the decision about the applicant and its implementation. Here the consequences of invalid decisions are the most decisive issue. For example, if an applicant is deported who is in fact entitled to protection, the consequence is that the State violates Article 3 of the European Convention on Human Rights ('prohibition of torture'). If (groups of) applicants are admitted who are not eligible for protection, this amounts to ineffective border control. Finally there are the cases of failed applicants whose purported country of origin refuses to admit them. Evidence about the frequency of such cases and the details of the experiences of the individuals involved would count as valuable evidence in investigating the validity of the conclusions of language analysis.

In summary, then, validation of language analysis involves checking the strength of each of the links in the chain. Each logical inference can be potentially faulty; one weak link can destroy the usefulness of the whole chain, as the ultimate decision about the applicant, which may have far-reaching consequences for the applicant, and for the society which is going to host him/her, depends on the strength of each link.

What we have discussed so far represent only one aspect of the validation of assessments, according to Messick. It represents what he terms 'construct validity'. But there are three more facets of validity, as set out in a famous matrix:

	Test interpretation	Test use
Evidential basis	Construct validity	Construct validity + Relevance / utility
Consequential basis	Value implications	Social consequences

Figure 2. Facets of validity (Messick, 1989, p. 20)

We can elaborate the distinctions present in the matrix in a form more relevant to the context of language analysis, as follows:

	What language analysis reports are assumed to mean	When language analysis reports are actually used
Using evidence in support of claims: the fairness of language analysis reports	What reasoning and empirical evidence support the claims we wish to make about individuals based on an analysis of their spoken language?	Are these interpretations meaningful, useful and fair in particular contexts?
The social context of using language analysis in the determination of origins	What social and cultural values and assumptions underlie the constructs used in language analysis and the inferences we make about individuals in relation to them?	What happens in the larger social context when we use language analysis in the determination of origin?

Figure 3. Understanding Messick's validity matrix (adapted from McNamara & Roever, 2006)

We will comment briefly about each of the other cells in the matrix. The second cell, on the top line, suggests that an analysis which is valid for one context may not be valid for another. This arises most clearly when language analysis is used as part of the procedure of deporting a person whose asylum application has failed. It is one thing to determine if a person is or is not from a region they claim to be from; it is another to determine positively which region a person is from.

The third and fourth cells introduce questions which were not previously part of psychometric orthodoxy, as they consider the broader social, political and cultural context within which the practice of language analysis is situated. The third cell considers the policy context in which language analysis is used. The fourth deals with the intended and unintended social consequences of the practice of language analysis.

We may make the following distinction: the first two cells (on the top line) deal with the technical quality of the assessment procedure and its relevance to its context, raising issues of what we may call test *fairness*. The last two cells (on the bottom line) invoke the broader social context of the use of the assessment, and raise issues of what we may call the *justice* of the procedure (McNamara & Ryan, in press).

There is no time to address these issues here, except to say that language analysis is subject to:
- laws designed to provide protection for refugees under international conventions;
- the administrative procedures of bureaucracies with limited time and resources;
- and the political pressure to reduce the extent of immigration through successful asylum applications and to limit the number of those 'sans papiers'.

This puts pressure on those involved in administering and conducting language analyses in ways that may compromise the validity of the procedure. The broader context also has to be acknowledged, that many asylum applications fail, and often involve those who do not have a reasonable fear of subjection to persecution, but for whom the asylum route is the only way to escape often poor social and economic conditions. The very refugee law that language analysis seeks to implement is of course itself the product of social and political compromise at a particular historical period, and the values implicit within it are clearly contestable.

A Research Map and a Research Agenda

Validation does not happen by itself: it involves careful research. Thinking of language analysis as a form of language assessment, and of what is involved in the validation of assessments, as set out in this paper, provides a useful framework for a research agenda, and for mapping research that has already been done, to identify significant gaps. Different researchers may have different motivations. For those wishing to develop quality standards for the work of those engaged in language analysis, the emphasis will be on the threats to validity adumbrated under the first cell of Messick's matrix. This represents a focus on the *fairness* of the procedure. We have seen above how the issues may be elaborated in terms of Kane's 5 steps. Of these, empirical research can focus on the first four steps.

For step 1, we need to explore the impact of the variables involved in the elicitation of the language sample to be analysed. Here a series of comparative studies, studying differences in the material available for analysis under each condition, and its impact on asylum decisions, would appear to be a priority. Each of the dimensions of variability – speech genre, other participants, channel, code and length – merit separate investigation, and studies of combinations of variables will also be needed. Some research has become available, directed at improving practice (e.g. de Graaf and van den Hazelkamp, 2006; Olaf and Meyer, 2008).

For step 2, the very contentious issue of the qualifications of the analyst could be explored in a study comparing the process of analysis and the outcomes of the analysis for the same data set under a number of conditions: e.g. native speaker non-linguistically trained analyst, with or without the supervision of a non-specialist linguist, vs linguistically specialized analyst, either native speaker or non-native speaker. A first experimental study was carried out by Wilson (2009).

For step 3, generalizability studies are conceivable, although as discussed earlier their feasibility may be limited, except for high frequency cases where there is a sufficient supply of suitable experts.

For step 4, an appropriate task might be to try define the minimum criteria that should be available for a language analysis to be feasible in a particular context, and the establishment of a taxonomy of threats to the meaningfulness of the sociolinguistic construct involved which would need to be taken into account by those interpreting the results of analysis.

Research on the lower two cells of Messick's matrix would focus on the justice of LADO, its social, administrative and political context. This is likely to be of less interest to administrative bodies within governments, or of those conducting contra-analyses within the constraints of the existing law, not because they are not interested in justice, but because they are necessarily constrained to work within current policy settings, however unreasonable these may be. But this research will be of interest to those who wish to develop and promulgate a critical understanding of the values implicit in, and the consequences of, the highly contested and highly consequential social practice represented by LADO. Research of this kind is already going on, and much more can be done.

Conclusion

This paper has suggested the usefulness of conceptualising language analysis as a form of language assessment, and of using the conceptual and empirical tools familiar within validity theory to develop and prioritise a research agenda for this area. We look forward to participating in and furthering the resulting program of research.

References

Bachman, L.F. (1990) *Fundamental considerations in language testing*. Oxford: Oxford University Press.
Bachman, L.F. (2004) *Statistical analyses for language assessment*. Cambridge: Cambridge University Press.

Bond, T.G. & C.M. Fox (2007) *Applying the Rasch model: Fundamental measurement in the human sciences.* 2nd Edition. Mahwah, NJ: Erlbaum.

Graaf, A. de & C. van den Hazelkamp (2006) Language analysis as a method to determine national origin in asylum cases. *Thema's en trends in de Sociolinguïstiek, Toegepaste Taalwetenschap in Artikelen (TTWiA),* 76, p. 101–110.

Kane, M. T. (2001) Current concerns in validity theory. *Journal of Educational Measurement,* 38(4), p. 319-342.

Linacre, M.J. (1989) *Many-faceted Rasch measurement.* Chicago, IL: MESA Press.

McNamara, T. (1996) *Measuring second language performance.* London: Longman.

McNamara, T. & C. Roever (2006) *Language testing: The social dimension.* Malden, MA & Oxford: Blackwell.

McNamara, T. & K. Ryan (in press, 2011) Fairness vs justice in language testing: The place of English literacy in the Australian Citizenship Test. *Language Assessment Quarterly.*

Messick, S. (1989) Validity. In R.L. Linn (Ed.), *Educational Measurement* (3rd ed.) New York: American Council on Education & Macmillan, p. 13-103.

Olaf, B. and L. Meyer (2008) *Research project on LINGUA interviews: proceedings and results.* Workshop on Linguistic Analyses within the Asylum Procedure, Lausanne, 2008.

Verrips, M. (in press, 2010) Language analysis and contra-expertise in the Dutch asylum procedure, *Internation Journal for Speech, Language and the Law.*

Wilson, K. (2009) *Language Analysis for the Determination of Origin: native speakers vs. trained linguists.* MSc dissertation, University of York.

Language Variation and LADO

*Peter L. Patrick**

This paper reviews, for non-specialists, some of the contributions to the theory and practice of Language Analysis for Determination of Origin (LADO) which may be made by employing the variationist approach to language structure, use and change developed and advanced by William Labov (2001) and colleagues (Chambers et al. 2002, Bayley & Lucas 2007). I briefly consider, in turn:
- Variation: a natural fact about all languages
- The variationist approach to linguistics
- The concept of the speech community
- Variationist methods and the research base
- Examples of variation in LADO reports
- Why variationist work should contribute to LADO

Where useful, I will relate the discussion to specific recommendations made in the *Guidelines for the Use of Language Analysis in relation to Questions of National Origin in Refugee Cases* (Language & National Origin Group, 2004), a document co-authored by an international group of 19 linguists (three of them variationists, including myself, many with forensic and LADO experience) to 'assist governments in assessing the general validity of language analysis in the determination of national origin', and to advise 'whether and in what degree language analysis is reliable' (2004: 261). The *Guidelines* have been endorsed by a dozen national and international linguistic organisations, numbering many thousand members and representing the profession in Australia, Europe, the US, the UK, and around the world.

Variation: A Natural Fact about All Languages

Variation occurs when speakers alternately use forms which do not make a linguistic difference to the meaning (e.g. the contrasting final nasal sounds in *talking*/*talkin'*). Such variation is ubiquitous in speech, and not confined to any subgroup of a population, particular dialects, or casual/informal occasions – contrary to popular beliefs. Because the word-meaning remains the same no matter which variant form is used, the choice among variants is free to take on social connotations associated (if not always accurately) with certain speakers or contexts. Thus a choice often expresses a difference along social dimensions (e.g. education, formality, politeness), or correlates with factors characterizing groups of speakers (e.g. social class, gender, ethnicity). Though quantitative patterns

*   Thanks to Enam Al-Wer, Diana Eades and Maaike Verrips for comments on a draft. Any errors are my own.

demonstrating such correlations are easy to find, speakers are unaware of how, when, and why they vary.

It is well known that all natural languages change. All natural languages also show *inherent variation*: i.e., alternation of forms exists as a part of the language system or grammar. Speakers use it expressively in response to, or to manipulate, social context. The choice among variant forms is also typically constrained by linguistic factors internal to the grammar: e.g., although both forms occur with a range of word-types, *–ing* is more frequent in nouns, and *–in'* in verbs. Language change is always foreshadowed by variation, as a form expands or contracts its social distribution – though there may be stability of patterns for generations or centuries. The pronunciation of /r/ has changed considerably across Western Europe and North America since 1800, but variation between *–ing* and *-in'* (which is a thousand years old in English) has remained stable for generations. Scholars of language variation have innovated methods of discovering whether contemporary variation indicates only differences of usage by age-group, or genuine changes in progress.

The Variationist Approach to Linguistics

Incorporating this seemingly simple and empirically verifiable idea about inherent variation, and the social functions it serves, into a scientific model of language has provided a challenge to the generative grammar approach which was dominant in linguistics towards the end of the 20th century. The study of language variation and change historically arose in the USA from combining traditional (i.e. largely rural) dialectology (Hazen 2007) and historical linguistics (Weinreich, Labov & Herzog 1968) with urban social science methods. Although early efforts focused on creating adequate descriptions of the complex structure of urban speech communities (Labov 1966, McCafferty 2001), it has also illuminated the structure of isolated rural varieties (Rickford 1986), and spearheaded the investigation of disrespected varieties and speakers - including both ethnic minorities (Wolfram & Thomas 2002) and majorities (Patrick 1999) in urban Western societies, and also indigenous peoples (Stanford & Preston 2009). For example, it has demonstrated that African American English has a systematic, rule-governed grammar, has unique properties as well as ones shared with other vernacular English dialects, and is historically linked to Creole languages which developed under Atlantic slavery (Rickford 1999, Mufwene et al. 1998).

Correlation of linguistic features with social factors, such as those noted above distinguishing speakers or characterizing contexts, was at the heart of the earliest 'socially perspicacious linguistic studies' (Chambers 2002: 6). Both network and accommodation studies examine effects of interlocutors on speech. A speaker's web of acquaintances (= network) constrains and influences her vernacular speech over time (Milroy 2002). In the moment, people normally adapt their speech towards or away from (= accommodate) that of their interlocutors, both consciously and unconsciously (Giles et al. 1991). This occurs in response to factors in their environment (e.g. bureaucratic interviews which have the power to decide their fate), their perception of the relationship they are in (e.g. being of the same nation – but perhaps not same native dialect – as LADO interviewers who are strangers), or the desire to express features of personal identity (e.g.

a co-operative, sympathetic face in an institutional process; an educated person, able to use a national language even if it is not her native variety). Such research has shown, e.g., how low-prestige dialects are maintained under pressure from the standard (Milroy 1980 for Belfast).

All the basic levels of traditional language description have been incorporated into a variationist perspective on language: phonetics, phonology (accent), lexicon (vocabulary), morphology (word structure), semantics and pragmatics (meaning), and syntax (grammar). Practitioners have invented and refined a set of powerful descriptive concepts and analytical tools, both qualitative and quantitative in nature, and have integrated them with earlier and contemporary linguistic knowledge and theory. The concept of *linguistic variable* was developed, quantified and extended (Labov 1969, Wolfram 1993, Fasold & Preston 2007) to measure individual and community usage norms, and constraints within the linguistic system itself.

A variationist view of speech is probabilistic. Some features of language do not involve choice – they are invariant and wholly predictable – but this is not true of all, as other linguistic theories assume. Rather, the default position is to expect variation, and to look for multiple constraining and explanatory factors in the context – both linguistic ones (e.g., surrounding sounds and structures) and social ones (e.g. sex, age, class, ethnicity, style). Multivariate analysis is a basic tool for modelling speaker choices; complex interaction among contextual factors is anticipated. Quantitative analysis is used because actual patterns of speech are too complex to perceive without them. The goal is not prediction of what sentences are *(im)possible* in language, as in other theories, but rich description, interpretation and explanation of empirical speech data-sets: what people actually do with language, and why.

A large empirical research base has been created, consisting of thousands of studies over hundreds of languages. The variationist approach has become one of the most influential paradigms for describing contemporary languages and dialects, partly because of its ability to explain changes in them, and partly because of its many methodological innovations. The study of language variation has revolutionized the fields of historical linguistics, corpus linguistics, language contact, and dialectology, etc.; witness statements such as, 'It is plausible to view [variationist] sociolinguistics as a refocusing of dialectology' (Chambers 2002: 6), and 'Nearly a century [after Saussure 1916]... historical linguistics and the study of language change [are] inconceivable without an awareness of language variation' (Montgomery 2007: 110).

The Concept of the Speech Community (1): Linguistic Uniformity

'The way that people speak has a strong connection with how and where they were socialized' (Guideline #2). The speech community is a socially-based unit of linguistic analysis, used to model speech in cities, villages, small nations, clans, etc. (Patrick 2002). It is 'the natural unit of sociolinguistic taxonomy' (Hymes 1972: 43), as it addresses the relationship of linguistic systems to speakers' collective behaviour. Because of this, it is crucial to the notions of native-speakerhood, competence in one or more languages, and linguistic boundaries – concepts basic to carrying out LADO properly.

The variationist concept of speech community is informed by a focus on vernacular languages, inherent variation, and social variability. It postulates the uniformity of speech on different occasions by different speakers, and the identity of a group based in language practices, such that one can 'say the same thing twice' in 'our language'. The speech community is also the locus of *socialization* into one's native language: it is where, with and from whom, language is learned, including acquiring and passing on structured variation in language. A much-discussed concept, it may serve the *correlation problem* (linking language behaviour to social structure) better than the *indexical* one (accounting for how the social meaning of language forms arises and changes; Patrick 2002: 576).

Speech community members' language competence overlaps significantly: i.e., members essentially share the same grammar, lexicon, stylistic norms, phonological inventory, and vowel system, and are affected by the same sound changes (with appropriate caveats in each case). The convergence of speakers across these sub-systems of a language amounts to linguistic uniformity, and has been demonstrated even for such highly diverse settings as Caribbean Creoles (Rickford 1987, Patrick 1999) and Deaf signing communities (Lucas et al. 2001).

However, a range of heterogeneity in speech is normal. Inherent variation always occurs, due to linguistic and social contexts; people make expressive choices, consciously and unconsciously. No single categorical reference norm exists for most living languages; that is, no prescriptive standard exists that is powerful enough to stamp out variation in everyday speech (though it is often stigmatized, and this goal often promoted). The range of inter-speaker variability and intra-speaker variation within a speech community is routinely established by empirical methods.

The variationist understanding of this core concept can thus be encapsulated in (1):

(1) *Axiom of the Speech Community*:
Speakers who share language socialization are alike enough in their linguistic production and evaluative norms to be identified as members of the same speech community.

The issue for language analysis in the asylum context is this: Given that language is indexical of origins, (how)[1] can LADO reveal whether a speaker is *alike enough* to other speech community members to permit his or her identification with them?

Variationist principles are often applied to characterize a single language or dialect, e.g. the complex urban distribution of English in New York City (Labov 1966). They have also been used to explain regional dialect mixing (Norwich, Trudgill 1974) and change, including re-studies (Martha's Vineyard, Blake & Josey 2003); ethnic dialects (African American English in Detroit, Wolfram 1969), maintenance of working-class dialects (Belfast, Milroy 1980), and more. Such *speech community studies* emphasize linguistic uniformity and shared norms within a population seen as a unified community, and tend to focus on vernacular dialects of standard, powerful languages.

---

1   Under what circumstances, using which data and methods, for what types of language contexts, etc.

However, since the 1970s they have steadily expanded to include multilingual and code-switching contexts (Fought 2002, Mougeon & Nadasdi 1998), second-language varieties (Preston 1989), and a wide range of language contact situations, including Creole communities (Sanchez 2008), sign languages (Lucas 2001), and endangered languages (King 1989). While multilingualism and language contact are dealt with elsewhere in this volume (see Muysken's contribution), there are many points in common between variation and style-shifting within a single language, and choice among different languages, which have been elucidated in variationist research. Evidently, this perspective is sensitive to the issues raised in Guideline #10 concerning LADO in a variety which is not the speaker's first language: i.e. cases where 'an international *lingua franca...* is the language of asylum seeker interviews... call for particular care', since 'An interviewee with limited proficiency in the language of the interview may – simply because of language difficulties – appear to be incoherent or inconsistent, thereby leading the interviewer to a mistaken conclusion concerning the truthfulness of the interviewee' (Language & National Origin Group 2004: 265).

The Concept of the Speech Community (2): Social Considerations

Complementing the objective and descriptive aspects of linguistic uniformity, social, subjective and perceptual factors also play an important role in defining a speech community. Members also broadly share a set of norms for interpreting the social meaning of variation in speech, as well as a complex system of affective language attitudes (Garrett 2010), hierarchical language ideologies (Irvine & Gal 2000), pragmatic conventions for working out implicit or cultural meanings, etc. Among these are the biases that attach to particular social factors or identities as they are signalled in speech, which have been widely investigated in both experimental and ethnographic studies since the 1960s.

Native speakers imbibe these during socialization into the speech community, but are generally unaware of how they relate to objective linguistic factors. Attitude studies show they are systematically unable to separate language bias from the facts of their own or others' language use, which often aren't accessible to introspection. Under the influence of ideologies that rank social groups, variable features are regularly misinterpreted as categorical; features widely used across groups, but at different frequencies, are mistaken as exclusively used by one group, and assigned on the basis of their social worth rather than actual usage. Native speakers without linguistic training also often have folk views of the number, extent and relationship of dialects and varieties in their own and neighbouring speech communities that are shaped by social, political and cultural beliefs, grounded in prescriptive biases (especially educated speakers), and based upon underlying constructs significantly at odds with the facts described by linguistics (Preston 2002, Preston & Long 2002).

For these and other reasons, native speakers lacking expertise in sociolinguistics frequently cannot reliably identify social characteristics of speakers from their own or similar speech communities (as shown in matched-guise and other test results, Garrett et al. 2003) – though they commonly believe that they can. Such characteristics may relate to ethnicity, social class, education, region, and nationality among others (age and gender too, though acoustic cues may assist here). Educated speakers are likely to be more bi-ased (Baugh 1996), due to having invested their schooling and career in standard-language ideology. Other sorts of production-perception asymmetry also exist, e.g. na-tive speakers are able to produce subtle distinctions of sound changes in progress (vowel near-mergers) within a speech community, but unable to reliably judge them as differ-ent, even in their own speech (Labov 1994).

Considering native-speaker competence in variationist perspective, then, several types of evidence support the finding that degrees of socially-based bias typical of non-expert native speakers (NENS) interfere with their ability to accurately judge the speech of others, even from their own or neighbouring speech communities. There is no doubt that the vernacular speech *production* of NENS authentically represents part of their native speech community's range, and is the typical object of variationist linguistic study; however, NENS *perception* of speech is systematically influenced by social norms, attitudes and ideology beyond their conscious awareness or ability to control. Very little of the wide-ranging research on this topic has yet been applied to the LADO context (Fraser 2009). For these reasons, the *Guidelines* caution that, 'The expertise of native speakers is not the same as the expertise of linguists... people without training and ex-pertise in linguistic analysis should not be asked for such expertise' (Guideline #7).

Variationist Methods and Research Base

The study of language variation and change is a method- rather than theory-driven ap-proach to linguistic science. Standard works, manuals and textbooks describing the evolving methods include Labov 1972 and 1984, Chambers & Trudgill 1998, Milroy & Gordon 2003, Chambers et al. 2002, Ammon et al. 2004, Bayley & Lucas 2007; these also cite a sampling of the thousands of speech community studies comprising the varia-tionist research base. Given the basic insight into the nature and functions of language variation in the 1960s, a radical revision of working procedures and assumptions about the nature of speech data and its analysis was necessary. Variationist linguists are trained in recording spoken data across a variety of contexts, including but certainly not limited to interviews. In accordance with Guideline #5, 'Language analysis requires useful and reliable data', we are competent to collect or advise on collection of such data to a high standard.

The primary object of investigation is vernacular speech – defined as one's native variety, acquired in one's home community and peer group, before school, literacy and exposure to other norms – hence the most systematic and unmonitored level of speech. (This is also the object of most LADO analysis; though it has been argued that speakers can be identified solely on the basis of a second or later-acquired language, cf. Simo Bobda et al. 1999, there is good reason to be wary of such an assumption, see Guide-lines #10 and #11.) When a speaker moves away from their vernacular to other styles, dialects or varieties in their linguistic repertoire, whether because of a conscious deci-sion or unconscious response to factors in the social context, their speech becomes less systematic, more prone to idiosyncrasies and external influences (Labov 1972). Ac-commodation to the speech of their interlocutor is only one such effect, with a large literature (Giles et al 1991). Correspondingly, it becomes more difficult to ascertain precisely the nature of their native speech variety – i.e., to perform LADO accurately.

A wide range of factors which make such shifts likely have been systematically investigated by variationists and other sociolinguists. These include the topic of conversation, the identity of the interlocutors (including relevant parameters such as sex, age, ethnicity, class, region of origin, in-group membership), genre of speaking (e.g. less- or more-structured interview, conversation with known peers or strangers, narrative, etc.), degree of shared knowledge, and so forth. Many of the features which occur in LADO interviews with asylum applicants are explicitly studied in empirical, comparative fashion in the sociolinguistic literature – e.g.,

(2)
- the bureaucratic context in which they occur,
- the unequal power relations among the persons involved,
- the necessity for language choice and interpretation,
- the coupling of purely linguistic issues with social and cultural information,
- the general existence of ethnic/class/racial conflicts which occur in and affect cross-cultural communication,
- pressures on minorities to assimilate linguistically to majorities,
- the prevalence of language contact, code-switching and language mixing,
- the manifestation of inappropriately prescriptive language attitudes and ideologies,

and many more. The methods used to study such contextual factors and their effects on speakers range from experimental to observational to ethnographic. In contrast, 'national origin, nationality and citizenship are all political or bureaucratic characteristics, which have no necessary connection to language' (Guideline #2).

To mention just one area in which social science methods have been extended to variation research, attention has been paid to sampling of speakers, and criticisms levelled at other linguistic approaches which naively assume a simple relationship between one or few speakers and the complex structure of their speech communities. Standard methods in research on language variation and change have included random, stratified or judgment sampling of populations, sized from 12-300 speakers, who can be identified on independent social grounds as sharing social characteristics such as those in (3) which are crucial for acquisition of vernacular language:

(3)
- Lifelong local residence
- Native speaker of the relevant variety
- Parents' local residence
- Few/no years lived outside community
- Shared social networks
- Recognised as local by others
- Sample stratified for age, sex, social class, ethnicity, education, other factors

The key is scientific comparison of heterogeneous groups, made with accountable, replicable, and validated methods. Similar metrics for methodology are routinely applied also to the recording of data, its transcription, qualitative and quantitative analysis, and so on. Such standards are recommended and used by forensic linguists also, some of whom employ a variationist approach.

By comparison, the research base often referred to in LADO reports, especially those I have seen produced by commercial agencies on government contract, is distinctly impoverished. I have examined a range of cases, which can be organized on a continuum according to increasing use of the resources upon which everyday scientific linguistics depends.[2]

(4)

i. No meaningful, empirical comparison is made at all.

ii. A NENS analyst compares speech data to his own competence in a relevant language (not always the same language variety as the asylum speaker), a competence which remains minimally documented or not documented.

iii. A NENS analyst appeals to general knowledge of other NENS as to what 'speaking X' is like.

iv. One or two research products are cited (*Ethnologue*, a grammar, a dictionary), typically treated as a <u>prescriptive</u> norm.

v. The report's content shows evidence of intervention by a supervising linguist, but a NENS analyst's prescriptive views, ideology, bias and folk-beliefs may still influence the resulting report.

vi. A qualified linguist – who holds expertise in the target language, is aware of the issues above, and demonstrates familiarity with a range of variation native to the speech community by citing attested empirical research – performs the analysis (usually with, but sometimes without, consultation with a native speaker).

This last case should in my opinion be the minimal requirement. While it is routine for some agencies, it is a pinnacle of expertise never approached by others.

It needs to be said that in many respects, the study of language variation and change builds on and incorporates earlier approaches to descriptive and theoretical linguistics, including much of the structuralist and some of the generativist models that dominated the 20th century. Its results are broadly compatible with those frameworks. Thus, the existence and some of the patterning of variation is often detectable (though often not in much detail) in descriptions of language situations which are analyzed from other points of view.

Examples of Variation in LADO Reports

It is therefore possible to reanalyze and interpret such language phenomena in the light of principles and findings of variation studies. This is frequently possible with descriptions of little-studied languages generally, and is also useful in LADO.

---

2   My data base currently consists of over 50 reports from four commercial LADO agencies. It is not a sample representative of LADO practices generally (no such sample yet exists). I have also discussed practices and methods with immigration bureau representatives from half a dozen European governments which conduct LADO.

Single variable features may play an important part in differentiating dialects from each other. Most North American English dialects typically pronounce /t/ between vowels as a flap [ɾ], with the sound in *butter* being closer to a /d/ than in most British English dialects, where a common vernacular pronunciation is a glottal stop [ʔ].[3] Finer distinctions can be made between closely-related dialects on the basis of the environments in which such sounds occur (Wells 1982), and even finer ones on the basis of typical frequencies across such environments (Straw & Patrick 2007, also on British /t/) – a common contribution of variation studies.

However, the number of features that show systematic variation even within a single dialect is probably at least in the scores if not hundreds, potentially allowing for secure and highly detailed identification of speech samples to well-studied speech communities. This approach has been used in descriptive and forensic linguistic applications and could be extended to LADO. Studies may need to be commissioned for many language varieties commonly spoken by asylum seekers, but they already exist in some cases (e.g. Liberian English contact varieties, Singler 2004a, 2004b). The co-occurrence of patterns of variation is also central to *language style* models, which relate variation within an individual's speech to larger social patterns across the speech community (Bell 2001, Schilling-Estes 2002).

Clearly, an approach that systematically analyses a large number of features across several domains of language, especially those that tend to co-occur in everyday speech, will be preferred to one which picks out a few features in isolation. The reality of analysis in LADO reports often appears to resemble the latter. Only a small number of features may be typically attended to, in more or often less detail. Particularly 'where related varieties of the speaker's language are spoken in more than one country,' as is commonly the case in LADO, Guideline #8 recommends that 'an analyst should be able to specify in advance whether there exist linguistic features which can reliably distinguish regional varieties, and what they are.' The reason for this is to ensure objectivity and prevent 'fishing expeditions'; however, it is certainly not always the case that such methods are adhered to.

Examples which demonstrate variation are not difficult to come by. In a typical agency report submitted as evidence to the UK courts in 2009, a NENS analyst writes that speaker X 'pronounces alternately open [a] and close-mid vowel /e/, depending on in which position it stands'. Similar statements are made for vowels [a] and [ai]. No further description of linguistic context is given, and such a vague reference to 'position' does not meet everyday standards of description by practicing linguists. The same report says that X 'uses certain words.. typical of.. NE Somalia.. e.g. *garanaayo* 'know of'.. [and] uses certain S Somali words, e.g. *kasaa* 'know of.' In other words, there is alternation here: the speaker knows and uses both words, both sounds, with the same linguistic meaning.

While this information is enough to attest to alternation, it is insufficient to determine (or to allow other experts before the courts to determine) whether it amounts to switching between two distinct dialects, or a mixed dialect (possibly due to the

---

3   The International Phonetic Alphabet, widely used by linguists, permits precise universal descriptions of a wide range of sounds. Its use in LADO reports is recommended by Guideline #3.

speaker's linguistic history, e.g. parents of different dialect groups), or systematic inherent variation within a single variety – three diagnoses which are unlikely to all be equally plausible or coherent with an asylum seeker's account of her life history. The result of faulty analysis may be to assign a speaker to the wrong region, wrong ethnic group, wrong side of a national border, or even to declare her unable to speak her native variety at all (a result noted several times in the UK when an asylum seeker later gives fluent oral evidence before a judge, through a court-appointed interpreter, using the language variety she was deemed unable to speak).

On the basis of the data above, a variationist linguist might well have concluded that X's speech shows evidence of switching, or dialect mixing, or variation (both sets of items are said to belong to branches of the Somali language), distinguishing these possible outcomes carefully, and determining what sort of data would allow one to choose between them in a principled fashion. The 2009 report however simply says:

(5) X 'speaks w/certain phonological features typical of a variety of Somali spoken in NE Somalia', but 'has at certain moments some features typical of a variety spoken in southern Somalia'

It goes on to give this surprising overall conclusion: 'The person speaks a variety of Somali found *with certainty not* in S Somalia', but rather '*with certainty* in NE Somalia, with features of a variety of S Somali.' It seems to imply that the alternation of regional dialects could plausibly link a speaker to one of the two relevant regions, but can safely be ruled out for the other.

However, especially considering the very small amounts of data provided (e.g. only two words as evidence for one feature), most variationist linguists would probably find it difficult to agree, particularly as to the degree of certainty which is expressed. Such evidence in isolation is not capable of resolving a speaker's dialect origin. The report fails to distinguish variable phenomena from categorical (obligatory) ones, and to recognise that regional dialect variation is to be expected. Moreover, it fails to provide an explicit (general linguistic or variationist) line of reasoning for its strong conclusions, or to consider possible counter-arguments, thus going against the spirit of scientific methodology, which can be defined as 'a careful, serious search for error in one's own work' (Labov 1972: 99).

Why Variationist Work Should Contribute to LADO

One must remember that the conclusions expressed in reports, and the degree of trust placed in them by bureaucrats and judges, may be the determining factor in an asylum decision, potentially a matter of freedom from persecution and danger. In such circumstances, quite ordinary in LADO cases, one needs to be highly confident of correctly answering the basic question, which is a sociolinguistic one:

(6) 'How does an applicant's linguistic performance in a LADO context correlate with their history of language socialization and speech community membership?'

To this end, a linguistic method and analytic practice should ideally be able to:
-   Specify strong criteria for identifying a language variety in advance;

- Collect data of quantity and quality required to support robust investigation;
- Elicit speech across a range of contexts, varying the relevant social factors;
- Identify and separate the facts of language distribution and use from normative responses, thus eliminating native perceptions and biases;
- Quantify the data appropriately in order to discover patterns of variation;
- Employ analysis techniques compatible with other linguistic perspectives;
- Demonstrate awareness of the significance of social context in interpretation;
- Compare results to a large research base using similar established methods; and
- Distinguish idiosyncratic patterns from what is a normal range of variation for a speech community.

There are doubtless other desirable criteria worth advancing for a suitable linguistic method, but I believe it is clear that the principles, methods, analytical techniques, and research base which characterize the general study of language variation and change satisfy the above criteria.

Variationist research uses empirical, accountable, replicable methods to produce descriptions of language structure and use that correspond to the social reality of speech communities. Moreover, the kinds of social distinctions relevant to asylum judgments (e.g., region of origin, clan membership, education/literacy, multilingual repertoire, etc.) are amenable to study using existing sociolinguistic variationist procedures. Such development would supplement, and not supplant, the other essential core areas of linguistic science (phonetics, syntax, morphology, etc.) which should inform analysis.

An argument against recommending variationist methods in LADO might be the small research base of descriptions for relevant languages. However compared to the existing research base often used in LADO, this is not especially convincing. A single good research article, MA or PhD thesis could provide a better basis of comparison than is often utilised by analysts, and increase the validity of reports. Ideally, governments will find it worthwhile and reasonably quick to support and even commission work (through typical academic processes such as peer-review, research council funding, etc., of course, to guarantee scientific standards), in order to improve the soundness of their decision-making. (The Swiss government LADO unit Lingua collaborates with reputable outside researchers to study the quality of their interview and analysis methods.) The problem of finding genuine reference speakers is a difficult but not an insoluble one, especially given that variationist researchers have a track record of collecting high-quality data in adverse circumstances. Linguists have responded quickly to calls for studies of endangered languages (which some LADO cases are); states fund and perform fact-finding COI missions.[4] Why not similar missions for crucial LADO data, using variationist methods?

Another objection that might be moved is that many asylum seekers plausibly have complex linguistic biographies due to a series of disruptions and dislocations, sometimes early in life. It could be argued that a focus on unified speech communities does not respond to such stories. However, these intricate life (hence, language) experiences and

---

4   Country of Origin Information (COI) is regulated by international guidelines in Europe (EU 2008); no such standards have been signed up to for provision of reliable language information.

trajectories are difficult to model in any existing type of linguistic description (Blommaert 2009), and they are likely to involve dialect and language contact, loss, and acquisition – areas well represented in studies of language variation and change.

Scholars are trained in this perspective across the Americas and Europe, as well as in the Anglo-Pacific and some Asian nations, so that a large variationist workforce speaking a range of native languages constantly turns its attention to new situations and language ecologies. There is also a strong tradition of applied work in a range of institutional contexts (e.g. educational, forensic, medical), with care applied to methods of data collection and ethical treatment of native speakers. As a discipline it has been established in forensic practice for several decades, and has features which make it a persuasive choice in this context.

For these reasons, the application of a variationist perspective to problems of LADO seems to me very promising.

References

Ammon, Ulrich et al. (2004) *Sociolinguistics: An international handbook of the science of language and society*, 2nd ed., Walter de Gruyter.

Baugh, John (1996) Perceptions within a variable paradigm: Black and white racial detection and identification based on speech, in E.W. Schneider (ed.), *Focus on the USA*, John Benjamins, p. 169-182.

Bayley, Robert & Ceil Lucas (eds) (2007) *Sociolinguistic Variation: Theories, methods and applications*, Cambridge University Press.

Bell, Allan, Back in style: Reworking audience design, in P. Eckert & J.R. Rickford (eds), *Style and sociolinguistic variation*, 2001, p. 139-160.

Blake, Renee, & Meredith Josey (2003) The /ay/ diphthong in a Martha's Vineyard community: What can we say 40 years after Labov?, *Language in Society* 32, p. 451-485.

Blommaert, J. (2009) Language, asylum & the national order. *Current Anthropology* 50(4), p. 415-441.

Chambers, J.K. (2002) Studying language variation: An informal epistemology, in J.K. Chambers, P. Trudgill & N. Schilling-Estes (eds.), *The handbook of language variation and change*, Blackwell, p. 3-14.

Chambers, J.K. & Peter Trudgill (1998) *Dialectology*, 2nd ed., Cambridge University Press.

Chambers, J.K., P. Trudgill & N. Schilling-Estes (eds) (2002) *The handbook of language variation and change*, Blackwell.

Eades, Diana & Jacques Arends (eds) (2006) Language analysis and determination of nationality, *International Journal of Speech, Language & the Law: Forensic Linguistics* 11(2), p. 179-266.

European Union (2008) *Common EU guidelines for processing Country of Origin Information (COI)*, April, http://www.unhcr.org/refworld/docid/48493f7f2.html.

Fasold, Ralph W. & Dennis R. Preston (2007) The psycholinguistic unity of inherent variability. In Robert Bayley & Ceil Lucas (eds), *Sociolinguistic Variation: Theories, methods and applications*, Cambridge University Press, p. 45-69.

Fought, Carmen, Ethnicity, in J.K. Chambers, P. Trudgill & N. Schilling-Estes (eds) (2002) *The handbook of language variation and change*, Blackwell, p. 444-72.

Fraser, Helen (2009) The role of 'educated native speakers' in providing language analysis for the determination of the origin of asylum seekers, *International Journal of Speech, Language & the Law* 16(1), p. 113-138.

Garrett, Peter (2010) *Attitudes to language*, Cambridge University Press.

Garrett, Peter, Nikolas Coupland & Angie Williams (2003) *Investigating language attitudes: Social meanings of dialect, ethnicity and performance*, Cardiff: University of Wales Press.

Giles, Howard, Nikolas Coupland & Justine Coupland (eds) (1991) *Contexts of accommodation: Developments in applied linguistics*, Cambridge University Press.

Hazen. Kirk (2007) The study of variation in historical perspective, in Robert Bayley & Ceil Lucas (eds), *Sociolinguistic Variation: Theories, methods and applications*, Cambridge University Press, p. 70-89.

Hymes, Dell H. (1972) Models of the interaction of language and social life, in J.J. Gumperz & D.H. Hymes (eds.), *Directions in Sociolinguistics*, Holt, Rinehart & Winston, p. 35-71.

Irvine, Judith & Susan Gal (2000) Language ideology and linguistic differentiation, in Paul V. Kroskrity (ed.), *Regimes of language: Ideologies, polities and identities*, Santa Fe, New Mexico: School of American Research Press, p. 35-83.

King, Ruth (1989) On the social meaning of linguistic variability in language death situations: Variation in Newfoundland French, in N.C. Dorian (ed.), *Investigating obsolescence*, Cambridge University Press, p. 139-148.

Labov, William (1966) *The social stratification of English in New York City*, Center for Applied Linguistics.

Labov, William (1969) Contraction, deletion and inherent variability of the English copula, *Language* 45, p. 715-762.

Labov, William (1972) Some principles of linguistic methodology. *Language in Society* 1, p. 97-120.

Labov, William (1984) Field methods of the Project in Linguistic Change and Variation, in J. Baugh & J. Sherzer (eds), *Language in Use: readings in sociolinguistics*, Englewood Cliffs: Prentice-Hall, p. 28-53.

Labov, William (1994) *Principles of linguistic change, Vol. 1: Internal factors*, Blackwell.

Labov, William (2001) *Principles of linguistic change, Vol. 2: Social factors*, Blackwell.

Language and National Origin Group (2004) Guidelines for the use of language analysis in relation to questions of national origin in refugee cases, in Diana Eades & Jacques Arends (eds), Language analysis and determination of nationality, *International Journal of Speech, Language & the Law: Forensic Linguistics* 11(2), p. 261-66.

Lucas, Ceil (ed.) (2001) *The sociolinguistics of sign languages*, Cambridge: Cambridge University Press.

Lucas, Ceil, Robert Bayley & Clayton Valli (2001) *Sociolinguistic variation in American Sign Language*, Gallaudet University Press.

McCafferty, Kevin (2001) *Ethnicity and language change: English in (London)Derry, Northern Ireland*, John Benjamins.

Milroy, Lesley (1980) *Language and social networks,* Basil Blackwell.

Milroy, Lesley (2002) Social networks, in J.K. Chambers, P. Trudgill & N. Schilling-Estes (eds), *The handbook of language variation and change*, Blackwell, p. 549-572.

Milroy, Lesley & Matt Gordon (2003) *Sociolinguistics: Method & interpretation*, Blackwell.

Montgomery, Michael (2007) Variation and historical linguistics, in Robert Bayley & Ceil Lucas (eds), *Sociolinguistic Variation: Theories, methods and applications*, Cambridge University Press, p. 110-132.

Mougeon, Raymond & Terry Nadasdi (1998) Sociolinguistic discontinuity in minority language communities, *Language* 74, p. 40-55.

Mufwene, Salikoko S., John R. Rickford, Guy Bailey & John Baugh (eds) (1998) *African American English: Structure, history and use*, New York: Routledge.

Patrick, Peter L. (1999) *Urban Jamaican Creole: Variation in the Mesolect*, John Benjamins.

Patrick, Peter L. (2002) The speech community, in J.K. Chambers, P. Trudgill & N. Schilling-Estes (eds), *The handbook of language variation and change*, Blackwell, p. 573-597.

Preston, Dennis R. (1989) *Sociolinguistics and second language acquisition*, Blackwell.

Preston, Dennis R. (2002) Language with an attitude, in J.K. Chambers, P. Trudgill & N. Schilling-Estes (eds), *The handbook of language variation and change*, Blackwell, p. 40-66.

Preston, Dennis R. & Daniel Long (eds) (2002) *Handbook of perceptual dialectology*, John Benjamins.

Rickford, John R. (1986) Some principles for the study of Black and White speech in the South, in M.B. Montgomery & G. Bailey (eds), *Language variety in the South*, Tuscaloosa: University of Alabama Press, p. 38-62.

Rickford, John R. (1987) *Dimensions of a Creole Continuum*, Stanford University Press.

Rickford, John R. (1999) *African American Vernacular English: Features, evolution, educational implications*, Oxford: Blackwell.

Sanchez, Tara (2008) Accountability in morphological borrowing: Analyzing a linguistic subsystem as a sociolinguistic variable, *Language Variation & Change* 20(2), p. 225-253.

Schilling-Estes, Natalie (2002) Investigating stylistic variation, in J.K. Chambers, P. Trudgill & N. Schilling-Estes (eds), *The handbook of language variation and change*, Blackwell, p. 375-401.

Simo Bobda, A.S., H.-G. Wolf & P. Lothar (1999) Identifying regional and national origin of English-speaking Africans seeking asylum in Germany, *Forensic Linguistics* 6(2), p. 300–319.

Singler, John V. (2004a) Liberian Settler English – Phonology, in B. Kortmann, E.W. Schneider, C. Upton, R. Mesthrie & K. Burridge (eds), *A Handbook of Varieties of English, Vol. 1*, Mouton de Gruyter, p. 65-75.

Singler, John V. (2004b) The Morphology and Syntax of Liberian Settler English, in B. Kortmann, E.W. Schneider, C. Upton, R. Mesthrie & K. Burridge (eds), *A Handbook of Varieties of English, Vol. 1*, Mouton de Gruyter, p. 879-897.

Stanford, James N. & Dennis R. Preston (eds) (2009) *Variation in indigenous minority languages*, John Benjamins.

Straw, Michelle & Peter L. Patrick (2007) Dialect acquisition of glottal variation in /t/: Barbadians in Ipswich, *Language Sciences* 29(2-3), p. 385-407.

Trudgill, Peter (1974) *The social differentiation of English in Norwich*, Cambridge University Press.

Weinreich, Uriel, William Labov & Marvin Herzog (1968) Empirical foundations for a theory of language change, in W. Lehmann & Y. Malkiel (eds), *Directions for Historical Linguistics*, Austin: University of Texas Press, p. 95-189.

Wells, John C. (1982) *Accents of English* (3 vols.), Cambridge University Press.

Wolfram, Walt (1969) *A sociolinguistic description of Detroit Negro speech*, Center for Applied Linguistics.

Wolfram, Walt (1993) Identifying and interpreting variables, in D. Preston (ed.), *American dialect research*, John Benjamins, p. 193-221.

Wolfram, Walt & Erik R. Thomas (2002) *The development of African American English*, Oxford: Blackwell.

Multilingualism and LADO

Pieter Muysken

1.   Introduction[1]

In this paper I will present the main notions pertaining to 'multilingualism' that may be relevant to the LADO community. The paper will be organized in brief sections, under the following headings:
-   Background readings
-   Multilingualism in the world
-   Definition of multilinguals
-   Dimensions of multilingualism
-   Recognition of multilingualism
-   Diglossia
-   L2 acquisition
-   L1 or L2 attrition
-   Bilingual simultaneous acquisition
-   Interference
-   Lingua francas, Pidgins, and Creoles
-   References
-   Multilingualism and LADO

The relevant background question, of course, is to what extent the fact that many of the countries from which asylum seekers originate are multilingual affects our capacities to successfully determine someone's place of birth and/or childhood socialization.

Before going on I should point out that I am using the word 'multilingual' to refer to someone who uses either two (a 'bilingual') or more languages.

2.   Background Reading

There are a number of introductions and handbooks on multuilingualism available. Early influential but still highly readable texts include Grosjean (1983), Appel and Muysken (1987), Romaine (1994). More recent specialized books are Winford (2003), Bhatia and Ritchie (2005), Myers-Scotton (2005), and Altarriba and Heredia (2008), while Grosjean (2010) takes up the theme of his earlier book again. Journals include *Bilingualism: Language and Cognition* (Cambridge University Press, 1998-), the *International*

---

1   A more rudimentary version of this paper was presented at the NIAS workshop. I am grateful to comments from the participants and the co-editors, in particular Maaike Verrips.

Journal of Bilingualism (Sage, 1999-), and *International Journal of Multiilingualism* (Routledge, 2003-).

3. Multilingualism in the World

There are over 6000 languages (depending how you count, since the distinction between language and dialect is far from simple to draw) and over 200 states, so there is an average of at least 30 languages per state. Many languages, of course, are spoken in several states, the so-called cross-border languages. These languages are particularly frequent in Africa, where national boundaries were drawn by the colonial powers. However, there is an enormous variation in the degree of multilingualism of the individual states, ranging from single language states (the prototypical example often cited is Iceland, which now has several immigrant languages, however) to countries like Nigeria with hundreds of languages. The only countries with only one reported language are North Korea (perhaps understudied), the Vatican (with Latin), the Falkland Islands (with English), Saint Helena, and the British Indian Ocean Territory.

There are two major contrasting perspectives on global multilingualism: the 'diversity' perspective and the 'language system' perspective. In the diversity perspective all languages are viewed as more or less of the same status, equivalent manifestations of the potentials of the human spirit (e.g. Haspelmath et al. 2005). Typically, many linguists will adopt this diversity perspective.

In the system perspective, languages are viewed as part of a hierarchy of more or less centrally used languages (e.g. de Swaan 2001), with English as the most frequently used, 'central' language. Thus in Kenya we find the hierarchy in A. between three languages (an international prestige language, an intermediate status, and a low status local language) and in B. the same for Peru.

A. *Kenya* B. *Peru*
   English   Spanish
   Swahili   Quechua
   Luo   Amuesha

In the system perspective, championed by the sociologist De Swaan, and adopted by many social and political scientists, it is not so much the properties of the languages as such that are central, as the position these languages have within societies and their attractiveness as useful systems to know for wider communication.

The fact that English and Spanish are high up in these hierarchies is reflected in the fact, among other things, that many people want to learn these languages as a second language while 'tribal languages' like Luo and Amuesha are not frequently taught or learned as second languages.

The following overview lists some countries with a tradition of asylum seekers and language numbers as reported in the *Ethnologue* (Lewis 2009).

Nigeria	521
Congo	217
Senegal	46
Liberia	31

In West Africa, Nigeria is clearly the country with most languages (in fact, it ranks third world wide, after Indonesia and Papua New Guinea), but many languages in the region have many languages.

Sudan	134
Ethiopia 88	
Kenya	74
Eritrea	18
Somalia	15

In northeastern Africa, Sudan and Ethiopia stand out in terms of their language diversity.

Iran	79
Pakistan	77
Afghanistan	52
Turkey	45
Iraq	26
Syria	22

In the Middle East, there is a surprising amount of language diversity, with figures which do not diverge very much once population is taken into account.

Notice that countries will often not portray themselves as bilingual. Some readers will be surprised that a country like Turkey harbors 45 languages, while the Turkish government until recently insisted that only one language was spoken there. More on this below.

A further important point is that languages are often linked to specific regions in a country, and the nature and degree of multilingualism may vary accordingly. Languages 'low' on the status hierarchy are often local, while intermediate status and high status languages are often regional or even cross-border languages.

A final important point is that, although I have cited the *Ethnologue* here for convenience sake, it is not as reliable as the exactitude of its figures suggests. Speaker numbers are notoriously hard to come by (based on self reports? based on linguistic research?) and sometimes partly political in nature. To label something a 'language', a 'dialect', a 'variety' is likewise often politically determined. The *Ethnologue* sometimes also contains information about multilingualism, but it more often than not impressionistic.

4.   Definition of Multilinguals

What counts as a 'multilingual'? When do we call someone a multilingual? In most current definitions two features stand out:
(a) 'Use' is central rather than 'knowledge'. Use implies knowledge, but not vice versa. Knowing many languages (as reported e.g. of the archeologist Heinrich Schliemann, the discoverer of Troy) makes one a polyglot, but using all these languages makes one a multilingual.
(b) A multilingual need not know all languages she or he uses with perfection.

Thus we can define a multilingual as '*someone who uses more than one language, however imperfectly, in daily life*'. The inclusion of the criterion 'in daily life' also points to the social dimension of multilingualism: using these multiple languages in daily life in not something one does on one's own.

5.   Dimensions of Multilingualism

It will be clear from the above that multilingualism is a complex phenomenon. In fact it has many dimensions, both psychologically and socially.

Hierarchy and symmetry. First of all, the different languages very often do not have the same position and status, neither in the life of the individual nor in society. It is rare that languages are exactly equal for the speaker. Relevant factors are age of acquisition (childhood versus school age versus later in life), competence (active and fluent versus only passive or rudimentary), domain of use (home versus work, see below), etc.

Societal versus individual. Multilingualism may exist on the societal level, without this implying that all or most members of a society are multilingual. Belgium is a multilingual country, with German, French, and Dutch as officially recognized languages, but that does not mean that Belgians will typically be multilingual in those languages. In fact, they may know Lingala or Arabic next to French, but no Dutch or German, or English next to Dutch, but no French.

Written versus oral multilingual traditions. People may use several languages in their daily lives, but not all languages in a written form. In most cases this is because a particular language may not have a tradition of written use; sometimes because a speaker may not have access to the writing system associated with that language. Speakers themselves may only 'count', in self-reports about their knowledge or use of languages, those languages that they can write in.

Legal recognition, status, and prestige. In the background to everything said so far, there is the important question of status and legal recognition. It is very rare (South Africa is an exceptional case in point) that a state will recognize all languages spoken within its borders, and even in South Africa languages of immigrants are not recognized.

Territoriality. In the highly multilingual nation of Paraguay, the two main languages, Spanish and Guarani, are not linked to a specific territory, while a language like Enhlet (also termed Lengua or Mascoy) is spoken in a specific region. In other countries, like Belgium and Switzerland, most languages are predominantly tied to a region, with only a few regions officially or de facto multilingual. Thus multilingual profiles are often territory- or region-specific.

6. Recognition of Multilingualism

We know of these 6000+ languages in the world because mostly Western academic linguists and missionaries have been studying these languages in many places for centuries now, in the wake of the colonial expansion. Currently, an evangelical Christian organization , originally from the U.S. but now global, called Summer Institute of Linguistics International, maintains a database of all languages, the already cited *Ethnologue*, because it feels the New Testament needs to be translated into every language spoken.

It is certainly not the states that have been spreading the word about multilingualism; state ideologies are more often attuned towards idealized monolingualism. It must be recognized, however, that partly with UNESCO support many countries have now published inventories of the languages spoken in their territory. Again, this rarely includes languages of economic immigrants or refugees.

7. Diglossia and Functional Specialization

In many multilingual language settings there is a 'complimentary social distribution' between languages. Each language has its own niche and sphere of use. Typical contrasts are those between the language of the office and the language of the home. The first then is a language of prestige, while the second has much less prestige. The language of the office typically is a second language for many speakers, while the home language is a first language, learned in childhood. This contrast between two varieties, each with a separate sphere of use, is termed *Diglossia*. Often, more than two varieties are involved, however.

In some areas in northern Morocco, as many as seven languages can be heard, each with their distinctive sphere of use:

Language use in areas in northern Morocco	
Dutch	AMONG IMMIGRANTS TO THE NETHERLANDS AND FLANDERS ON SUMMER HOLIDAYS
English	TOURISM AND BUSINESS
Spanish	WITH RESIDENTS OF SPANISH ENCLAVES AND TRADERS
French	HIGHER EDUCATION, SOME MEDIA
Classical Arabic	RELIGION AND OFFICIAL COMMUNICATION
Moroccan Arabic vernacular	IN THE REGION AND IN THE CITIES
Local Berber variety	AT HOME AND IN THE VILLAGE

Speaking more generally, when there are several languages in a community, they all tend to have their distinctive spheres of usage. Recall that this profile will only hold for parts of northern Morocco; in other parts other configurations can be found.

When speakers are interviewed in a formal setting, they will feel most comfortable and speak and act most naturally when the choice of language conforms to their expectations of the social appropriateness of a particular language choice.

8.   L2 Acquisition

While the vast majority of children grow up with one or more languages that they acquiire as first languages (L1 acquisition), not everyone, but perhaps half the world's population, also learn one or more languages later in life (L2 acquisition).

There are vastly different degrees of success in L2 acquisition. Poland-born Joseph Conrad learned English well enough to become a highly regarded novelist in that language, while Diego Maradona's English is nothing to write home about. A number of factors influence one's success in learning a second language.

Starting age. Perhaps the most important factor is the age at which one starts learning a second language. Scholars disagree about the exact turning point and the reasons for the difference, but it is clear that starting at thirty is harder than starting at fifteen, for example.

Individual differences. It is also clear that individuals differ greatly in the ease with which they pick up a second language, although there is less clarity about the nature of the psychological traits that make for the difference.

Nature of the input and interaction. A third factor concerns the nature of the input to which a learner is exposed and of the interaction in which the learner is engaged. Just seeing the news makes learning much harder than having a neighbor who likes to chat with you in the second language.

Ambitions, attitudes, expectations. A fourth cluster of factors concerns the ambitions, attitudes, and expectations that a learner brings along. Having the dream of becoming an integral part of a new community and the feeling that this will be possible makes it much more likely that one will learn a new language than if the community of the new language is despised and if the learner has no intention of becoming part of it.

Clearly these factors will interact and sometimes they will reinforce or counterbalance each other, but it is clear that they all play a role.

9.   Bilingual Simultaneous Acquisition

Often languages are acquired (almost) simultaneously by the child rather than in succession with intervals. The circumstances under which this occurs differ widely, however. At the one extreme, there is the bilingual French-German family in Hamburg (mother French, father German) where both parents pursue a conscious one-parent one-language policy, and the child grows up bilingually knowing well that with her mother and close associates of her mother good French is the norm, and with the father and perhaps also in Kindergarten good German is called for.

At the other extreme there is a child growing up in a compound in Lagos, Nigeria, with one parent natively speaking Igbo, the other Yoruba, but other people around using Nigerian Pidgin English or yet other languages, and the child feels her way around trying to make sense of the diversity and high variability in the ways of speaking surrounding her.

Research in setting such as the one in Hamburg has shown that children are very well capable, after a very early mixing period, of keeping the two languages apart. These children also tend not show too much interference between the languages. French is French, German is German.

On the other hand, in the compound in Lagos, there is extremely frequent language mixing (see below), also acquired by the child, and the norms for the different languages are fairly flexible, as are the norms, if any, for the Pidgin. Interference between the languages is the norm rather than the exceptions.

Between these extremes, there are many intermediate situations. The degree of 'interference', mutual influence of the languages spoken, varies widely depending on the situation. Here a few more settings are illustrated (M = mother, F = father, S = siblings, DL = dominant language, OL = other languages):

Hamburg	Los Angeles	Amsterdam	Lagos
M: French	M: Spanish	M: Turkish, Dutch	M: Yoruba
F: German	F: Spanish	F: Turkish	F: Igbo
S: bilingual	S: Spanish, English	S: Dutch, Turkish	S: multilingual
DL: German	DL: English	DL: Dutch	DL: Pidgin
OL: none (English)	OL: none (Korean)	OL: none (English)	OL: Hausa, English

10. Interference and Language Mixing

This brings us to the general issue of interference. The first language (L1) may influence the (L2), and vice versa. The same holds for the L3, L4, etc. In fact all languages an individual uses influence each other, as is shown by language research of psychologists. If I use a Dutch word that resembles an English word, both words are involuntarily 'activated' by neurons in my brain at the same time. However, bilinguals often manage to keep their languages pretty well separate, with occasional influence or interference. The domains in which this mutual influence is typically found include sentence intonation, phonetic detail (how a [v] or an [r] is actually pronounced), expressions and word meanings, and occasionally the order of the words in the sentence.

However, speakers are not aiming to keep their languages entirely separate, but for some reasons they combine them in the sentence, a phenomenon referred to as 'language mixing', 'code mixing', or 'code switching'. Bilingual speakers will mix their languages most often when speaking to someone they know from the same bilingual community. Only rarely do they do this when outsiders are present, unless they are desperately trying to make themselves understood and are trying out various languages with their interlocutors.

11.   L1 or L2 Loss or Attrition

Can speakers 'loose' a language? The answer is yes, but only to some extent. All languages can become 'deactivated' in the brain when not used. Dutch immigrants in Australia sometimes report having 'lost' most of their Dutch. Tsou (1982) reports on the extreme case of women having migrated from China to the US in the early part of the 20th century and forgetting their Chinese, without however acquiring adequate English. He refers to these women as SWONALS (=speakers without a native language).

For the L1, activation generally possible, however, as far as known. People who have 'forgotten' a language often can relearn it very quickly when brought into contact with other speakers of the same language.

Presumably, people must have spoken the L1 for quite some time in their youth. The situation may be different for children who have only used their L1 for a few years before migrating, e.g. adoption children. While age at which the L1 stopped being spoken certainly is a key factor in language loss, I do not know precise studies about the possible cut off point here. Neither am I familiar with research on the role of traumas in this respect.

12.   Lingua Franca's, Cross-border Languages, Pidgins, and Creoles

In many places a lingua franca is used, a common language (also termed *working language* or *bridge language*), not necessarily well-known by everyone, but sufficiently known to be of use. Sometimes these lingua franca's are colonial and imported languages, such as Spanish in Middle America or Arabic in the Middle East. Sometimes they are larger languages indigenous to a region. Thus in Africa Berber (North West Africa), Hausa (West Africa), and Swahili (East Africa) have been and still are important lingua franca's.

Lingua franca's typically are cross-border languages, although in specific cases a cross-border language may be just that: a language spoken on both sides of a particular border, without extensive regional use. Kurdish is a cross-border language (spoken in several varieties in Turkey, Syria, Iraq, Iran) but not a lingua franca in most regions where it is spoken.

Sometimes this lingua franca is a Pidgin (no one's native language, simplified grammar and lexicon), such as Fanagalo in the mines of Johannesburg in the earlier part of the 20th century and Tok Pisin in Papua New Guinea and surrounding areas at least from WWII onward.

Not every lingua franca is a Pidgin, however, and not every Pidgin has lingua franca status.

There may be pidginized varieties of the lingua franca, next to non-pidginized varieties, as is the case with Swahili, which is spoken in its full form on the coast of East Africa and the island of Zanzibar, but spoken in more rudimentary form elsewhere, including the mining areas of eastern Congo.

Next to Pidgins, there are Creoles, languages for which we can date their origin precisely. Typical Creoles are spoken e.g. in Caribbean countries that used to be sugar producing slave colonies. Many Creole languages have indeed emerged out of earlier

Pidgins, and may be used as lingua franca's in a more Pidgin form, as is the case with Creole English in West Africa.

In many highly complex multilingual states, such as Nigeria, a network of non-standard lingua franca's will occupy the intermediate range in the functional hierarchies outlined above under the term diglossia, between the home languages and the official language of the state. In some border areas, the lingua franca's compete with each other, and people may know more than one lingua franca.

13.   Multilingualism and LADO

After all these tidbits of information, we need to ask ourselves what the consequences of multilingualism are for LADO. If everyone were monolingual in the specific single language of their country and no languages crossed national borders, LADO would be simple: the language spoken would be a unique window on someone's origin and identity.

However, the world is not simple. The consequences of multilingualism in some cases are profound and affect at least three dimensions:

(a) Actual proficiency of the asylum seeker may differ considerably for different languages, and there may be mixture and interference. This mixture in turn, depends on the interlocutors. Speakers are unconsciously or consciously very sensitive to the speech situation in which they find themselves, and a LADO interview is a very sensitive and sociolinguistically 'special'situation;

(b) The perception of an asylum seeker of her or his own language competence and proficiency may not reflect reality, since factors of status and functional differentiation intervene. Speakers may overrate their knowledge of more prestigious, and underrate their knowledge of less prestigious languages;

(c) Since in multilingual communities languages are organized in diglossic (functional differentiation with status differences) systems, the choice of a particular language in an admission interview and performance in that language is affected by status considerations;

(d) Patterns of multilingual usage are very local and individual. A national language or lingua franca with wider usage may be known in a provincial town by local male traders or functionaries, but not in the surrounding villages or by women farmers. If expected multilingual competence plays a role in LADO, it must be based on very detailed expertise, expertise often not available.

Things obviously get even more complicated if the asylum seeker has travelled a lot, lived in refugee camps, etc. but this is a topic outside of the area of this brief overview. In any case I hope to have made clear that understanding the natural of multilingual communities as such as such and the sociolinguistic profiles in particular areas is crucial for understanding the nature between the identity of an individual and her or his multilingual proficiency.

14. References

Jeanette Altarriba & Roberto R. Heredia (eds) (2008) *An Introduction to Bilingualism. Principles and Processes*, London: Routledge.

Appel, René & Pieter Muysken (1987) *Language Contact and Bilingualism*, London: Edward Arnold, republished by Amsterdam University Press.

Bhatia, Tej K. & William C. Ritchie (eds) (2005) *The Handbook of Bilingualism*, Oxford: Wiley-Blackwell.

Grosjean, François (1983) *Life with Two Languages: An Introduction to Bilingualism*, Cambridge, Mass.: Harvard University Press.

Grosjean, François (1983) *Bilingual: Life and Reality*, Cambridge, Mass.: Harvard University Press.

Haspelmath, Martin, Matthew S. Dryer, David Gil & Bernard Comrie (eds) (2005) *The World Atlas of Language Structures*, Oxford: Oxford University Press.

Lewis, M. Paul (ed.) (2009) *Ethnologue: Languages of the World*, sixteenth edition, Dallas, Tex.: SIL International. Online version: http://www.ethnologue.com/.

Li Wei & Melissa Moyer (eds) (2008) *Blackwell Guide to Research Methods in Bilingualism and Multilingualism*, Oxford: Wiley-Blackwell.

Myers-Scotton, Carol (2005) *Multiple Voices: An Introduction to Bilingualism*, Oxford: Wiley-Blackwell.

Romaine, Suzanne (1994) *Bilingualism*, 2nd edition, Oxford: Wiley-Blackwell.

Swaan, Abram de (2001) *Words of the world*, Cambridge: Polity Press.

Tsou, B.K. (1982) The language of SWONALS (speakers without a native language): A study on semilingualism and accelerated creolization, in H. Baetens-Beardsmore (ed.), *Aspects of theory on bilingualism*. Brussels: Didier, p. 125-167.

Winford, Donald (2003) *An introduction to contact linguistics*, Oxford: Wiley-Blackwell.

Speech Technology for Accent Identification and Determination of Origin

Dirk Van Compernolle

Introduction

Speech Technology has become an element in our daily lives over the past two decades. Speech compression was one of the essential ingredients in the development of mobile phones. Speech Synthesis is pervasive in public announcement systems and route planning devices. Speech Recognition is used for access of information over the phone and has become popular for dictation in a number of specific situations, e.g. when the user is not sitting behind his desk while inputting the information. The most successful application of speech recognition today is likely the dictation of medical reports by radiologists who do this standing up in front of a backlit display. Automatic language identification is incorporated in every modern text processor and spoken language identification may be found in customer service centers for switching customers to the right operator. Some of the most sophisticated usage of speech technology is found in the military and intelligence community. Speech-to-speech translation has been deployed for assisting non native doctors in first-aid posts in foreign countries. Language identification combined with keyword spotting is used to identify which calls may be worth listening to for intelligence purposes.

In this contribution we want to focus on one subarea of speech technology, i.e. automatic accent identification, as it is the technology that is the most pertinent to the problem of determining the origin of the speaker. Accent identification may be used for speaker (origin) identification but is also interesting in the context of speech recognition. Automatic speech recognition systems tend to degrade rapidly when subjected to highly accented speech. Dedicated pronunciation models for specific classes of accents (native or non-native) may bring performance back to acceptable levels.

In order to understand how automatic accent identification works we will first give a brief introduction to speech recognition in general as all language and accent identification schemes rely on speech recognition technology for part of the solution. Then in the second part we focus on specificity of the accent recognition problem. Using Language for determining the origin (LADO) of the speaker is one particular usage of such accent identification systems. However, practical usage often involves "under-resourced" languages, i.e. languages for which little of the speech and language resources required to build these automatic systems are available. In the last part we review the impact of limited resources on typical LADO situations.

Automatic Speech Recognition

The Speech Signal, a Bearer of Multiple Information Sources

In everyday conversations we may pay little attention to the fact that speech sounds contain much more information than the underlying words. Nevertheless, unconsciously and implicitly we are aware of it. Functionally speaking, we may say that any speech signal depends on:

- CONTENT: WHAT is being said, as given by a plain transcription
- META INFORMATION: additional information on HOW it is said and which might be added in an enriched transcription
    - o (physical, long term) speaker characteristics: gender, pitch range, voice properties
    - o (learned, time varying) speaker/speaking characteristics: accent, pronunciation details, intonation, tempo, stress pattern, moodiness, ..
- CHANNEL: HOW and WHERE we hear the signal or where it is recorded
    - o reverberation characteristics of the room, background noise
    - o recording equipment

SPEECH RECOGNITION is the technology that converts a speech signal to a transcript. SPEAKER RECOGNITION identifies the speaker. Closely related technologies are GENDER and ACCENT identification which cluster the speakers into a small number of groups based on voice properties.

Looking at this wealth of information from an information theoretic viewpoint only draws our attention even more to the richness of the acoustic signal beyond its content. One intuitive way of getting insight into this, is to look at the bit rates of popular encodings and to see which information is preserved in an undisturbed manner for each of these schemes.

SIGNAL COMPRESSION	QUALITY	BIT RATE
uncompressed, wideband (CD)	highest quality audio	705. 6 kbits/sec
audio compression, wideband (MP3)	highest quality audio	100.0 kbits/sec
digital telephony (ISDN)	good quality on narrowband signals	64.0 kbits/sec
speech compression, telephone BW	good quality on single voice	8.0 kbits/sec
ultra compressed, telephone BW	understandable for single voice	1.2 kbits/sec
phonetic transcription	content	0.05 kbits/sec

One could state that the task of SPEECH RECOGNITION is to perform the ultimate form of data compression on a speech signal while preserving the corresponding transcription with 100% accuracy.

A Model for Speech Production and Recording

The previous paragraph highlights different contributions to structural variability in a speech signal. Understanding these contributions, however, does not imply that we can build a simple model of speech in which all of these effects can be manipulated independently in a straightforward manner. E.g. the precise pronunciation of a sound is the result of a complex mix of sound identity, the speaker's accent, the phonetic context and some random variability.

Notwithstanding these reservations, a simple model of speech generation and recording exists, that separates a number of the influences and tells us quite a bit as to how other effects may influence the speech signal. This model is shown in Figure 1.

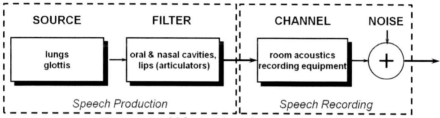

Figure 1: Model for Speech Production and Recording

Production of a speech sound is initiated by energy released from the lungs; then, this raw energy passes the glottis either unaltered or modulated after which it is filtered by the articulators. This resulting clean speech sound then travels through the air before it is captured by someone's ears or recorded by a device. On its way it gets further filtered by the acoustic channel and the recording equipment. Finally extraneous noise coming from other acoustic sources may be injected into the recording as well.

Let's first focus on clean speech as generated by the speech production model and what properties of the signal can be understood from the production model. In Figure 2 we see different waveform and spectral representations of the word "be". The left pane shows the time-varying nature of speech (1.2 seconds is shown in total); the right pane focuses on a 30msec snapshot, extracted from the middle of the sound at around 0.65sec. Three types of information are shown: (i) the time waveform (top picture in both panes), (ii) a detailed spectral analysis (middle picture at the left) showing all harmonics in the signal (fundamental is 100Hz in this case), (iii) a wideband spectral analysis (bottom picture at the left) giving a smooth representation of the spectral envelope. In the main picture in the right pane a single spectral slice is presented in which narrowband and wideband representations are overlaid.

The jagged curve is the narrowband spectrum; it shows a spectrum with sufficient resolution such that the individual pitch harmonics can be seen. It is the spectrum obtained when using analysis parameters derived from the human auditory system. The spectral envelope shows a spectrum in which individual pitch harmonics are not visible anymore but only a smooth overall picture of the energy distribution over frequencies. One may think of it as obtained by putting a veil on top of the narrowband spectrum.

In practice this is done by applying complex smoothing techniques such as cepstral analysis[1]. It may alternatively be obtained by applying a wideband spectral analysis directly on the signal, though this method has a number of undesirable side-effects and is typically not used anymore in today's systems.

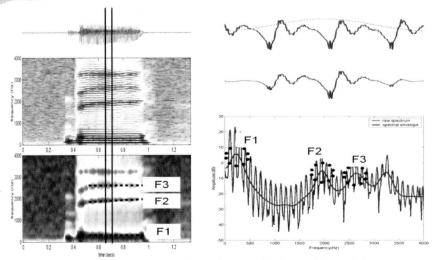

Figure 2: Time Waveform and Spectra for the English word 'be'

Now, how do the different components in the speech production model relate to the (spectral) characteristics of a sound?

- the overall *amplitude* is a function of the energy release in the lungs and will shift the spectral envelope up and down, but will not affect its shape; the amplitude level only influences overall loudness and has no direct impact on content; variation over time may be relevant, mainly to convey the right intonation
- the harmonic structure (as seen in the narrowband analysis) is due to the vibrations of the glottis; the rate of vibration can be matched 1-to-1 with *pitch* perception, i.e. the ranking that we give a sound on a musical scale; the global pitch range is person specific; within sentence pitch variations relate to intonation (question/statement) and within syllable/word pitch variations carry content information as well in tonal languages (Mandarin, Thai, Vietnamese, ..); the spectral envelope on the other hand is independent of the pitch
- *spectral envelope* (as given by the wideband analysis) is fully determined by the position of the articulators while uttering sounds; moreover, perception is dominated by the peaks (called Formants: F1, F2, F3, ..) in the envelope; however, such peak analysis is only easy and valid for vowels, for consonants other shape characteristics may be required; relating formants to sounds is not as trivial as one might hope as formants are heavily influenced by neighboring sounds (look at the onset of the

---

1   Cepstral analysis not only performs the required smoothing to produce a smooth spectral envelope but simultaneously generates cepstral features which are a very compact representation of that envelope and therefore a popular feature set for speech recognition

sound [i] in /be/) , also formants are speaker dependent as the shape of the vocal tract differs from person to person and formants will be influenced by the accent of a person as well

In conclusion, the spectrum a speech signal can be decomposed into amplitude, pitch and spectral envelope of which the latter carries almost all articulatory, thus also phonetic, information.

A Pattern Matching Approach to Speech Recognition

All of today's automatic speech and speaker recognition systems use a statistical pattern matching approach, though detailed algorithms may differ substantially from one system to another.

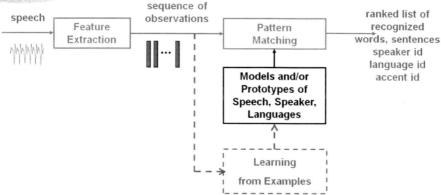

Figure 3: Speech Recognition by Pattern Matching

First features are extracted from the raw signal which ideally should have following dual property: (i) they contain all information necessary for the target classification problem and (ii) they are as compact as possible, i.e. they avoid redundancy and contain no irrelevant information and no noise.

During a training phase (dashed components) statistical properties are learned for each of the defined classes (these classes can be phonemes or abstract sub-phonetic units, but also speakers, languages, accents, ..). These properties are stored in the models representing the classes. Then, during recognition, an incoming feature stream is matched vs. all models or possible model sequences and the best match is selected as the recognized one.

It is important to understand some of the basic limitation of ALL statistical pattern matching systems:

- the ultimate system can never be better than the data that it learned from during the training phase; peculiarities absent in the data can by no means be reflected in the trained models

- the ultimate system can never be better than the underlying model; i.e. we need to use sufficiently relevant features, the correct classes and understand the statistical distributions of the features in all classes
- finally, we need enough data to train all of the parameters in the model accurately; in practice we often need to make compromises, i.e. the number of the parameters in the system may be dictated by the amount of available training data rather than by the intrinsic understanding of the problem; a well known adagio is "there is no data, like more data"

The dramatic improvements in speech recognition accuracy, during the 1980's and 1990's, was to a large extent due to rather straightforward scaling of the existing paradigm. Improvements in computer technology allowed scientists to train more complex models based on more and more data. State-of-the-art systems in the mid 80's relied on databases of maybe 20 hours, while database sizes grew to over 100 hours in the mid 90's and up to several thousands of hours today. While further improvements with more data are slower and slower, there is no real bottoming out effect yet.

Feature Extraction & Normalization

The goal of feature extraction is to extract a compact set of relevant features from the raw data in view of the back-end classification task. Hence, depending on the task the extracted features may be different. To give a simplistic example: eye color is a relevant feature if trying to determine race or country of origin of a person, but utterly irrelevant if gender classification is the target application. As illustrated by the speech production model it is the smoothed spectral envelope that carries the phonetic information (except for tonality) and is a parametric representation of this envelope that will be computed and used as features in a speech recognition system.

In most situations we don't have access to the clean speech signal (a close talk microphone is required for that) as it is filtered by the recording channel and obscured by background noise in the final recording. This filtering is reflected into the measured spectral envelope. Rather adequate compensation schemes have been developed for situations where channel and background noise are stationary, i.e. when they don't change over time. The applied concept is "measure-and-correct". We make use of the fact that speech sounds are short and come in almost random sequences, making that the long term average spectrum of speech is a constant. Hence the measured long term average spectrum is a combination of the long term average clean speech spectrum, and the presumed constant channel and background influences. Moreover, speech comes with pauses during which we observe only the background noise only. Combining these two observations allows us to measure the impact of these stationary disturbances quite accurately and use them to transform a noisy spectrum into a good estimate of the clean speech spectrum. In non-stationary situations compensation schemes are considerably more complex and less effective. The reason why we want to feed estimates of 'clean speech' to the pattern recognition system is obvious: the extracted parameters should be the same independent of the recording conditions otherwise the statistical pattern matching system will fail.

Accent Identification

About Dialects and Accents

Dialects can differ from each other in many different ways. Word usage may differ substantially or the pronunciation of certain words may deviate heavily from one dialect to another. Sometimes dialects can be identified on the basis of specific words or specific phoneme strings. However, the occurrence of such words or constructs may be unpredictable and not happen for a long time in any given conversation. Hence, while such specific phenomena are often good indicators, their occurrence may be too rare to be of great practical use in automatic systems.

Apart from these specific phenomena, regional variation normally implies systematic pronunciation variability as well. Such systematic variations often come in two flavours: chain shifts and mergers. In order to preserve the same average distinction between sounds, one sound cannot change without forcing its closest neighbours to another place in acoustic space as well, and so on. Such chain shift might take the effect of a rotation of the vowel triangle in the F1-F2 formant space, as documented in some studies by Labov (Labov, 1996). Mergers is a quite different type of phenomenon in which two distinctive sounds are mapped to a single sound in a specific accent; obviously, this is only possible if such systematic merge will introduce only very few confusable homophonic pairs.

These systematic variations are of much greater interest to automatic systems, as they occur in a persistent way, independent of the content. Moreover, most speakers cannot hide or fake this, even when trying to speak "standard" language. Systematic changes in the average formant positions for vowels /I/, /A/, /u/ as in the Dutch words, "dik", "dak", "doek" are illustrated below. The regions are clustered into 3 classes for visualization (Antwerp+Brabant, Limburg, West and East Flanders). Apart from a notable rotation we may also observe contraction and elongation of the vowel triangle.

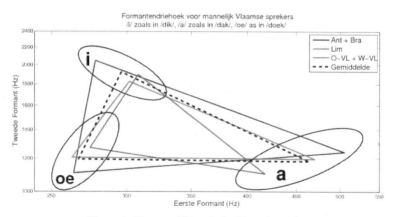

Figure 4: Formant Triangle for Flemish Dialects

Concerning Dutch, Knops (Knops, 1984) investigated if listeners from Flanders and the Netherlands could identify whether semi-spontaneous speech fragments were spoken by a person from Belgium or from the Netherlands, and, if possible, could specify the regional identity of the speaker. Country identification was nearly perfect (96%). Identification was mainly done on pronunciation (90%), morphology (42%) and on intonation for the Dutch listeners (44%). Identifying the region (open choice, 10 regions) was much more difficult; only 16% of all speakers were classified correctly by the Belgian listeners while 18% were classified correctly by Dutch listeners. Results are significantly better (~45%) if Flemish listeners only need to identify Flemish accents and Dutch listeners only Dutch accents.

The ESAT Automatic Accent Identification System

At K.U.Leuven-ESAT we developed a system for automatic accent identification for a similar task (Wu, 2008). We used read speech from the COGEN corpus consisting of 174 Flemish speakers – all instructed to speak 'standard' Dutch - and tried to identify their region of origin. As region classes we used the 5 provinces, which correlate well with accent, but whose boundaries definitely are not identical to where a dialectologist would place them. The fuzzy class definition in combination with 'read, standard' speech makes this task particularly hard. In an informal setup 8 untrained native listeners classified on average only 45% correctly. A simple classifier using cepstral features as input and a mixture of Gaussians for the modeling the class distributions works very well (>95%) for distinguishing male vs. female or Dutch vs. Flemish, but when used for the accent identification task the result is only slightly better than chance which is another indication of the complexity of the task. With the ESAT system we achieved over 70% accuracy in a semi-supervised setup (the semi-supervision exists in the fact that we assume a rather accurate transcription to be available at the work level, alternatively that the Phoneme Recognizer in the picture below has a near perfect accuracy).

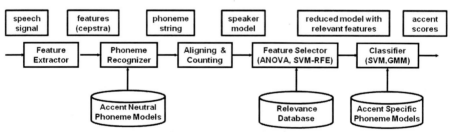

Figure 5: The ESAT Accent Identification System

The ESAT system (Figure 5) has the following components:
1. In a first step a speaker model is computed containing the average pronunciation of each phoneme in the language; the parameters in such speaker model typically are cepstra, similar to what is being used in speech recognition technology.
2. From the raw speaker model (1482 parameters) the most relevant parameters (only some 120) are extracted for accent identification. The rest is discarded.
3. Finally the accent classifier using SVM (Support Vector Machines) determines the speaker's accent.

The second step in this process was found to be crucial. How should we understand this? Typically a recognizer works better if it gets more (relevant) information; however, if the additional information is too noisy the impact on performance may not be neutral and even negative. Clearly for accent identification, the system wants to focus on a few consistent anomalies in the pronunciation. Some sounds are not susceptible at all to accent variation, others are only in minute aspects of them. In order for the system to perform optimally we first need to discover which are the relevant features. This information is stored in a relevance database (Figure 6) that was obtained from the COGEN training database containing 174 speakers. The same database had been used to train the accent independent speech recognizer.

The relevance database for Flemish dialects tells us the following:
- all diphthongs (ei, oei, aau, …) are highly relevant;
- many consonants (e.g. f,v,s,z,m,n) are utterly irrelevant;
- for the relevant consonants (e.g. t,k,ch) only the very broad spectral features (represented by c2 and c3) are retained for classification.

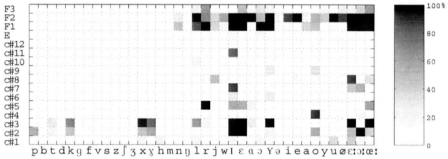

Figure 6: Relevance Database for Flemish Accent Identification (the gray scale is an indication of the amount in which a feature may contribute to accent identification; features shown are cepstra 1-12, Energy and Formants 1-3)

In our work we found that it was easiest to work with features derived from speech recognition technology, that sadly enough do not always translate easily into linguistically inspired features. Linguistically inspired features, while interesting from an interpretative viewpoint, may not always be extracted in a robust manner and ultimately lead to lower performance.

The same approach was tested for the classification of Dutch vs. Flemish. Compared to the Flemish accent identification this is an easy task. This is reflected in many different ways. Almost all features can be determined as relevant and in not too bad acoustic settings a performance of over 96% can be achieved.

Resources and Speech Technology

Technologies based on a pattern matching paradigm, as the ones described in this contribution, invariably need significant resources for development:
- Basic linguistic resources (dictionaries, phonetic dictionaries) are a prerequisite

- Large databases (hundreds of speakers, hundreds of hours) are required for training the acoustic models; ultimate performance will depend on size but also on speaker selection, diversity of recordings, etc.

Moreover there is no easy answer to 'how much data is enough data?'. Till today we see that performance keeps improving with ever growing database. State-of-the-art systems use thousands of hours of speech and billions of words of text to make acoustic and language models. Obviously such resources are only available for large languages with a high economic potential (English, Mandarin, Spanish, ...). Some governments (US in particular) have sponsored campaigns to collect the required materials for other languages that they consider of strategic importance e.g. to develop speech-to-speech translation systems for emergency and first line medical aid in countries like Iraq and Afghanistan.

It is clear that these resources are not in place for many of the languages spoken by a large number of economical and political refugees around the world; let alone that resources would be sufficient to model all regional variants of these already under-resourced languages.

Conclusions

In this paper we have shown that speech technology in principle can be used to distinguish even beyond rather subtle accent differences. Two important remarks need to be made immediately. First of all, the potential performance of such systems will greatly vary from case to case. Some regional variants can be distinguished in an automatic way with almost perfect accuracy (e.g. Dutch vs. Flemish), others may have too high an error rate for practical applications with a judicial impact (e.g. Flemish provinces). This remark is equally valid for technology as for human experts. Moreover in some situations target regional differentiation may align poorly with existing language and accent differences.

Secondly, for automatic accent identification technology to be developed considerable resources (knowledge, databases and manpower) are required. For many languages of interest (in a LADO context) these resources are not available today and it is uncertain that LADO as an application is capable to mobilize the necessary funds to implement these technologies.

Finally, it should also be understood that a technological approach has some great advantages over the use of human experts. The performance of automatic systems is quantifiable and known in advance, whereas very little is known concerning the performance of human experts in this context. Also, once available, a technological system can be deployed more flexible in the field. So despite the early stage of development that this research is still in, it is our opinion that automatic accent Identification is a technology that is capable to perform or support in the not so distant future the determination of the region of origin of people.

References

Knops, U. (1984) Cognitieve en evaluatieve reacties met betrekking tot regionale standaard-variëteiten. Een vergelijking tussen Vlamingen en Nederlanders, *Taal en Tongval* (36), p. 25-49 and 117-142.

Labov, W. (1996) *The organization of dialect diversity in North America*, first presented at the International Conference on Spoken Language Processing; with an extended version available at: http://www.ling.upenn.edu/phono_atlas/ICSLP4.html.

Wu, Tingyao, Jacques Duchateau, Jean-Pierre Martens & Dirk Van Compernolle (2010) Feature Subset Selection for Improved Native Accent Identification, *Speech Communication* (52) February, p. 83-98.

Part Three: Language and Origin: Three Case Studies

Part Three begins with the paper by *Katrijn Maryns*, who focuses on multilingual interactions between individuals and institutions. Marijns discusses data from her research on interviews with asylum seekers in Belgium. *Vincent de Rooij* discusses some aspects of LADO regarding Swahili – a language probably spoken by around 50 million people. *Judith Rosenhouse* presents dialects of Arabic from Iraq, with detailed information on the complexities of Arabic dialect variation in these regions. Each case illustrates potential problems for reliably identifying people's origins.

Identifying the Asylum Speaker: Reflections on the Pitfalls of Language Analysis in the Determination of National Origin

Katrijn Maryns

This paper investigates LADO practices in the Belgian asylum procedure. It explores the ways in which linguistic expertise is called in to assist asylum determination agencies with the task of fact-finding on the basis of speaker identification. LADO is conducted in different ways in the Belgian asylum application process: (a) the use of bilingual language tests in asylum interviews and (b) language examination at the language analysis desk, a governmental information service that applies LADO practices to inform the Belgian asylum agencies. It is argued that although language plays a key role in a person's socialisation and leaves traces of identity, it bears no transparent relation to the social history and the origin of a person. In this respect, this paper takes up a very cautious stand on LADO practices in the Belgian asylum procedure: it advises against the use of bilingual language testing and encourages the development of reliable, linguistically informed research methods.

This paper was published earlier as a contribution to the special issue on language and the determination of national origin of asylum seekers (IJSLL 11/2, 2004). Although the Belgian asylum procedure was reorganised in 2007 by reducing the number of authorities investigating asylum applications, fact-finding and identity assessment techniques are still quite the same. Data analysis and recommendations in this paper are therefore still relevant to the current field of LADO research. Unfortunately however, the Belgian language analysis desk became the victim of its own ambition to reach high quality standards. The desk was very selective about what cases to accept for analysis, but despite its high standards of quality, it was whistled back on the basis of its low productivity and eventually shut down.

Introduction

Early forensic linguistic work was mostly concerned with two domains, voice identification and comparison of handwritten data, both of which are mainly used for the linguistic investigation of authorship for forensic purposes. Forensic linguists consider as one of their tasks the identification of authorship on the basis of sophisticated linguistic analysis. Such analysis may concern linguistic discrepancies such as double negatives, substandard forms of verbs and relative pronouns, mixed constructions, syntactic phenomena such as word frequency or sentence complexity, pronunciation, the syntactic complexity of written records and the phonetic/phonological analysis of spoken data (Labov 1998, French 1994, Gibbons 1994, Kniffa 1996).

Over the last few years a new subdiscipline has come into existence: forensic discourse analysis (Coulthard 1992, Shuy 1993, Sarangi and Coulthard 2000, Gibbons 2003). Forensic discourse analysis mainly deals with collaborative documents, collaboration which is not approved by one of the co-authors, in which the authenticity of the statements is investigated on the basis of analysis in terms of consistency and coherence, repetitions and parallelisms or terms of address. It is mainly applied in the field of police records of interviews with suspects and witnesses, where it is the task of the analyst to investigate on the basis of linguistic analysis what parts of the interviews are faithful reports of the originally produced discourse and what statements have been consciously or unconsciously modified on the basis of trigger notes or simply from memory.

This kind of forensic discourse analysis could equally be applied to official records of narratives produced by asylum seekers in the course of the procedure whose purpose it is to decide whether or not asylum will be granted. Refugee narration appears to articulate a particular blend of linguistic and narrative variation which takes the shape of small textual details, the narrative outcome of which indexes significant aspects of speaker identity and voice (Maryns and Blommaert 2001, Silverstein and Urban 1996). In order to meet the demands of bureaucracy, however, the original discourse needs to be transformed into institutional, written reports. This transformation takes place in the course of the text trajectory from one institution to another in the form of long and complicated entextualization processes, the result of which may be that original meanings are altered or even left out altogether (Maryns and Blommaert 2002). And this is where the demand for a forensic narrative analysis comes in: a micro-analysis of these narratives may reveal a variety of contextualizing information used by applicants to motivate their case, but at the same time this information tends to lose its functionality as the narrative is transformed into an institutionalized written report. As a considerable amount of this crucial information about speaker intentions and identity is contained in small linguistic and narrative details, it requires on the part of the analyst 'consciously attending to the "little" things that most people ignore as they try to understand the "big" things they hear' (Shuy 1993: xviii).

The intention of this article, however, is not to focus on the transformations of applicants' narratives nor to explore overall patterns of linguistic–narrative fusion and micro-shifting (Maryns and Blommaert 2001). Rather, I will – though without leaving the realm of narrative mixing and shifting behind – focus on one particular aspect of forensic linguistic analysis, viz. the use of language analysis in the Belgian asylum procedure in the identification of national origin. The notion of *origin* occupies a central place in the assessment of asylum applications. Yet, although it is a key element in the procedure, given the increasing number of applicants who arrive without any documents to prove their identity, national origin is very hard to determine. In order to live up to the institutional demand for objectivity, the asylum agencies often resort to language analysis for the determination of citizenship. This article explores to what extent a phenomenon as variable as language lends itself to decision making as is the aim of language analysis. It investigates the validity of language analysis in two sets of data, translation practices in the application interview and language analysis at the official language desk, a governmental information service that uses language analysis in order to inform the three Belgian immigration agencies about asylum seekers' origins. The next section provides some background on the Belgian asylum procedure. The third section discusses practices of fact-finding in the procedure. What follows next is the analysis of the two data sets, and a subsequent discussion of the validity of linguistic analysis in the determination of citizenship and, finally, the last section addresses the responsibilities of linguistics in the asylum procedure.

Seeking Asylum in Belgium

Seeking asylum for fear of persecution is an inviolable right, which has been internationally laid down in the 1951 Geneva Convention (see Eades and Arends, this issue). However, since the early 1980s, the asylum policies of many European countries have been characterized by a significant tightening of their regulations. In Belgium, the assessment of asylum cases had always been a responsibility of the United Nations High Commissioner for Refugees (UNHCR). In 1987 this task was taken over by three institutions, the Dienst Vreemdelingenzaken or DVZ (Aliens' Office), the Commissariaat Generaal voor de Vluchtelingen en de Staatlozen or CGVS (Commissioner General for Refugees and Stateless Persons) and the Vaste Beroepscommissie voor Vluchtelingen or VBV (Permanent Commission of Appeal for Refugees). The examination of the asylum application proceeds in two phases: (a) the examination of admissibility: at this stage it is decided whether or not the application is under consideration for further investigation, and (b) the investigation of the merit of the application: this stage involves a thorough investigation of the application on the basis of which the status of refugee is to be adjudged or not. At each of these stages, interviews between asylum seekers and officials about the applicant's motivation for seeking asylum in Belgium occupy a central place in the assessment of the case and each stage involves possibilities of appeal. Given the fact that only a minority of the applicants is able to submit official documents, experiential narration is basically the only tool for explaining and supporting the application. Direct interaction between applicants and officials forms the input for long and complicated textual trajectories across the different stages of the investigation: applicants tell their narratives to officials, who transform them into institutional, deeply modified written reports. These reports are then entextualized – de- and recontextualized (Silverstein and Urban 1996) – as they move from one stage in the procedure to the next and, in this way, the text trajectories are in fact co-narrations of the applicant's account (Blommaert 2001, Maryns 2004).

Since the late 1980s, the number of asylum applications has witnessed a remarkable development. Until about 1984, the number of applications was fairly low, totalling about 3000 applications a year. Between 1989 and 1993, the number increased considerably, from about 12 000 applications in the year 1990 to 25 000 applications in 1993. As a result, the asylum institutions could no longer keep up with the increasing number of applications. It was in this context that public opinion began to demand a tightening of the asylum regulations, one of the basic adaptations being a thorough reconsideration of the asylum regulations to keep economic asylum seekers out of the procedure (OCIV 1997). The number of asylum applications rose to a new high with more than 40 000 applications in 2000. As a reaction to this increase, the Belgian government hurriedly decided to modify both its asylum procedure and its system of administration and social integration of refugees. It was felt that, due to its financial support for applicants combined with the long duration of the procedure, Belgium had gained a reputation of being a very attractive country for seeking asylum. This was also one of the reasons why from January 2001 onwards asylum seekers could no longer look to the government for financial support. Legally speaking, the asylum procedure was not modified; the changes mainly concerned its implementation. In January 2001, the DVZ and the CGVS introduced four new techniques in the handling of applications (BCHV, OCIV and CIRE 2001):

- the *Last In First Out principle*: new applications are given priority over applications made before 3 January 2001. In this way, the treatment of applications filed prior to 2001 falls behind, so that many refugees are kept in a state of suspense or even never gain the recognition they deserve – these files are often ironically referred to as 'first in never out'
- the examination of admissibility is given absolute priority over the investigation of the merit of the application by the CGVS: all means available are deployed to tighten up the first selection of applications and the number of applications that need a thorough investigation increases
- a radical speeding-up of the procedure and an increase in the assessment of the officials' individual productivity
- quota restrictions, phrased in terms of 'special attention to particular nationalities or groups' showing a particularly high increase in the number of applications.

These changes in the asylum procedure were aimed at dissuading refugees from seeking asylum in Belgium. And it worked: in the course of 2001, the number of applications decreased drastically, from 42 000 to 25 000. But the question is to what extent the logic of management and efficiency affects the quality of the procedure (cf. BCHV, OCIV and CIRE 2001, Maryns 2004). It is against the background of this turbulent period – which is also the period during which I collected my data – that the practices described in this article need to be seen.

Identifying the Asylum Speaker: Authentic Self versus Productive Other

Article 52 of the Belgian Immigration Law (1980) lists a number of criteria for determining admissibility. Within this set of criteria, two types can be distinguished: (a) legal-technical criteria, and (b) intrinsic criteria, i.e. criteria concerning the content of the application. As to the latter type, two categories are particularly relevant to my research: (a) compliance with the Geneva Convention ('motives which don't qualify for asylum'), and (b) evidence indicating persecution ('obvious unfoundedness'). The latter criterion implies that the credibility of the case has to be assessed. In this respect, the task of the DVZ/CGVS/VBV official could be conceived of in terms of a twofold investigation, consisting of two equally important subtasks, (a) testing the evidence against the Geneva Convention, and (b) weighing the sufficiency and credibility of the evidence.

A considerable number of non-Convention refugees – mainly economic refugees claiming to be political refugees – enter the asylum procedure and it is one the officials' main tasks to distinguish 'true' from 'false' applications. It is generally believed that there is a tendency among applicants, in their attempt to live up to institutional expectations, to try to fill the gaps between their personal narrative and the institutionally recognized narrative by constructing a 'productive other' through discourse (Barsky 1994: 4):

> the constructed Other stands in the place of the original claimant as a doormat would stand in the place of a house; it bears little semblance to the interior space in which lived experience occurs, but rather fits into too-easily accepted bureaucratic procedure that requires a façade of self-justification rather than veritable representation.

Some of the officials working at the CGVS explained to me that they are often faced with 'rehearsed stories', stories that are prepared and 'constructed' in accordance with the convention criteria. Therefore, in order to assess credibility, interviewers are taught certain identification techniques in the course of their training: in addition to questions about the location of buildings, airports, railways, the distance between towns, the names of streets, rivers, mountains, and motorways or the colour of number plates, asylum seekers whose identity is a matter of dispute are also being tested on the language(s) they speak.

In the course of my fieldwork period, it gradually became clear to me that determining refugee status is not so much a problem of assessing whether the case is compatible with the refugee convention as it is a matter of investigating the veracity of the claim and, in the case of a negative evaluation, of demonstrating that this is so. In other words, it is one thing to decide that the applicant's statements comply with the refugee convention, but quite another to find out whether these statements are reliable. After all, officials are procedurally obliged to provide objective elements in their motivation of each case. This demand for objectivity explains why officials make such a strong appeal to the method of linguistic identification in their assessment of asylum applications. But the question is to what extent a phenomenon as variable as language lends itself to truly objective analysis and decision making. This will be our main subject in the Discussion section below. Before that, however, I shall take a look at some data.

Data Analysis

The data concern (a) an extract taken from an interview at the CGVS in which the interviewer tries to determine the applicant's nationality on the basis of a translation test, and (b) a case of linguistic analysis conducted at the language analysis desk of the Belgian migration agencies.

Translation Tests in the Application Interview

The extract below is taken from a three-hour interview at the CGVS.[1] The asylum seeker (AS) is a 17-year-old boy who claims to come from Sierra Leone. After having

---

1   Transcription symbols are: dots for pauses, xxx for unclear parts of the utterance, = for overlaps and self-corrections and ★★★ for the sound of the official touching the keyboard.

been refused at the DVZ, the asylum seeker has lodged an appeal with the CGVS. The interviewer (I) explains that before asking the applicant about his motivation for seeking asylum in Belgium, he would like to ask some questions about the applicant's identity: who he is and where he is from. In this extract, the interviewer wants to find out, on the basis of a Krio test, whether the applicant comes from Sierra Leone. As the interviewer does not speak Krio himself, he makes use of a standard test:[2] first, he gives some English words and asks for the Krio equivalent, then, realizing that this does not work very well, he switches to a list of Krio words and asks the asylum seeker to give the English translation.

Extract from Interview between Asylum Seeker and CGVS Official

(1) I: What dialects =dialects do you speak?

(2) AS: She? (pointing towards researcher)

(3) I: You

(4) AS: Mende

(5) I: ★★★★★★★★★★★★★★★★★★★★★★★★★★★★★★★ Other dialects?

(6 AS: .... I= IIsabi other dialect Kuku xxxxxxxxxxxxxx no

(7) xxxxxxxxxx no no no no

(8) I: but you mentioned something about Gugu . wha =what's that

(9) AS: I say I don't sabi it

(10) I: (facial expression: doesn't understand)

(11) AS: I don't know it .. I don't know other dialect

(12) I: ★★★★★ and do you know Krio? Do you speak it?

(13) AS: Krio . I don't speak Krio well well ... well well ... because .

(14) because xxxxxxxx

(15) I: ★★★★★★★★★★★★★★★★★★★★★ will we talk some words . we do some

(16) words

(17) urm in Krio . ok? I say some words in English and you try to

(18) translate them in Krio ..

(19) ★★★★★★★★★★★★★★★...... money . how would you translate it in Krio ..

(20) AS: money? .. in Mende orrr..

(21) I: in =in Krio ★★★★★★★★★★★

(22) AS: this Krio I say I don't know Krio well well

(23) I: ★★★★★★★★★★ but do you know what money is in Krio?

(24) AS: money

(25) I: ★★★★★★★★★★★★★★★★★

(26) AS: xxxxxxxxxxxxxx (inaudible between AS and his adviser)

(27) I: ★★★★★★★★★★★★★★★★★★★

(28) AS: I don't know how you call it

(29) I: ★★★★ do you know what onion is in =in =in Krio

---

2   The translation test is used by several asylum agencies in Europe. Although its actual origin is hard to determine, the hypothesis is that the Belgian agencies have borrowed this method from foreign language desks.

(30) AS: xxx anja

(31) I: ★★

(32) AS: anja

(33) I: anja

(34) AS: anja

(35) I: ★★★★★★ were you working on the farm with your parents?

(36) AS: yeah

(37) I: what kind of vegetables were you growing?

(38) AS: we grow rice

(39) I: ★★★★★★★★★★★ do you know what urm plenty is in =is in Krio

(40) AS: xxxxxxxxxxx call planting

(41) I: plenty

(42) AS: (sighs) no

(43) I: ★★★★★★★★★★★★★★★★★★★★★★★★★★★ do you know what rice is in

(44) =in Krio ★★★★★★★★★★★★★★★★★★★★

(45) AS: ne the thing is this if da Mende he talk yeah is better xxx I say

(46) I do kn =I don't sabi Krio well well

(47) I: ★★★★★★★★★★★★★★★★★★★★★★★★★ urm .... were people speaking

(48) Krio in you area sometimes xxxx

(49) AS: no .. Mende

(50) I: it's a language that is much spoken in =in Sierra Leone you

(51) know?

(52) AS: Mm

(53) I: Mm ... so don't you have some basics of it?

(54) AS: urm . the place I live he . the place I live . place we urm =I

(55) grow up he

(56) I: ★★★★★★★★★★★★★★★★

(57) AS: xxxx speak too much Krio ... people speak their =their

(58) dialect

(59) I: ★★★★★★★★★★★★★★★★★★★★★★★★★ in the places where you lived

(60) they =they only spoke the dialect?

(61) AS: more people speak their dialect . they don't sabi this .why

(62) they don't like this Krio is this . because the bush .. is the

(63) very strong people

(64) I: ★★★★★★★★★★★★★★★★★★★★

(65) AS: with another dialect

(66) I: ★★★★★★★★★★★★★★★★★★★★★★★★★★★★★★ how are you? xx how

(67) would you translate this in Krio? ★★★★★★★★★★★

(68) AS: how you de? .. how you de? (louder)

(69) I: ★★★★★★★★★★★★★★★★★★★★★★★★ could you repeat that?

(70) AS: how you de? How you de?

(71) I: ★★★★★★★★★★★★★★★★★★★★★★★★★★★★★★★★★★★ how you de?

(72) ★★ I =I'll tell

(73) you some words in Krio and could you try to translate them in

(74) =English

(75) .. now?.. do

(76) you understand? ....
(77) AS: (no reaction)
(78) I: I say some words in Krio
(79) AS:yeah
(80) I: and you try to translate them in English ★★★★
(81) AS: yeah yeah
(82) I: ok? ... poda poda ....
(83) AS: poda poda ....
(84) I: poda poda
(85) AS: wha you say you say in Creole?
(86) I: Yes .. that's Krio ★★★★★★★★★★
(87) AS: I don sa = I dono you call it
(88) I: ★★★★★★★★★★★★ titi ★★★★★★★★★★★★★★★
(89) AS: titi is xxx is woman girlfriend . that's titi .. they say ma titi .
(90) titi
(91) I: uhu
(92) AS: this woman my girlfriend or so
(93) I: ★★★★★★★★★★★★★★★
(94) AS: titi
(95) I: ★★★★★★★★★★★★★★★★★★★★★★ well ★★★★★★★★★★
(96) AS: well
(97) I: well
(98) AS: yes xxxx I don't know .. maybe you put it ... in something
(99) xxxxxxxx where you could see it
(100) I: mmm .. but it = they are just basic words
(101) AS: basic wor .. I don't know how you would say well .. how do
(102) you say . xxxx
(103) I: hm .. it's just small words . like titi
(104) AS: yeah
(105) I: and urm .. and it's not = you don't have to see them in a
(106) context . you understand? .. it's like
(107) mampama . do you know what that is? ..
(108) AS: mampama ...
(109) I: ★★
(110) AS: I no sabi

The applicant is not able to provide the desired Krio equivalents of the English words. On the other hand, his performance can be identified as 'translingual' (Woolard 1998), containing some variety of West African Pidgin English or Krio. His expression 'I don't sabi Krio well well' (line 46) contains words that are used in Krio as well as in other West African (pidginized or creolized) varieties of English: 'sabi' is also a word in Nigerian Pidgin, Ghanaian and Cameroonian, and the reduplicated 'well well' is also used in Nigerian Pidgin. On the basis of this elementary piece of performance, however, it is very hard to state which variety or varieties the applicant is using: it is not clear whether we are dealing with forms of speech accommodation, codemixing or 'bivalency', the use of words that could simultaneously belong to both codes (Woolard 1998). In other words, whereas he cannot deal with the translation test, the applicant paradoxically re-ports this lack of linguistic competence using a West African Creole that could be iden-tified as Krio. The interviewer, however, does not understand the word *sabi* (line 9) so that the applicant has to translate it into English, thereby perfectly fulfilling the demands of the official's original test (lines 11, 87). Unfortunately, this spontaneously produced 'language test' is not picked up by the interviewer and does not play a role in the as-sessment.

Turning to the official's conception of Krio, it has become clear from an interview I had with him that he holds the following assumptions: (a) somebody who claims to come from Sierra Leone should have a basic understanding of Krio; (b) a basic under-standing of Krio implies being familiar with words and expressions such as 'how are you', 'money', 'girl', etc.; (c) not being able to explain the meaning of these words casts doubts on a person's Sierra Leonean identity. Whether or not the official is able to un-derstand spontaneously produced stretches of Krio is no longer relevant here, given the belief that, if an asylum seeker really comes from where s/he claims to come from, s/he should be able to translate a list of basic words and expressions, i.e. to perform a specific communicative task in Krio that is perceived as evidence for 'full' competence. At least two issues can be raised here: (a) the issue of testing bilingualism, and (b) the issue of linguistic variation.

As to the first question, what from a linguistic point of view can be considered problematic in the interaction is the way in which linguistic proficiency is assessed. The applicant's competence is tested on the basis of a very specific linguistic task: his ability to translate isolated words from one language into another. In fact, rather than examin-ing whether Krio belongs to the applicant's linguistic repertoire, the official's task is to test his bilingual competence. In the literature on 'bilingualism' and 'multilingualism', however, it has been amply documented that bilingual or multilingual competence does not necessarily imply full competence in the different language varieties making up the repertoire of the speaker (Harris 1997, Haviland 2003, Rampton 1995). In this re-spect, multilingual speakers should not be assumed to be able to perform translation tasks from one language into the other. Therefore, it is not possible to make reliable as-sessments using this type of linguistic identification.

A second question that can be raised here is whether the official's familiarity with the linguistic landscape of Sierra Leone forms a reliable basis for distinguishing 'true' from 'false' applications. The official displays a rather simplistic conception of the use and distribution of Krio in Sierra Leone, a conception that ignores any form of social, regional and domainrelated variation. Sierra Leone's linguistic landscape is a very com-plex one and although Krio has come to gain unofficial recognition as a national lan-guage, it does not occupy an equally important place in the linguistic repertoire of every Sierra Leonean citizen (Eades and Arends, this issue, Maryns 2000). Factors such as interference from the applicant's repertoire of codes other than Krio or the appli-cant's limited exposure to Krio – which may be confined to a particular domain such as selling on the market – are not taken into account in the elementary translation test. As a result of that, the official is not in a position to make a reliable linguistic judgement about the applicant's origin.

Language Analysis in the Belgian Asylum Procedure[3]

In April 2001, the Belgian documentation and research centre CEDOCA established an impartial language analysis desk. CEDOCA is a French acronym for 'Centre de Documentation pour les Différentes Instances d'Asile Belge' (Documentation Centre for the Different Instances of Belgian Asylum). It is a governmental organization that consists of a research team (part of the CGVS) and a library (which belongs to all three agencies: DVZ, CGVS and VBV) and it refers to itself as an information service for the officials working for the DVZ, the CGVS and the VBV. The research team is subdivided into seven regional desks and the language analysis desk. The main concern of the language analysis desk is to use language analysis in order to inform the three Belgian immigration agencies about asylum seekers' origins. Being aware of the fact that linguistic and national boundaries do not necessarily coincide, the language desk explicitly states that it does not analyse language in order to determine citizenship. Rather, it aims at determining the speaker's socialization environment (see also Singler, this issue). The main focus is on the repertoire used by the asylum seeker and as much attention is paid to *how* something is said as to *what* is said during the recorded conversation. The language desk admits that the quality and efficiency of its work are inextricably constrained by its tight budget. Because of that, it confines itself to particular areas/language varieties for which there is a network of analysts available: Arabic (Iraq, Syria, Morocco, Egypt and Jordan), Kurdish (North Iraq, Syria), Russian (North Caucasus) and Armenian (Armenia and the Armenian diaspora). Owing to this focus on particular linguistic profiles, the language desk has committed itself to co-operate with foreign language desks to contract out the analysis. Foreign language desks are addressed for a second opinion on particular cases, both during the intake procedure of new analysts and for cross-checking the results of their analyses.

In the language analysis process, three stages can be discerned: (a) the selection of workable files, (b) the implementation (recording the conversation, performing the analysis) and (c) the implementation of the analysis. The first stage in the investigation involves the selection of files that qualify for linguistic identification. A number of criteria are to be considered here:

- the migration history of the applicant and/or the community s/he belongs to
- the linguistic identity of the applicant: what varieties does s/he use in what context and for what purpose?
- the relation between national and linguistic boundaries (many languages cross national boundaries)
- the question whether the regional and/or (socio)linguistic profiles of the applicant and the analyst overlap (taking into account the impact of language ideologies, e.g. the issue of socially or politically charged language variation).

In case a file qualifies for further investigation, the applicant is invited to the CGVS for a short interview. This interview is entirely different from the interview held during the

---

3   The data and the argument presented in this section benefited greatly from my co-operation with Aldona Van Haesevelde.

standard procedure in the sense that it is a conversation rather than an interrogation. What the applicant wants to talk about takes priority over what the interviewer wants to hear. During the conversation, the applicant is instructed not to talk about his/her motivation to seek asylum. Rather, in order to avoid extra stress and repetition, conversational topics tend to be addressed that are closely related to the applicant's way of life and his/her personal interests. After all, the investigation does not merely focus on features of speech, it also takes into account the sociolinguistic situation of the applicant and his/her familiarity with the customs in his/her region of origin. For this purpose, the actual conversation is preceded by a short 'metalinguistic interview', in which the applicant is asked about his/ her linguistic repertoire and patterns of language use. During the conversation, the applicant and the official are assisted by an interpreter who has a good command of the language used by the applicant during the conversation. In order to obtain high-quality recordings, officials are instructed to record 30 minutes of conversation on minidisk. The identity of neither the applicant nor the analyst is revealed in the recording.

Once the conversation between the applicant and the CGVS official has been recorded, the disk is sent to the language desk to be analysed. The applicant's statements about his/her place of origin form the main point of departure for the investigation. It is on the basis of the applicant's claimed place and language(s) of origin that an analyst is selected to perform the linguistic analysis. The language analyst has to meet a number of criteria (the relevance of these criteria will be discussed below). He/she should:

- be a native speaker of the language(s) used by the applicant during the conversation
- be familiar with the sociocultural background of the language(s) concerned
- originate from more or less the same region/country as the applicant
- have received academic schooling (preferably a linguistic training) and/or hold a certificate of higher education
- be competent in one of Belgium's national languages (Dutch, French or German) or English in order to ensure that the analysis requires no further translation
- not work as an interpreter for any of the Belgian asylum agencies.

Language analysts work on a freelance basis and are remunerated per analysis. Depending on their academic and linguistic schooling, they are assisted by a staff member of the language desk. The analysts are expected to lay down their observations in a formal report. The presentation of the findings is organized in terms of a number of linguistic categories: phonology, lexicon, syntax, followed by an additional category of 'other features', such as idiomatic expressions and interjections. These categories have been established by the language analysis desk and mainly serve as an instrument for classifying and organizing the data analytically. The report also allows for meta-linguistic remarks concerning such matters as the mutual intelligibility of the applicant and the interpreter or the content of the conversation. Finally, analysts are asked to formulate their decision and to indicate its degree of certainty. When the analyst is unable to make a decision, this is also stated in the report.

The language desk emphasizes that linguistic analysis is but one of the many elements in the determination of refugee status; its value should not override the value of the other methods used. In more concrete terms, it states that (a) in case of a negative decision, the language analysis has to be used in combination with other arguments and

(b) in case of a positive decision, the language analysis can be used as a decisive criterion. The language desk also states that, whereas in some cases the analysis may be illuminating, it is important to accept that in other cases it may be very hard to reach a conclusion owing to the complexity of the linguistic situation at issue. In such a case, even if the constraining factors only become clear in the course of the analysis, the results of the analysis should be dismissed as unreliable, notwithstanding all the efforts made to perform it.

Let us now turn to a concrete example of linguistic identification as it is being practised at the language analysis desk. The analysis took place in May 2002. The basic criterion for selection was the analyst's disproof of the applicant's claimed origin.

The analysis in question concerns the Kurdish language, and more particularly the Kurmanji variety of Northern Kurdish that is spoken in Turkey (4 million speakers), northern Iraq (2.8 million), Syria (500 000), Armenia (100 000) and Iran (100 000) (Campbell 1991). The data were provided by Aldona Van Haesevelde, who is employed as a supervisor at the language analysis desk. The applicant claims to have been born in Mardin, a city in eastern Turkey, and, because of the political situation there, to have fled his country to Kirkuk in northern Iraq. In spite of having lived in Iraq for more than thirty-five years, he claims to have retained his Turkish Kurmanji accent. The analyst, who claims to come from Aqrah, a city in northern Iraq, conducted the analysis under the supervision of two qualified linguists. The analytical procedure may be described as follows: the analyst first listens to the disk; then, he discusses his first impressions with the two linguists; subsequently, together they try to formulate their argumentation on the basis of representative examples from the disk; and finally, they fill in the standard form.

An Example of Language Analysis as performed by the Belgian Language Desk (my translation[4])

1. File number asylum seeker

2. Method of analysis
    Indirect analysis
    Duration of the conversation: 30 min
    Quality of the recording: ok

3. Languages used
    Language(s) of the applicant: Kurmanji
    Language(s) of the interpreter: Kurmanji and Bahdini
    Language(s) of the analyst: Kurmanji and Bahdini

---

4   This is a word-for-word translation of the Dutch report. As I have chosen to give a faithful rendering of the original version, the inconsistencies and obscurities characterizing the original report have not been adjusted in the translation.

4. Analysis
    The analysis should be based on various linguistic elements:
    Phonology (pronunciation)

    [?_d]   instead of in North Iraq: [a_d] (feast)
    [klet¹]   instead of in North Iraq: [kletça] (sort of pastry for feast)
    [nn]   instead of in North Iraq [n_n]
    [hurkeren]   instead of in North Iraq: [h_rkeren] (to hack)
    [tann_r]   instead of in North Iraq [tann_r]

    Lexical (word choice)
    - layzin (to play)   not used in North Iraq (rather: yar_)
    - mah (month)   is in North Iraq: heyf
    - 'azzeb_n (to suffer) is in North Iraq: zahmat
    - zal_m (husband)   in North Iraq: m_r

    Syntax (grammatical structure)
    Tenebbu: prefix -te indicates Turkish influence: is *not* used in North Iraq: neb-
    bu

    Other (idioms, interjections, …) Taf (always) is used by the applicant as a sort of
    filler and is not used in North Iraq

    Remarks
    Apart from the Arabic words that generally typify Kurmanji, the applicant uses
    no Arabic words that are typical for North Iraq, whereas all speakers of Kur-
    manji in North Iraq show this kind of Arabic influence in their language.

5. Conclusion
    On the basis of the analysis above I can

    x with certainty
    0 most probably
    0 presumably

    0 confirm
    x exclude★
    that the asylum seeker comes from the region and language- and culture com-
    munity he claims to come from, North Iraq.

    0 or it is not possible to arrive at a conclusion because:

    ★ In case of exclusion I can
    0 with certainty
    0 most probably
    x presumably
    indicate that the asylum seeker comes from the following region: Turkey.

The analyst concludes that the applicant does not come from the region and language community he claims to come from, viz. North Iraq (exclusion with certainty). In addition, the analyst suggests that the applicant comes from Turkey.

6. Professional declaration I have carried out the analysis above in an objective way. The report is formulated by order of the Commissioner General for Refugees and Stateless Persons. I am sworn to secrecy with regard to this report and any other information about the asylum seeker that I became acquainted with through the analysis of the cassette recording.

The Belgian language desk is very selective about what cases to accept for analysis and its productivity is rather low compared with that of language desks operating in other countries. This critical stance is mirrored in the high quality of its methodology: the analyst is a university-educated native speaker of the North Iraq variety of Kurmanji, he is assisted by two qualified linguists, and his analysis is linguistically motivated. At the same time, that does not take away the fact that we are dealing with a rather tricky case of linguistic identification here. The analyst identifies several linguistic cues pointing towards Turkish influence, which may be the result of migration. Combined with the absence of any Arabic influence in his speech and with the way in which he resolutely sticks to particular words that, according to the analyst, are not used in northern Iraq, this leads the analyst to conclude that the applicant did not live in the region in which he claims to have spent a substantial part of his life. This conclusion is based on the idea that after 35 years of socialization in a particular community – the applicant claims to have been socially active in North Iraq, it is where he lived and worked, where his children went to school, etc. – a speaker's linguistic behaviour inevitably displays some degree of influence from the language variety(ies) spoken in that community. On the other hand, it could be argued that the conclusion 'exclusion with certainty' needs some qualification as we are dealing with a case of mixed socialization here. A more reasonable conclusion would probably be to point to the striking absence in the applicant's speech of any of the features that distinguish North Iraq Kurmanji from Turkish Kurmanji, and on the basis of this to state that the applicant's linguistic behaviour is not consistent with what is known about the linguistic profile of that area. Language may leave traces of identity, but it bears no transparent relation to the social history of a person. Its inherently social and variable nature will be the subject of the next section.

Discussion

In determining refugee status, Belgium appeals to the United Nations' 1951 Geneva Convention. In its definition of 'refugee' the Convention refers twice to the applicant's country of origin: it states that a refugee is 'a person who is outside *his/her country of origin* and is unable or unwilling to avail himself/herself of the protection of *that country*'. Consequently, the applicant's origin plays a central role in the assessment of his/her asylum application. Yet, although it is a key element in the procedure, national origin is very hard to determine. The institutional demand for objectivity in deciding eligibility for refugee status is translated into an attempt at 'scientification'. Based on the idea that language is a fundamental element in a person's socialization, the asylum procedure appeals to the discipline of linguistics in trying to determine national origin. Although it is currently being used by several European governments, language analysis as a tool for testing the validity of nationality claims still causes a great deal of controversy. Indeed, this is not a black-and-white issue and nor is it my intention to reflect upon the issue in black-and-white terms. Rather, I shall address some established linguistic ideas that are difficult to evade, while at the same time adding some qualifications to the validity of the use of language analysis in the determination of national origin.

As current developments in sociolinguistics show, the idea that language should not be treated as an abstract category but as a socially anchored and deeply contextualized phenomenon can no longer be denied. Hymes (1996) points to the meaningful development in sociolinguistics from a definition of the speech community in terms of a single language to a conception based on mixed repertoires of codes, containing different sets of socially, regionally and situationally defined varieties. This view of language behaviour in terms of multiple code use renders the practice of linguistic identification problematic. The phenomena of language mixing and shifting challenge the kind of translation tests illustrated in the data extract discussed earlier. While they are communicating, speakers move around in their mixed repertoire of codes, yet without necessarily being competent in any of the single codes in their repertoire, nor having the ability to draw clear boundaries between the different codes used (Auer 1998, Matras 2000, Meeuwis and Blommaert 1998, Rampton 1995, 1998, 1999, Woolard 1998).

Multilingual language behaviour equally poses a problem for the second type of linguistic speaker identification. Code mixing and shifting seriously complicate the search for competent interpreters and experts for linguistic analysis. It can be argued that assessing one of the varieties making up the repertoire of a speaker is in no way representative of that speaker's overall competence. In other words, both the interpreter's and the analyst's repertoire should be the best possible reflection of the applicant's repertoire. To push the issue even further, one might suggest that the social variability characterizing interlocutors inevitably causes their speech to be subject to individual variation. No two individuals belong to exactly the same social networks, share exactly the same experiences and therefore draw from exactly the same discursive repertoires. Ultimately, this would rule out the possibility of any objective speaker identification. Moving from this radical perspective to the reality of language analysis, one could argue for a certain degree of moderation and responsibility on both sides. Although it would be unrealistic to aim at scientifically 'objective' results on the basis of linguistic evidence, it is clear that in some cases and in combination with other types of evidence the identification of particular linguistic cues does reveal significant information about a speaker's socialization environment and his/her spatial trajectories across communities, which may assist migration agencies in making a decision about national origin. Yet, some further qualifications are necessary here:

National borders and speech communities In order to meet institutionally defined criteria for obtaining asylum in Belgium, many applicants apparently claim a false nationality, which in many cases concerns a neighbouring, often war-stricken, country. The fact that this often concerns a neighbouring country increases the possibility for different varieties of one and the same language being involved. Consequently, in such situations, language is a poor indicator of national origin.

127

The perception of language and language varieties The practice of determining regional identity on the basis of indexical cues should take into account how the language varieties in question are perceived by the interlocutors in the interaction. One cannot expect every applicant to be able to handle the distinction between 'language' and 'dialect', between 'pidgin' and 'creole', or between 'English', 'West African English', 'West African Pidgin English' and 'Krio', etc. Even for trained linguists such distinctions are sometimes difficult to make, given the fact that these different varieties of the same language should not be seen as separate units but as gradations on a continuum, with fuzzy boundaries between them (Maryns and Blommaert 2001). In other words, what an applicant identifies as a particular language variety is not necessarily recognized as such by the interpreter and/or the analyst and vice versa.

Expert knowledge In order to be able to assess regional identity on the basis of language, a first requirement for analysts is to be native speakers of the variety or varieties in question. Their expertise, however, should also include the ability to make their knowledge explicit using standard systems of transcription and discourse representation and to motivate their conclusions on the basis of the available documentary evidence.

How to define 'region' The evaluation of regional identity on the basis of consistency between the applicant's repertoire and that of the analyst cannot be isolated from the definition of 'region'. The language desk responsible for the analysis should always try to find 'the man next door' to carry out the analysis. The way the applicant and the analyst are related regionally should be made explicit in the analysis and needs to be taken into consideration when assessing the validity of the analysis.

Style shifting and speech accommodation Language analysis cannot be isolated from the context in which the discourse operates. According to the situation, speakers select the appropriate language forms from their repertoire. Institutional pressures and uncertainty about what might strengthen or weaken their application, may cause the applicant to accommodate his/her speech to that of the official carrying out the interview. Therefore, it is very important to explain clearly the actual purpose of the conversation.

Individual migration history Applicants' individual migration patterns need to be taken into account. After all, we are dealing with refugees, people with migration histories that are mirrored in complex relations between speech and spatial trajectories. Migration, mixed socialization and intermarriage, combined with the fact that some individuals are more susceptible to language accommodation than others, are factors that weaken the reliability of linguistic cues in the determination of speaker identity.

Noise Undoubtedly, there are many more factors that play a role in the determination of regional identity, some of which may be combined in a final category of 'contingency factors' that produce 'noise' in the process of analysis. The impact of particular language ideologies – such as the 'monoglot ideology' (Silverstein 1996) – on language description and the fact that some languages or varieties are better described than others (Blommaert 2004), inevitably constrain the potential for and the validity of particular analyses. Also, the applicant's fluency, the analyst's skills in expressing his/her thoughts and naming particular phenomena, even the state of mind and the feelings of the interlocutors about the conversation, and so many other variables that characterize any form of social evaluation, will always stand in the way of a perfectly objective and reliable practice.

The Responsibilities of the Language Analyst in the Belgian Asylum Procedure

In this article, the main task of the asylum agencies has been summarized in terms of two equally important aspects: (1) testing the evidence against the refugee convention and (2) assessing the credibility of the evidence. Linguistic expertise is mainly called in to assist the asylum agencies with the latter issue of fact-finding and speaker identification. Still, analysis has shown that it is very difficult to devise reliable linguistically informed methods that are at the same time workable in the context of the Belgian asylum procedure. Yet, linguistics has much more to offer. While it may not be able to provide objective parameters for the identification of regional identity, linguistic expertise should be called upon at a much more fundamental level, the level of information exchange between applicants and officials in the standard procedure itself. After all, unlike the interviews carried out at the language desk, the interviews that make up the standard procedure are not recorded on disk. In other words, the interviewing official's written account of the hearing is basically the only element that plays a role as information input in the procedure. As a matter of fact, the quality of the interview and the accuracy of the report will make or break the validity of any decision made in the legal-administrative procedure later on. Throughout the procedure, linguistic expertise could be mobilized to facilitate the interaction between applicant and official and to make the authorities understand that ignorance of sociolinguistic variation may seriously hamper the exchange of detailed and sensitive information. Linguistic expertise may help (a) to make sure that second language varieties, let alone Creole or pidgin varieties of a language, are not simply treated as one and the same language; (b) it may help interlocutors identify the language(s) they are comfortable with; and (c) it may assist responsible agencies in selecting the appropriate interpreters. Narrative expertise may be called in to make officials understand that there are alternative narrative patterns that qualify for the expression of truth, patterns that do not necessarily coincide with Western narrative standards (Blommaert 2001, Maryns and Blommaert 2002). In short, whatever purpose linguistic expertise is mobilized for in the procedure, its main responsibility is to point to the widespread nature of language variation, multilingualism and styleshifting, in order to make the authorities understand that language is as complex and as variable as the social world in which it operates.

Acknowledgements

Research for this article was made possible by a personal research grant from the National Science Foundation, Flanders. I would like to thank Jacques Arends, Jan Blommaert, Chris Bulcaen, Chris Corcoran and Cécile Vigouroux for their comments and suggestions. I am particularly grateful to Aldona Van Haesevelde for providing data and sharing her experiences as a member of the Belgian language analysis desk. She also contributed significantly to the final shape of the argument of this article. I also want to thank other people working at the DVZ, the CGVS and the VBC for their cooperation and I owe the greatest debt to the asylum seekers who allowed me to examine their applications.

References

Auer, P. (1998) *Code-switching in Conversation: Language, Interaction and Identity*, London: Routledge.

Barsky, R. (1994) *Constructing a Productive Other. Discourse Theory and the Convention Refugee Hearing*, Amsterdam and Philadelphia, PA: John Benjamins.

Belgisch Comité voor Hulp aan Vluchtelingen (BCHV), Overlegcentrum Integratie Vluchtelingen (OCIV) and Coordination et Initiatives pour Réfugiés et Étrangers (CIRE) (2001) Rapport. *De werking van de Belgische asielprocedure*, unpublished report.

Blommaert, J. (2001) Investigating narrative inequality: "home narratives" from African asylum seekers in Belgium, *Discourse & Society* 12(4), p. 413–449.

Blommaert, J. (2004) Language policy and national identity, in T. Ricento (ed.), *An Introduction to Language Planning*, London: Blackwell, in press.

Campbell, G. L. (1991) *Compendium of the World's Languages*, Vols 1–2, London and New York: Routledge.

Coulthard, M. (1992) Forensic discourse analysis, in R.M. Coulthard (ed.), *Advances in Spoken Discourse Analysis*, London: Routledge, p. 242–57.

French, P. (1994) An overview of forensic phonetics with particular reference to speaker identification, *Forensic Linguistics* 1(2), p. 169–82.

Gibbons, J. (ed.) (1994) *Language and the Law*, London: Longman.

Gibbons, J. (2003) *Forensic Linguistics: An Introduction to Language in the Justice System*, Oxford: Blackwell.

Harris, R. (1997) Romantic bilingualism: time for a change?, in C. Leung and C. Cable (eds), *English as an Additional Language: Changing Perspectives*, Watford: National Association for Language Development in the Curriculum (NALDIC), p. 14–27.

Haviland, J. (2003) Ideologies of language: some reflections on language and U.S. law, *American Anthropologist* 105(4), p. 764–74.

Hymes, D. (1996) *Ethnography, Linguistics, Narrative Inequality: Toward an Understanding of Voice*, London: Taylor & Francis.

Kniffa, H. (ed.) (1996) *Recent Developments in Forensic Linguistics*, New York: Peter Lang.

Labov, W. (1998) The judicial testing of linguistic theory, in D. Tannen (ed.), *Linguistics in Context*, Norwood, NJ: Ablex, p. 159–82.

Maryns, K. (2000) *English in Sierra Leone: A Sociolinguistic Investigation*, Studia Germanica Gandensia 14, Ghent: Ghent University.

Maryns, K. (2004) Displacement in asylum seekers' narratives, in M. Baynham and A. de Fina (eds), *Dislocations/Relocations: Narratives of Displacement*, Manchester: St Jerome Publishing.

Maryns, K. (2004) Identifying the asylum speaker: Reflections on the pitfalls of language analysis in the determination of national origin, *IJSLL* 11/2, p. 240–260.

Maryns, K. and J. Blommaert (2001) Stylistic and thematic shifting as a narrative resource: assessing asylum seekers' narratives, *Multilingua* 20(1), p. 61–84.

Maryns, K. and J. Blommaert (2002) Pretextuality and pretextual gaps: on de/refining linguistic inequality, *Pragmatics* 12(1), p. 11–30.

Matras, Y. (2000) Mixed languages: a functional-communicative approach, *Bilingualism, Language and Cognition* 3, p. 79–99.

Meeuwis, M. and J. Blommaert (1998) A monolectal view of code-switching: layered code-switching among Zairians in Belgium, in P. Auer (ed.) *Codeswitching in Conversation: Language, Interaction and Identity*, London: Routledge, p. 76–99.

OCIV (1997) *Vluchtelingenonthaal in de praktijk*, Brussels: OCIV.

Rampton, B. (1995) *Crossing: Language and Ethnicity among Adolescents*, London: Longman.

Rampton, B. (1998) Crossing and the redefinition of reality, in P. Auer (ed.), *Code-Switching in Conversation: Language, Interaction and Identity*, London: Routledge, p. 290–317.

Rampton, B. (1999) Deutsch in Inner London and the animation of an instructed foreign language, *Journal of Sociolinguistics* 3(4), p. 480–504.

Sarangi, S. and M. Coulthard (eds) (2000) *Discourse and Social Life*, London: Pearson.

Shuy, R. (1993) *Language Crimes: The Use and Abuse of Language Evidence in the Courtroom*, Oxford: Blackwell.

Silverstein, M. (1996) Monoglot "Standard" in America: atandardization and metaphors of linguistic hegemony, in D. Brenneis and R. K. S. Macaulay (eds), *The Matrix of Language: Contemporary Linguistic Anthropology*, Boulder, CO: Westview Press, p. 284–306.

Silverstein, M. and G. Urban (eds) (1996) *Natural Histories of Discourse*, Chicago and London: University of Chicago Press.

Woolard, K. (1998) Simultaneity and bivalency as strategies in bilingualism, *Journal of Linguistic Anthropology* 8(1), p. 3–29.

Language Analysis for the Determination of Origin (LADO): A Look into Problems presented by East and Central African Cases

Vincent A. de Rooij[*]

Introduction

In this chapter, I will first discuss some of the problems in using language analysis for determining the origin of asylum seekers claiming to hail from East and Central Africa. Taking Somalia and Burundi as case studies, I will then present and evaluate language analyses made by the Office for Country Information and Language Analysis (Bureau Land en Taal) of the Netherlands Immigration and Naturalization Service, and by independent (counter)experts, including myself. I will argue that in the cases discussed and ones that are similar to these, LADO as currently practiced does not allow for categorical conclusions pertaining to language origin.

Assumptions Underlying LADO and African Linguistic Realities

East and Central Africa are characterized not only by widespread multilingualism, but also by economic and political crises causing massive migratory movements. Pervasive language contact and low levels of schooling among parts of the population result in vernacular ways of speaking that may dramatically differ from national or official languages. Assumptions underlying LADO run counter to these sociolinguistic realities in East and Central Africa (and other regions in the world for that matter). So, before looking into the cases of Burundi and Somali, a critical examination of the assumptions underlying LADO is in order.

LADO, as practiced by the Bureau Land en Taal (Office for Country Information and Language Analysis) of the Netherlands Immigration and Naturalization Service, is based on the assumption that "when someone spent the bigger part of his life, and especially his youth (in which early language acquisition occurs) in a specific area, he may be expected to speak at least one of the language varieties current in that area" (Bureau Land en Taal 2007: 1). It is assumed, then, that there is a fixed link between a particular language and a particular delineated geographical space in which this language is spoken. In other words, speakers can be located in space because the language they speak can be located in space. This idea of assigning each language its own territory is a perva-

---

[*] I thank the editors for their comments on an earlier version of this chapter. Of course, they cannot be held responsible for any errors or the opinions expressed in it. I also want to thank Anna de Graaf for translating the OCILA report in the Appendix.

sive practice in linguistics and African linguistics in particular. From colonial times until today (see e.g. the way Bantu languages have beenneatly mapped at the SIL website at http://www.sil.org/silesr/2002/016/bantu_map.htm) African languages are neatly mapped in a way that simply denies multilingual practices and language mixing. The belief that languages, and hence its speakers, can be mapped is connected to 19th century ideas of the linguistically homogenous nation state and has since become common sense. In reality, neither languages nor their speakers can be mapped in such a static manner because people and the languages they speak are constantly moving through space, crossing borders (Blommaert 2009). In the process, the languages people speak change through contact with speakers of other languages. In today's world, the connection between language and territory is further complicated by transidiomatic practices (Jacquemet 2005) resulting from transnational migration processes and ongoing developments in media and communication technologies.

Mapping Languages: The Example of Swahili

Not only is the idea of mapping languages and their speakers problematic for the reasons just outlined, mapping languages is also subject to various biases. This may be illustrated by a map, reproduced below as Figure 1, at the Swahili Language pages of the Stanford University website showing the part of Africa where Swahili is spoken.

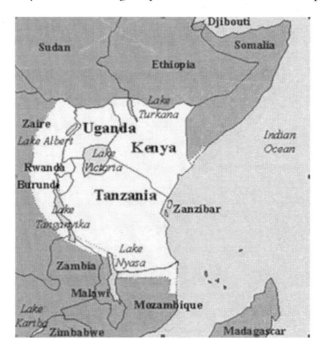

Figure 1: 'Where Swahili is spoken' (grayscale adaptation from the color image at: http:// swahililanguage.stanford.edu/where%20swahili%20is%20spoken.html)

Of course, such a map may give the false impression to a Western audience that the area in yellow is monolingually Swahiliphone territory. The author of the text accompanying the map seems aware of this pointing out that '... even in the East African countries, the language [i.e. Swahili, vdr] is not used equally'.

Another fundamental problem with this map, however, is that the entire Southeastern Katanga province of DR Congo is left grey while Swahili is spoken by millions of people in that region, often as a first language (de Rooij 1996). I can only speculate why these Swahili speakers are made invisible on this map. Swahili scholars at Stanford may be ignorant of studies of Katanga Swahili going back several decades (see Fabian 1986) or they may know about these studies and not regard Katanga Swahili as authentic Swahili, in spite of the fact that they explicitly mention that different varieties of Swahili are spoken in different regions. The erasure (Irvine & Gal 2000) of Katanga Swahili from this map may have to do with the view originating in colonial times that Swahili in Katanga is a 'corrupted' variety of Swahili (Fabian 1986).

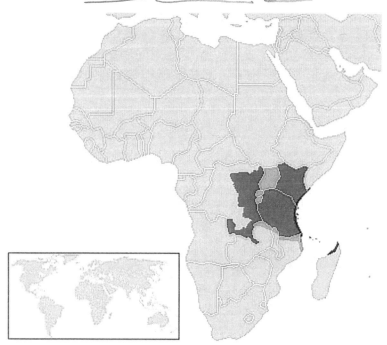

Figure 2: Areas of Swahili speakers (adapted from: http://upload.wikimedia.org/wikipedia/commons/archive/a/ae/20060708100133!Maeneo_penye_wasemaji_wa_Kiswahili.png

An alternative mapping of Swahili is found on Wikipedia (see Figures 2 and 3, which are grayscale adaptations form the original Wikipedia color images). Here, we see that the Swahili speaking area does include parts of Katanga in the oldest version (Figure 2) and the entire Katanga province in the more recent version (Figure 3). And that is not the only difference; the Wikipedia map also distinguishes between different kinds of speakers and functions of Swahili in different countries and regions. Native speakers according to the Wikipedia maps (see the explanation on the file history page:

http://en.wikipedia.org/wiki/File:Maeneo_penye_wasemaji_wa_Kiswahili.png)   are
found only the dark grey area, the East Coast and the islands off this coast, including the
Northwestern tip of Madagascar. In the mid grey areas, Kenya, Tanzania, and parts of
East and Southeastern DR Congo, Swahili is an official language. The light grey
patches, Rwanda, Burundi, the Northern tips of Mozambique, Malawi and Zambia,
and, on the map in Fig. 2, Uganda, indicate areas where Swahili is in use as a 'common
language.' I am not going to discuss the validity of the choices made by the map mak-
ers; the purpose of presenting these maps here is simply to show how a label for a linguistic object, Swahili in this case, is apparently interpreted in different ways by different (groups of) people.

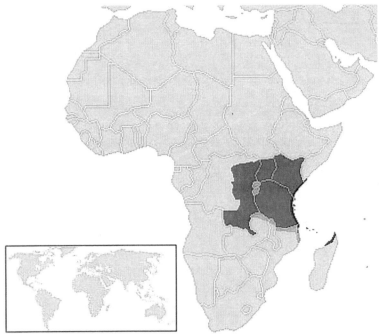

*Figure 3 Areas of Swahili speakers (source: http://upload.wikimedia.org/wikipedia/com-
mons/a/ae/Maeneo_penye_wasemaji_wa_Kiswahili.png.*

Political, Scientific and Folk Labels of Languages

Divergent opinions on the use of language labels, where a language is spoken, who
counts as native speakers (and who don't) are motivated by political concerns, identity
politics and language ideologies that may not seem relevant to the practice of LADO.
However, how people label languages and how ideas on what specific language labels
refer to diverge, is a matter of crucial import in LADO. Do we really know what it is
that asylum seekers refer to when they say they speak 'Swahili', 'Bajuni', 'Arabic', et ce-

tera? Derek Nurse, in a contra-expertise report, asks himself this question in relation to the reported language use of a Bajuni asylum seeker from Kismayu, Somalia:

> On track 4 (O[fficial]R[ecording]), she says she speaks Swahili. Asked to say in Swahili which was the language used by her parents, she falters and stops entirely. This claim to speak Swahili is not otherwise tested.
>
> So what does she speak – Bajuni, Swahili, or both? In section 3.3, below, it is shown that the language used daily by many young Bajunis varies: at one end are those who have only Swahili with little or no Bajuni, while at the other end are those with good Bajuni, and a bit of Swahili added. In between are many with a mixture, using a Swahili matrix, and a smaller or larger admixture of Bajuni, depending on age, location, and on who they are talking to. *Consequently many have trouble labelling the language they are using.* That is her case – see the end of section 3, and also section 6, below. If young Somali Bajunis are asked what language they speak, some will say Swahili, others Bajuni, and they are both right (Nurse 2010: 3; italics mine, vdr).

If lay usage of language labels conflicts with usage by LADO practitioners, asylum seekers may be seen as imposters if this conflict goes unnoticed. Especially in countries that experienced massive displacements of peoples caused by political and social upheaval, the sociolinguistic situation on the ground often no longer corresponds with what is reported in the (socio)linguistic literature. New language varieties may have come into being and groups of speakers who once spoke language A may now be speaking language B or a new, possibly mixed, variety of A and/or B.

Recognizing Spectacular Speakers and Spectacular Vernaculars

If recent sociolinguistic and descriptive linguistic studies are absent, it is, therefore, always dangerous to make assumptions about the language(s) a person originating from a particular country should be able to speak. But even in relatively stable speech communities, we may find 'spectacular' speakers (Sweetland 2002) that remain invisible because they do not fit into established categories. And if they become visible, they may be seen as inauthentic speakers of the language they use. Delilah, the speaker reported on by Sweetland (2002) is such a spectacular speaker. Delilah defies American common sense notions on language and race: a white woman like Delilah is not supposed to speak African American Vernacular English. But, contrary to common sense, Delilah is recognized as an authentic speaker of AAVE by African Americans and white Americans.

The Bajuni asylum seeker referred to above could also be a spectacular speaker as she defies common sense assumptions expressed in the language analysis report by the Office for Country Information and Language Analysis of the Netherlands Immigration Service: 'The applicant speaks fluent Swahili as is common in Kenya. The applicant does not speak Bajuni and no Somali, and thus does not speak any language that is common within Somalia'. The problem with statements like these about people claiming to hail from countries that have been going through prolonged periods of political turmoil is that they seem to ignore the often dramatically changing linguistic realities on the ground caused by massive displacements of people and the breakdown of institutions, schools and government bodies, that normally propagate national languages or languages that have the status of official language. Many asylum seekers have spent time in refugee camps or have other complex migration histories before arriving in the country where they seek asylum. Under these conditions, the established 'traditional' patterns of language use will not, in all likelihood, be transmitted from older to newer generations. Young Bajuni in Somalia, as presented by Nurse (2010), seem to be caught up in a process of language shift, from Bajuni to Swahili, or one of contact-induced language change, possibly leading, or already having led, to a new language variety.

In cases like this, we should, in the absence of recent descriptive studies of language use in situ, be extremely careful in qualifying the language use of asylum seekers as characteristic of a particular country and or group of speakers. What we need is solid research that is regularly updated. Solid research entails prolonged sociolinguistic and ethnographic research in order to establish what languages are spoken by whom in different social contexts. In other words, we need to have up to date information on the sociolinguistic situation of relevant countries and on sociolinguistic profiles of speakers and speech communities in those countries. Of course, this type of research is hard to do for practical, ethical, and financial reasons: we are dealing here with terrains that are often hard to access and that present danger to researchers and informants. And there have to be parties willing to finance these projects. In the end, the matter boils down to the question of whether one wishes to do LADO in a scientifically valid way. If one wishes to do so, one is forced to invest in continuing field research at relevant sites. So-called fact finding trips as the one undertaken by Tolsma (2008) clearly do not meet the necessary requirements for this type of studies: Tolsma's field report provides no information on how speakers were selected, who these speakers are (what are their social and sociolinguistic profiles), how and in which contexts recordings were made, and whether and how speakers' language use varies across social contexts.

Involving native speakers in LADO (cf. Cambier-Langeveld, this volume) to close this gap in our linguistic and sociolinguistic knowledge actually introduces new and more problems. Although native speakers may certainly be helpful in the analytic process, one should also realize that their knowledge may be 'outdated', or restricted to non-relevant language varieties. Also, like any other observer, they are subject in their observations and judgments to bias informed by sociolinguistic stereotypes.

Practicing LADO under Less than Ideal Conditions: The Dutch Case

Unfortunately, we do not live in an ideal world, and LADO is being practiced in the absence of the kind of descriptive linguistic, ethnographic and sociolinguistic studies we would want to have at our disposal. In light of this, it is all the more important that we develop a highly critical stance toward received wisdom on the linguistic situation in African countries characterized by political and social unrest leading to ongoing migration, highly dynamic patterns of multilingualism, and low levels of schooling that hamper the spread and use of a standardized national language.

From my own experience as a contra-expert in about a dozen cases of asylum speakers claiming to be Swahili speaking Burundians, I can report that LADO as practiced by the Dutch Office for Country Information and Language Analysis was seriously flawed in several ways. First of all, during the interviews providing the data for language analysis the asylum seekers never talked for more than 12-15 minutes. Narratives of any length were virtually absent, so an inventory of important features such as tense-aspect morphemes could not be made. Another problem was the Standard Swahili speaking interpreter whose language clearly diverged from the varieties of Swahili spoken by the interviewees. For the analyst, any degree of stylistic variation then presents insurmountable problems of interpretation because given the paucity of data and not being able to compare the speech used in this situation with speech used in other more informal situations, it is impossible to know whether and to which extent the speech variation produced was the result of accommodating to the interpreter's speech. Interviewees able to accommodate towards the high prestige variety of the interpreter could then easily be mistaken for speakers of a variety of Swahili as spoken in Tanzania. Of course, some varieties of Swahili spoken in Burundi may resemble Tanzanian Swahili – we don't know because relevant studies are absent– but in that case, it becomes very difficult to decide whether the interviewee is from Burundi or Tanzania.

The problem with LADO as practiced by OCILA that is most 'visible' is the format and contents of their language analysis reports. One of these reports, translated into English, is reproduced in the Appendix. The case at hand concerns a Swahili speaker claiming to originate from Nyanza-Lac, Burundi. In his life story, he states that at the age of two, after the death of his mother, his aunt took him with her from Nyanza-Lac to Tanzania to live with her. Fifteen years later, he returned to Nyanza-Lac where he lived until 2005. Looking at the OCILA report, a trained linguist or any other scientific researcher for that matter will immediately notice two things. First, not only does the report present very few data, it also presents them without any interpretative analytic comments. The only qualification of the Swahili spoken by the asylum seeker is that '... he speaks Swahili with an accent that places him outside Burundi'. But how the examples presented led to this qualification is left entirely unexplained. The second striking thing about the report is the categorical statement of the analyst under the heading 'origin according to language analysis':

On the basis of the language analysis carried out by me, I am able to declare the applicant definitely not to belong to the speech and cultural community of Burundi.

Putting forward such an unequivocal conclusion can be done only if there is no indication of possible origin in Burundi. As I will show, the speech of this asylum speaker contains evidence forcing one to conclude that a possible origin in Burundi cannot be ruled out. In this case, as in other contra-expertise work, I tried to carefully document features that differed and resembled the well described Standard Swahili and then tried to draw several possible conclusions. A feature diverging from Standard Swahili usage that I encountered in this case was the pronunciation of Swahili /l/ as [r] or [ɾ]. Since Kirundi is one of several Central African Bantu languages in which /l/ has a marginal status, this use of [r] or [ɾ] may be attributed to Kirundi influence and, hence, the possibility of Burundi as the asylum seeker's origin could not be ruled out. Another non-

Standard Swahili feature was the use of vowel epenthesis as in 'muji mukubwa' (big city) where Standard Swahili would have 'mji mkubwa.' However, vowel epenthesis was not applied categorically in all possible contexts. I also paid attention to features in his speech that were similar to Standard Swahili. An interesting feature of his speech was the use of the verbal affix -me-, marking perfective aspect. This mix of Standard and non-Standard, so-called upcountry varieties of Swahili, makes it hard to draw firm conclusions. The similarities to Standard Swahili could be explained by the fact that the asylum speaker spent his youth in Tanzania. One could also argue that at least some Swahili speakers from Burundi speak a variety of Swahili that is close to the Standard variety. We do not have descriptive and sociolinguistic studies of Swahili as spoken in Burundi but we do know that there are pockets of muslim Swahili speakers in Burundi originating from the Swahili speaking East Coast of Africa (see e.g. Luffin 1999). The non-Standard features in combination with a few French loan words ('chauffeur', driver and 'douane', customs) can be taken as proof of his second stay in Nyanza-Lac. My conclusion in this case (and cases similar to it), was that the data did not allow me to rule out Burundi as a country of origin. Not a very neat conclusion but that was really all I could say on the basis of the evidence available.

In this and other related cases, the OCILA LADO reports, always conclude with one hundred percent certainty that speakers' origins were either definitely not Burundi or definitely a country other than Burundi. Such strong claims cannot be upheld if the data point in various possible directions, particularly so if data are left uninterpreted and argumentation leading to conclusion is kept hidden.

If LADO practitioners wish to be accountable as is normal practice in scientific work, they should make every effort to make their argumentation transparent and to present all data they rely on in their argumentation. This is clearly not the case in the Dutch reports. The reason for this is that the OCILA guidelines for drawing up language analysis reports do not specify that the reports should provide the line of argumentation that link the conclusion to the data. The guidelines only state that after providing the main conclusion, '… a selection is presented of representative examples of pronunciation, lexical choice and / or grammar supporting the conclusion' (Bureau Land en Taal 2007:2). The fact that the OCILA does not adhere to normal scientific practice is a direct consequence of their guidelines and reflects a choice not to provide transparent argumentation. By doing this, OCILA chooses not to be accountable in a scientific way, and in fact places itself outside the scientific community.

Conclusion

So what does all this mean? Is LADO at all possible in cases of refugees with complex life trajectories from countries that have been going through rough times and are characterized by complex sociolinguistic constellations? Paying respect to scientific principles we should ask ourselves which conditions should be satisfied for scientifically responsible LADO. As I have tried to argue, at least the following conditions should be met: data should be gathered in a way that ensures a rich set of data covering phonology, morphology, and syntax. Ideally, the interviewee should be stimulated to deliver extended narratives in which a broad range of linguistic features are used. LADO itself should be carried out in an accountable way in order to enable an orderly scientific debate on the validity of LADO claims. For OCILA, this would entail changing their reporting style in a dramatic way providing all relevant data used in the argumentation while the argumentation itself should be made completely explicit.

And last but not least, doing LADO in a scientifically responsible manner relies on the availability of fieldwork-based linguistic studies in relevant countries; these studies should also be updated at regular intervals since countries from which refuges hail from are most often in a continuous state of change.

References

Blommaert, Jan (2009) Language, asylum, and the national order, *Current Anthropology* 50(4), p. 415-441.

Bureau Land en Taal (2007) *Vakbijlage taalanalyse*, Ministerie van Justitie, Immigratie- en Naturalisatiedienst, Gemeenschappelijk Centrum Kennis, Advies en Ontwikkeling, Bureau land en taal.

Fabian, Johannes (1986) *Language and colonial power: The appropriation of Swahili in the Belgian Congo 1880-1938*, Cambridge: Cambridge University Press.

Irvine, Judith T. & Susan Gal (2000) Language ideology and linguistic differentiation, in: Paul V. Kroskrity (ed.), *Regimes of language: Ideologies, polities, and identities*. Santa Fe: School of American Research Press/Oxford: James Currey, p. 35-83.

Luffin, Xavier (1999) Muslims in Burundi: Discretion and neutrality. *ISIM Newsletter*, July 1999, p. 29.
    https://www.openaccess.leidenuniv.nl/bitstream/1887/11959/1/newsl_3.pdf (29 September 2010).

Nurse, Derek (2010) *Contra-expertise report* [in the case of a Bajuni asylum seeker from Somalia].

Rooij, Vincent A. de (1996) *Cohesion through contrast: Discourse structure in Swahili/ French conversations*, Amsterdam: Ifott.

Sweetland, Julie (2002) Unexpected but authentic use of an ethnically–marked dialect. *Journal of Sociolinguistics* 6(4), p. 514-538.

Tolsma, Gerard (2008) *Native Swahili of Buyenzi (Bujumbura): Preliminary results from a fact finding field trip to Burundi*, Powerpoint file accompanying a paper delivered at IAFPA 2008, Lausanne, 20-23 July 2008.

Appendix

English translation of OCILA language analysis report

LANGUAGE ANALYSIS REPORT

Date:	2007
Code of supervising linguist:	GT
Code of language analyst:	KIR 1

Declaration by expert

This report on the language analysis of the said asylum seeker has been drawn up under commission and supervision of "Bureau Land en Taal" of the Immigration and Naturalisation Service (IND). The language analysis that provides the basis of this well-founded report is carried out in an objective and professional manner. The report hereby issued has been subject to review by a linguist affiliated to aforementioned Bureau, as appears from the signature below. The work performed by language analysts is subject to constant quality control.

Origin according to applicant

....Burundi............................

Origin according to language analysis

On the basis of the language analysis carried out by me, I am able to declare the applicant
☐ definitely can
X definitely not
☐ probably can
☐ both/ and

to belong to the speech and cultural community of

....Burundi............................

☐ It is not possible to draw a conclusion based on the available data.

FURTHER DETAILS

1. Languages used

Language(s) or dialect(s) of the applicant	: Swahili
Language(s) or dialect(s) of the interpreter	: Swahili
Language(s) or dialect(s) of the language analyst	: Kirundi, Swahili, French

2. Details of the applicant

None.

3. Applicant's knowledge of the country

3.1 Applicant's account

The applicant stated the following during the conversation, among other things. The applicant claims that he was born in Nyanza Lac, Makamba, Burundi. He says that in 1980 he went to Rugufu, Kigoma, Tanzania, where he went to live with his aunt. He says that lived in Tanzania for fifteen years. From Tanzania he returned to Nyanza Lac, Burundi, where he [stayed]* until his departure to the Netherlands. He says that he attended school for two years in Tanzania. He says that he only speaks Swahili, and knows just a few words in Kirundi. He names the words of Kirundi that he knows and translates several words from Swahili to Kirundi. Several other topics are being discussed.

3.2 Analyst's comments

The applicant is unable to provide concrete and detailed information about his claimed region of origin.

4. Description of the language use of the applicant

4.1 General

- The applicant speaks Swahili with an accent that definitely places him outside Burundi.
- The applicant knows a few words of Kirundi, but is unable to pronounce these correctly.
- The applicant has no active knowledge of Kirundi, the national language of Burundi.

- There is nothing in the applicant's speech that points to an origin or a prolonged stay in Burundi.

4.2 Pronunciation

No particulars.

4.3 Word choice

radio [rediyo]	'radio'
college [kɔ lidʒ]	'college'
sokoni	'on the market'
kufahamu	'to remember'

4.4 Grammar

Watu wa bilimani wanazungumza Kirundi.
'People from the country side speak Kirundi.'

Alikuwa na magali mawill.
'He had two cars.'

Yiko nyota tatu.
'There are three stars.'

5. Result

The applicant definitely can<u>not</u> be traced to the speech community within Burundi.

6. Background language analyst

The language analyst originates from Burundi. His native language is Kirundi. In addition he masters Swahili and French fluently.

7. Additional remarks

None.

★ Verb missing in the original added by the translator.

LADO and Arabic: The Case of Iraqi Arabic as an Introduction to the Middle East

Judith Rosenhouse

Abstract

The goal of this paper is to discuss several linguistic aspects of LADO (Language Analysis for Determination of Origin), from the point of view of Arabic as used in Iraq, which is a major source of refugees in Europe and elsewhere. We first describe the background of Iraq and the outlines of its mainly modern history. Next, we mention the languages currently used in Iraq, since they are related to LADO. In the third section we present a few general language/dialect verification problems, based on Iraqi LADO cases. The background and examples lead to a discussion of the situation, bringing out the complexity of language analysis by merely a recorded speech sample, as well as our suggestions and conclusions.

1. Introduction: The History and Population Make-up in Iraq

Our goal here is to discuss several problematic aspects of Arabic LADO, from the point of view of Arabic spoken in Iraq, which is a major source of refugees in Europe and elsewhere. As way of introduction in section (1) we first briefly describe Iraq, its structure, its historical background, the make-up of its population and Arabic, the dominant language in this country. We will then proceed in section (2) to describe language use in Iraq, since Arabic is not the only language spoken there. Neither is Arabic a uniform entity, and therefore some elaboration is in order. The next stage in this paper, in section (3) will be a short discussion of dialect verification as part of forensic linguistics. To elucidate the complexity of Arabic-related dialect verification (DV) we present in section (4) a few examples of different kinds of problems encountered in LADO cases, in particular such that reflect real cases of applicants claiming to have come from Iraq. These examples will lead to section (5), which presents a discussion of DV in Arabic LADO and a few conclusions can be drawn.

Iraq is an important and large state in the Middle East. Historically, it was a cradle of civilization since the 6th millennium BC, and along history it was the center of several empires including the Accadian, Assyrian, and Babylonian empires in the pre-Christian era. It was an important part of the Greek and Roman empires, and later on – part of the Sassanid (in Persia), Arab, Turkish Ottoman, and British Empires.[1]

---

1   Britain had many interests in Iraq mainly due to Britain's world trade and Iraq's vicinity to Iran and the Indian colony.

Figure 1. Map of Iraq (from:_http://en.wikipedia.org/wiki/Iraq)

For speakers of Arabic Iraq is an important country (see Figure 1). Baghdad became the capital city of the Abbasid Arabic Empire (751 CE). Other cities, e.g., Basra and Kufa, were also important centers of learning and science in the 8-10 centuries. Historically and politically also Karbala and An-Najaf were and still are important, as the holy cities of the Shi'a Muslims. The wealth and prosperity of the Arab empire gradually disintegrated into smaller units ruled by local sultans (Nicholson, 1960, Hourani, 1991, Rogerson, 2007). Baghdad and what remained of the Arab empire was finally destroyed by the Mongols in 1258. After a few centuries of instability, the Turkish Ottoman Empire stabilized in the Middle East including Iraq (and Eastern Europe). During the following four centuries cultural stagnation spread in the Arabic Middle East. At the same time, Iraq was gradually re-inhabited by Bedouin tribes coming from the Arabian Peninsula. The first signs of Renaissance and westernization began in the Middle East in the beginning of the 19th century, more or less with Napoleon's journey to Egypt and the Holy Land (Tauber, 1995).

At the end of World War I and the fall of the Ottoman Empire, the League of Nations (the predecessor of the present UNO) granted the regions of Baghdad and

Basra (in 1921) and later also Mosul (in 1926)[2] to Britain as a Mandate. This act formed the territory of the modern Iraqi state. The country became an independent kingdom in 1932, with the British still present in Iraq. On April 1st, 1941, a *coup d'etat* led to the short Anglo-Iraqi War (May, 1941) which was followed by restoration of the monarchy and the British occupation. The British colonial administrators were the real rulers of the country during the Mandate and appointed members of the Sunni Arab elite for government and ministry offices. They also suppressed Arab and Kurdish rebellions against the occupation. The monarchy lasted until the revolution on 14th of July, 1958, which was led by Brigadier General Abdul Karim Qasim, who ruled Iraq for seven years (1958-1963) (Marr, 2004). But Iraq did not calm down. In 1968 the Arab socialist Ba'ath party took over, and Ahmed Hasan Al-Bakir was the first Ba'ath president of Iraq. The party gradually came under the control of Saddam Hussein al-Tikriti who in July 1979 acceded to presidency and control of the Revolutionary Command Council. Saddam Hussein's regime was notoriously brutal against many Iraqi communities (Kurds, Sunnis, gypsies and others). He led three wars: Iran-Iraq (1980-1988), 1st Gulf War (1991), and the 2nd Gulf War (2003). The latter began with an invasion of Iraq by the USA following the claim that Iraq was developing nuclear weapons. On April 9th, 2003, Saddam Hussein was militarily overthrown by the U.S.-led coalition and was later executed (30.6.2006). In June 2004 sovereignty was transferred to the Iraqi Interim Government. A new Constitution has since been approved by referendum and a new government has been elected.[3] The USA forces withdrew from Baghdad in June 29, 2009, and the full withdrawal of U.S. military forces from Iraq is scheduled for December 31, 2011.[4]

Islam was and is the official state religion in Iraq. Approximately 97% (about 22-28 million persons) of the Iraqi population is Muslim. 60-65% of them are Shi'a Muslims: Arabs, Turkoman, Fayli Kurds, etc., and 32-37% of them are Sunni Muslims (of whom ~18-20% are Sunni Kurds, 12-15% percent Arabs, and the rest are Turkoman). The remaining ~3% of the population consists of minorities: Christians (Assyrians, Chaldeans, Roman Catholics, and Armenians), Yazidis, Mandaeans, and a few Jews. The Iraqi Constitution did not provide for the recognition of Assyrians, Chaldeans, or Yazidis.

Shi'a Muslims are predominantly located in the south. They form a majority in Baghdad and have communities in most parts of the country. Sunnis form the majority in the center of the country and in the north. Shi'a and Sunni Arabs are not ethnically distinct, but their long-standing religion-based rivalry endangers the future of the country. Ethnically, the Kurds in the north, north-east and east of Iraq are the largest minority. Their biggest center is Mossul but even there they are a minority. The other minorities, too, are located mainly in the north and north east of Iraq.

---

2   At the same time Britain received the Mandate over Palestine and Jordan also.
3   Recently a new round of elections took place again in Iraq.
4   On the situation in Iraq after the American operation in Iraq see e.g. Stewart (2007).

2.   Language Use in Iraq

Arabic is one of the major world languages with more than 250 million speakers. Attention to it has been growing in the last decades not only in speech sciences. Native speakers of Arabic spread in the world from the Arabian Peninsula to the Middle East and North Africa and from there to the rest of the world. Arabic is known for its:

(1) numerous dialects. Classification criteria of Arabic dialects include at least: geography (east-west), religion (Muslims, Christians, Jewish etc.), habitation (nomadic vs. sedentary, the latter divided into urban vs. rural), gender (male, female) (Holes, 1995, Versteegh, 1997, Kaye and Rosenhouse, 1997).

(2) Diglossia. This term refers to the differences between the prestigious Literary Arabic (LA, also named Modern Standard Arabic, MSA) and the colloquial dialects of Arabic (Ferguson, 1959a, Bousoffara-Omar, 2006).

Arabic is the dominant and official language in Iraq. It is therefore the common language of its population, whichever ethnic or religious community they belong to. Proficiency in the local dialects – mainly the dialect of the capital, Baghdad, but also dialects of other local urban centers, such as the Maslawi Arabic dialect in Mossul – is therefore widespread for daily communication of all the minority communities when speaking with other minority speakers or with the Arab majority. Of course, proficiency varies among individual minority speakers according to the rate of their contacts with the Arabic speaking majority and/or their education (for schooling is conducted in Arabic).

Kurdish is the 2nd official language of the country (Allison, 2007), but due to the contact with Arabic in Iraq it is full of Arabic loanwords. (Arabic, on the other hand, is hardly thus influenced by Kurdish, except in the northern regions of the Kurds centers; Chyet, 2007). Several other languages, such as Turkic, and others, mostly descending from Aramaic, an old North-West Semitic language (Khan, 2007), are used by the smaller minorities.

The main geographical and communal language classification of Arabic in Iraq is between *gelet* and *qeltu* dialects (Blanc, 1964): *gelet* dialects are used by speakers descending from older Bedouin groups that gradually re-settled Iraq after its destruction by the Mongols in the 13th century; *qeltu* dialects are typically spoken by Christian and Jewish communities, who live mostly in the center and north of the country and had settled there before the *gelet* dialect speakers.

During Saddam Hussein's rule (1979-2003), as well as before him, deportations, forced population removals, refugee emigrations and sedentarization of nomadic groups took place in Iraq. The cultural situation changed in the 20th century also due to expanded school education rate in LA/MSA. All these factors have changed the linguistic landscape in Iraq (even compared to Blanc, 1964). The above events and factors, as well as the effects of LA (and foreign) style and vocabulary, level down, mix and change the original dialects: "The point has now been reached in Baghdad where dialects other than that of the Muslim majority are becoming invisible in public contexts and according to recent research even receding in domestic ones," writes Holes (2007: 133). Such a situation as we see in Iraq may eventually lead to the extinction of local dialects and languages, as happens in many other places around the world.

Minority languages in Iraq include mainly Kurdish, as noted, which is a language with several dialects and is used by Kurds and Yezidi speakers. The Turkoman community's mother tongue is Turkomanian (they mostly live in the North-East of Iraq, the same area as the Kurds; see Bulut, 2007). The Mandean minority uses Mandaic, the classical liturgical language, and speaks the Neo-Mandean language, which developed from the older Mandean. This language branched from old Aramaic (see "Mandean" in Wikipedia and its references). The Assyrian and Chaldean minorities also speak their modern versions of Aramaic (Neo-Eastern Aramaic – see, e.g., "Assyrian," "Chaldean" and "Armenian" in Wikipedia, and their references), while the Armenians speak their Armenian language – see Russell, 2004). As noted, however, all these minorities are bilingual or multilingual and use Arabic outside community boundaries.

3.   Dialect Verification

Dialect Verification (DV) is a growing field of forensic linguistics, due to the numerous asylum seekers whose origin needs to be verified (Coulthard &Johnson, 2007, De Graaf, Verrips & van den Hazelkamp, 2009). DV has in fact been part of forensic linguistics without this title, and not only in the context of asylum seekers. Suspects' voices may be analyzed within the field of speaker identification, when speakers are traced back to some definite location by the dialect features of the recorded speech sample (cf. Nolan, 1999, Hollien, 2002). A main distinction between speaker identification and DV is that in DV for official LADO tasks the speaker's identity is known but not her/his origin. The question in DV is how to verify or falsify applicants' claims to a certain origin using linguistic features. This issue is rather complex in many cases, due to linguistic as well as sociolinguistic factors, as the examples below will portray.

In DV the language expert has to work mostly with acquired knowledge of the language, and heated debates have been going on as to the quality of the work done by language specialists vs. native speakers, who are not necessarily qualified linguists (cf., e.g., Eades, 2003, Fraser, 2009), or computer programs (Rose, 2002). The quality of human speech analysis and recognition has also been questioned in the context of forensic linguistics (Hollien, 1990, 2002, Rose, 2002, Gibbons, 2003: 297-302). We see that no method is perfect for the time being, not even the quantitative/computerized approach, which routinely reports various levels of errors as part of system evaluation in studies of computerized language recognition/ identification (e.g., Shriberg et al. 2008, Broeders, 2001). For DV, Arabic is a particularly important language, due to the immense number of its dialects and Arabic-speaking asylum seekers all over the world.

The term 'Variety Switching' has also come into use (e.g., Tamer, 2006) indicating switching and mixing linguistic elements of different dialects. This process would be expected in a speaker's long-term socialization with speakers of different Arabic dialects, which may eventually lead to mother tongue gradual attrition. This process is already noticeable not only in the LADO framework.

4. Examples

Some examples of difficulties in DV (for Arabic-LADO) are presented here. They concern mainly speakers of Iraqi Arabic, but some of them reflect problems that are common to DV in other languages. The examples are classified into the following topics: (4.1) lack of documentation, (4.2) linguistic accommodation (including (4.2.1) the local prestige factor and (4.2.2) sex-based sociolinguistic considerations), (4.3) undergoing linguistic developments in (4.3.1) emphatics and (4.3.2) consonant palatalization, (4.4) lexical interference, (4.5) missing features and (4.6) too many features.[5]

4.1 Lack of Documentation

First and foremost, it should be taken into consideration that not all the linguistic details of all the Arabic dialects are known. This is the case in researched places as well as in many under-studied dialects such as in sub-Saharan Fringe dialects of Nigeria, Chad, Sudan, or Somalia. Accordingly, experts sometimes have no available information to rely on (cf. Coulthad and Johnson, 2007: 142). So, how can one verify or falsify a speaker's dialect if s/he claims to be from a village or a small town in, e.g., Iraq, which has never been linguistically studied? For certain dialects the general regional features may be known, but it may be difficult to determine that certain features are original rather than acquired from neighboring dialects.

4.2 Linguistic Accommodation

Basically, this issue is not unique to Arabic speakers (Trudgill, 1986, Shiri, 2009): It involves communication patterns of speakers of different social and socio-economic groups (urban/rural speakers, employers/employees, native/immigrant, etc.). In the context of LADO and Arabic, the effect of sociolinguistic factors cannot be overemphasized.

4.2.1 The Prestige Factor

Bedouin speakers (or other speakers of a nomadic-type or rural dialect), will tend to use sedentary (mainly urban) features outside their home, but an urban/sedentary speaker would not normally mix Bedouin features in her/his speech (Abu Haidar, 2006b). This linguistic behavior is due to the fact that the urban sedentary population has been for many centuries more prosperous and cultured and therefore socially more prestigious. Yet Bedouins are considered a prestigious group in Jordan and Bahrain, and many Iraqi sedentary dialects are descended from Bedouin dialects. So, if a speaker is a native of Iraq but says s/he has also lived in Jordan or Bahrain, the speech sample may include

---

5 Such difficulties and others have been encountered and solved in real cases, but the solutions were not based only on single features as presented in the isolated examples below.

Iraqi sedentary (*gelet*) as well as Bedouin features. How, then, should a linguist decide which is this speaker's original "mother tongue"?

4.2.2 Sex-based Sociolinguistic Considerations

In the Arabic speaking communities, men do not accommodate to female speech (for fear of being made fun of), but women usually accommodate to male speech. It should also be noted that in traditional Arabic-speaking communities the social distance between men and women who do not belong to the same family is usually larger than in the Western society. Thus, men are the prestigious group. Now, if a women speaking to a male stranger (say, the interviewer in a LADO recording session) uses /g/ (which is a male feature) instead of or in addition to /'/ (which is used by female speakers in certain non- Iraqi dialects):[6] Is she a native speaker of a /g/ dialect (a *gelet* dialect) or is she only accommodating to the interviewer's phonetic system (which differs from hers)?

4.3   Undergoing Linguistic Developments

4.3.1 Emphatic Consonants (/s', t' d', d̲'/)

The emphatic (pharyngealized) phonemes characterize Arabic at least since its Classical period. But some of them have been weakening in many Arabic dialects. Sociolinguistic factors characterize also this process (Royal, 1985, Rosenhouse, 1998). So, if there are few emphatics in a speech sample - what does it imply? Does the speaker want to be considered a native speaker of some Arabic dialect, though s/he is not? Or: Is s/he a native speaker of an Arabic dialect in which the emphatics are weakened? The question is relevant for Iraq, from where Kurdish applicants claim to originate, since Kurdish dialects have emphatics, but their distribution is different. Apparently, in such a case the occurrence of emphatics cannot be distinctive or decisive, whatever their frequency in the applicant's sample (but they should always be noted).

4.3.2 Consonant Palatalization (e.g., /t/> /ts/ or /t'/, /d/> d'/)

Consonant palatalization in dental stops such as /t, d/ characterizes female speakers in Cairo (Haeri, 1997, Royal, 1985). But it has been spreading in male groups both in Cairo and outside Egypt. Thus, also this feature is not absolutely distinctive for LADO goals.

4.4   Lexical Interference

As described in the introduction, many languages were in contact with Arabic in Iraq along history and have affected its vocabulary, e.g. Persian, Turkish, Italian, Kurdish, English, etc. Loanwords from such languages sometimes involve occurrence of pho-

---

6   /g/ and /'/ reflect LA/MSA /q/ in her dialect.

nemes that originally do not exist in Arabic, e.g., /p/, / tʃ/ or /ts/.[7] Now, how is one to interpret recurring occurrences of both /k/ and /tʃ/ in a speech sample? Do they reflect an original Bedouin-type dialect, an expanding foreign influence, or even hypercorrections?

Moreover, what is the implication of foreign words in a speaker's speech? Could English be the mother tongue of a speaker who says "o.k." frequently? And how should one consider sophisticated or technical words, which partly originate in LA/MSA? Such words, which sometimes have no equivalent terms in the vernacular dialects, are becoming part of the daily vocabulary, due to the spread of literacy. In such a case we may question whether the speaker could be using LA/MSA because s/he does not know the relevant word in the alleged 'mother dialect,' or because this word does not exist in the dialect.

4.5   Missing Features

Recorded speech samples hardly provide all the typical features of some dialect (its *shibboleth* features). *gelet* Iraqi Arabic, for example, has an indefinite article /fad/ 'a' and a verb prefix /da-/ indicating an ongoing action. But what should the linguist think if these characteristic features do not turn up in the recording? Is the speaker not a native speaker of the claimed dialect? Or, is s/he rather accommodating to the listener's dialect (by avoiding the use of this "marked" feature)?

4.6   Too Many Features

The opposite case is when one finds in a recording too many features, apparently representing several dialects or languages. Which is, then, the mother tongue and which is the speaker's acquired 2nd or 3rd language? Is s/he inconsistently accommodating to the interlocutor? Or (to use a professional term somewhat differently from its original meaning) is s/he code switching between several dialects in which s/he is more or less proficient at the same level (the noted Variety Switching)? In such cases it seems that only a detailed study and classification of the features might help solve the puzzle.

5.   Discussion and Conclusions

Language skills or rather mother tongue skills are considered important, for they have traditionally defined one's origin (cf. Patrick, 2009a, 2009b). But since immigration to almost all parts of the world has become relatively easy in the last half century or so, State authorities are obliged to check incoming immigrants for various social interests such as security, economy and culture. LADO is therefore considered by the governments an important tool, an essential and a positive framework. Still, it involves many implementation problems, as claimed in the literature mentioned here and elsewhere.

---

7   / tʃ / or /ts/ occur, however, in some modern Bedouin dialects as reflexes of LA/MSA /k/.

Improving results of LADO requires not only research for defining expertise, procedures, analysts and other participants in the process, but also applying results of such studies. At least for the language experts detailed questionnaires or protocols should be prepared concerning the specific features of each language and community which comes under study. This protocol will question details of existing, missing or erroneous features in the analyzed speech sample, which could yield a relatively "objective" picture of the recorded profile and could, for example, be also used to compare the speech of different applicants from the same dialect community. A large archive could keep these data which might be used in international cooperation for LADO cases. Linguistic features cannot serve as the sole means of identifying a speaker's origin, however, and sociolinguistic and social factors should always be taken in consideration side by side with the linguistic features.

We have surveyed here the case of Iraqi Arabic within LADO tasks. In the 20th century the importance of Iraq grew largely due to the economic benefits of its oil production and oil reserves. From the perspective of LADO, Iraq is a melting pot of local and foreign languages and dialects. Since Arabic is the major, dominant language of this country (and the Middle East) it affects speakers of minority languages in Iraq. This picture yields for many speakers at least the bilingual setting of an embedded language and a matrix language (Myers-Scotton, 1993), or even a multilingual setting. It is often difficult to distinguish the embedded language from the matrix language when a speaker uses much code-switching/code-mixing (cf. the quotation from Parkinson, 2003, in Bousoffara-Omar, 2006: 635). Constant bilingualism may cause a code switching amalgam which cannot be separated into mother tongue vs. second/foreign language (also in Morocco, for example, where Moroccan Arabic is mixed with French, Berber and LA/MSA, cf. Sadiqi, 2003). Indeed, most Arabic dialects developed (and are still developing) due to multiple influence sources, as described in cases of interaction, contacts and effects (see e.g., Miller et al., 2007, for recent urban Arabic). An applicant's recorded speech may thus reveal linguistic features - or not (Patrick, 2009a, 2009b).

Concerning Iraq, we do not find recent field work. Recent works on Arabic dialects do not include Iraqi dialects (e,g., Miller, 2007), while Abu Haidar (2006a), Jastorw (2007) and Holes (2007) are general descriptions and mainly rely on research from the 1990's or earlier (e.g., Abu Haidar, 1991). So, developments and changes in Iraqi Arabic dialects in the last two decades are practically unknown (at least to civil linguists). This means that information which may confirm asylum seekers' claims to Iraqi origin is not available to the language analysts.

Many factors cause linguistic changes. An applicant says in the recording that members of her/his community do not use their local dialect outside their own town, for fear of being derided by speakers of other (i.e., more prestigious) dialects. Avoiding the use of a typical 'shibboleth' feature as a strategy could then reflect accommodation to the interlocutor's speech, Koinèization (Ferguson, 1959b) or leveling (cf. Blanc, 1960). Above we presented several examples of questions that rise concerning applicants' sociolinguistic and linguistic behavior. This behavior apparently reflects modern dialect structures and forms the building blocks of language change in time.

A language analyst who does not have sufficient linguistic data is supposed to processes the LADO questions based on principles of linguistic features. According to the literature, LADO is usually performed without even semi-automatic programs, unlike some forensic linguistics fields. For tasks where linguistic details are not available, language analysts apparently use, partly at least, their *implicit knowledge* (e.g., Polany, 1958, 1966, Reber, 1993). *Implicit (tacit) knowledge* reflects skills and information acquired without conscious attention to (and awareness of) learning details and procedures. *Tacit knowledge* cannot, however, replace accurate details when they are available, and language analysts should rely not only on 'general impression' based on a recorded speech text. It seems that the best language analyst would be a native speaker of the applicant's dialect who is also a professional linguist and uses his/her *implicit knowledge* at work. But such experts are rare.

To sum up, Iraq has been multilingual for thousands of years. Mainly due to political circumstances and urbanization, asylum seekers with mixed dialects live outside Iraq in Arabic-speaking countries and elsewhere. Linguistic features cannot serve as the sole means of identifying a speaker's origin, and sociolinguistic factors should always be considered with the linguistic features (and provided to the language analysis). There is still no perfect human or automatic language analysis system (e.g., a uniform, coherent, computerized, statistical language analysis system). Thus, the issues involved in LADO will apparently continue to concern us for a long time yet.

References

Abu Haidar, F. (1991) *Christian Arabic of Baghdad*, Wiesbaden: Harrassowitz.

Abu Haidar, F. (2006a) Baghdad Arabic, in: K. Versteegh (ed.), *Encyclopedia of Arabic Language and Linguistics*, Leiden: Brill, Vol. I, p. 222-231.

Abu Haidar, F. (2006b) Bedouinization, in: K. Versteegh (ed.), *Encyclopedia of Arabic Language and Linguistics*, Leiden: Brill, Vol. I, p. 269-274.

Allison, C. (2007) 'The Kurds are alive': Kurdish in Iraq, in: J. N. Postgate (ed.), *Languages in Iraq Ancient and Modern*, Cambridge: British School of Archeology in Iraq, p. 135-158.

Blanc, H. (1960) Stylistic Variations in Spoken Arabic: A sample of inter-dialectal educated conversation, in C. Ferguson (ed.), Contributions to Arabic Linguistics, Cambridge, Mass.: Harvard University Press, p. 78-161.

Blanc, H. (1964) *Communal Dialects of Baghdad*, Cambridge, Mass.: Distributed for the Center for Middle Eastern Studies of Harvard University Press.

Broeders, A.P.A. (2001) *Forensic speech and audio analysis: Forensic Linguistics 1998 to 2001: a Review*, 13th INTERPOL Forensic Science Symposium, Lyon, France, October 16-19, 2001.

Bousoffara-Omar, N. (2006) Diglossia, in: K. Versteegh et al. (eds), *Encyclopedia of Arabic Language and Linguistics*, Leiden: Brill, Vol. 1, p. 629-6637.

Bulut, C. (2007) Iraqi Turkman, in: J.N. Postgate (ed.), *Languages in Iraq Ancient and Modern*, Cambridge: British School of Archeology in Iraq, p.135-187.

Chyet, M. (2007) Kurdish, in: K. Versteegh et al.(eds.), *Encyclopedia of Arabic Lnaguage and Linguistics*, Leiden: Brill, Vol. 2, p. 604-608.

Graaf, A. de, M. Verrips and C. van den Hazelkamp (2009), *Implementing the 'Guidelines for the Use of Language Analysis' when determining national or regional origin in asylum cases*, 9th IAFL Biennial Conference, Amsterdam, 6-9 July, 2009.

Eades, D., H. Fraser, J. Siegel, T. McNamara and B. Baker (2003) Linguistic identification in the determination of nationality: A preliminary report, *Language Policy*, 2 (2), p. 179-199

Ferguson, Ch.A. (1959a) Diglossia, *Word*, 15, p. 325-340.

Ferguson, Ch.A. (1959b) The Arabic Koinè, *Language*, 35, p. 616-630

Fraser, H. (2009) The role of 'educated native speakers' in providing language analysis for the determination of the origin of asylum seekers, *International Journal of Speech Language and the Law*, Vol. 16(1), p. 113-138.

Gibbons, J. (2003) *Forensic Linguistics: An Introduction to Language in the Justice System*, Malden, MA: Blackwell Publications.

Haeri, N. (1997) *The Sociolinguistic Market of Cairo: Gender, Class, and Education*, London: Kegan Paul International.

Holes, C. (1995) *Modern Arabic: Structures, Functions and Varieties*, London: Longman (and 2004[2] – Georgetown University Press).

Holes, C. (2007) Colloquial Iraqi Arabic, in: J. N. Postgate (ed.) *Languages in Iraq Ancient and Modern*, Cambridge: British School of Archeology in Iraq, p. 123-134.

Hollien, H. (1990) *The Acoustics of Crime: The New Science of Forensic Phonetics*, New York: Plenum Press.

Hollien, H. (2002) *Forensic Voice Identification*, San Diego: Academic Press.

Hourani, A.H. (1991) *A History of the Arab Peoples*, London: Faber and Faber.

http://en.wikipedia.org/wiki/Armenians_in_Iraq (accessed 22.5.2010).

http://en.wikipedia.org/wiki/Assyrian (accessed 22.5.2010).

http://en.wikipedia.org/wiki/Chaldean (accessed 22.5.2010).

http://en.wikipedia.org/wiki/Iraq (accessed on 11.3.2010).

http://en.wikipedia.org/wiki/Refugees_of_Iraq (accessed on 11.3.2010).

http://en.wikipedia.org/wiki/mandaic_language (accessed 21.5.2010).

http://www.reintegration.net/europa/download/Irak.pdf (accessed on 11.3.2010).

Jastrow, O. (2007) Iraq, in: K. Versteegh (ed.) *Encyclopedia of Arabic Language and Linguistics*, Leiden: Brill, Vol. II, p. 414-444.

Kaye, A.S. and J. Rosenhouse (1997) Arabic dialects and Maltese, in: R. Hetzron (ed.) *The Semitic Languages*, London: Routledge, p. 263-311.

Khan, G. (2007) Aramaic in the medieval and modern periods, in: J. N. Postgate (ed.) *Languages in Iraq Ancient and Modern*, Cambridge: British School of Archeology in Iraq, p. 95-114.

Marr, Ph. (2004) *The Modern History of Iraq*, Boulder, Colorado: Westview Press.

Miller, C., E. Al-Wer, D. Caubet and J.C.E. Watson (2007) *Arabic in the City: Issues in Dialect Contact and Language Variation*, London: Routledge.

Myers-Scotton, (1993) *Social Motivations for Codeswitching: Evidence from Africa*, Oxford: Clarendon Press.

Nicholson, R.A. (1960) *A Literary History of the Arabs*, Jerusalem: Kiryat Sepher (in Hebrew; translated into Hebrew by J.J. Rivlin).

Nolan, F. (1999) Speaker recognition and forensic phonetics, in: W.J. Hardcastle and J. Laver (eds), *The Handbook of Phonetic Sciences*, Oxford: Blackwell Publishing, p. 744-767.

Parkinson, D.B. (2003) Verbal features in oral *fusha* in Cairo, *International Journal of the Sociology of Language*, 163, p. 27-41.

Patrick, P.L. (2009a) *The linguistic human rights of asylum speakers*, presentation at 4th LangUE conference, University of Essex, 12.6.2009.

Patrick, P.L. (2009b) *Sociolinguistic issues in Language Analysis for Determination of Origins*, presentation at the workshop Seeking Refuge: Caught between Bureaucracy, Lawyers and Public Indifference?" The Centre of African Studies, SOAS, University of London, April 16th-17th, 2009.

Polanyi, M. (1958) *Personal Knowledge: Towards a Post-Critical Philosophy*, London: Routledge & K. Paul.

Polanyi, M. (1966) *The Tacit dimension*, Garden City: Doubleday.

Reber, A. (1993) *Implicit Learning and Tacit Knowledge: An Essay on the Cognitive Unconscious*. New York, Oxford: Oxford University press and Clarendon Press.

Rogerson, B. (2007) *The Heirs of Muhammad: Islam's First Century and the Origins of the Sunni-Shia Split*, Woodstock: Overlook Press.

Rose, P. (2002) *Forensic Speaker Identification*, London and New York: Taylor and Francis.

Royal, A. (1985) *Male/Female Pharyngealization Patterns in Cairo Arabic: A Sociolinguistic Study of Two Neighborhoods*, Ph.D., the University of Texas at Austin.

Rosenhouse, J. (1998) Women's speech and language variation in Arabic dialects, *Al-'Arabiyya*, 31, p. 123-152.

Russell, J.R. (2004) *Armenian and Iranian Studies*, Belmont, MA: Heritage Press.

Sadiqi, F. (2003) *Women, Gender, and Language in Morocco*, Leiden: Brill Academic Publishers.

Shiri, S. (2009) Speech accommodation, in: K. Versteegh et al. (eds), *Encyclopedia of Arabic Language and Linguistics*, Leiden: Brill, Vol. 4, p. 320-328.

Shriberg, E., L. Ferrer, S. Kajarekar, N. Scheffer, A. Stolcke and M. Akbacak, (2008) Detecting Non-native Speech Using Speaker Recognition Approaches, *Odyssey 2008*, Stellenbosch, South Africa.

Stewart, R. (2007) *The Prince of the Marshes and Other Occupational Hazards of a Year in Iraq*, Orlando, FL, USA: Harvest book, Harcourt, Inc.

Tamer, Y. (2006) Constraints and motivations of Varietal-Switching as a case of code-switching within the Moroccan triglossia, in: F. Monge and A. Vicente (eds), *Ciudades del Mediterraneo: Las Modernidades de un Viejo Mundo en un Nuevo Milenio, Program and Abstracts,* International Seminar of the International Union of Anthropological and Ethnological Sciences (IUAES), Commission on Urban Anthropology, 30.5 – 2.6.2006, Cádiz, Spain, p. 50-51.

Tauber, E. (1995) *The Formation of Modern Syria and Iraq*, Ilford, Essex, UK: Frank Cass (translated from Hebrew).

Trudgill, P. (1986) *Dialects in Contact,* Oxford: Basil Blackwell.

Versteegh, K. (1997) *The Arabic Language*, Edinburgh: Edinburgh University Press.

Part Four: Language in Asylum Procedures: A Country Survey

The fourth part surveys the role of language in asylum procedures in several different countries. *Silvia Morgades* discusses the situation in Spain and *Dirk Vanheule* the case of Belgium. *Claudia Pretto* demonstrates that in Italy language differences are only taken into account in some cases. Thus LADO is virtually not applied in Italy in any organized way. *Jens Vedsted-Hansen*, finally, presents the use of LADO in Denmark. Considerable variation appears in the degree to which LADO is integrated in the procedure and the extent to which it is used at all.

The Asylum Procedure in Spain: The Role of Language in Determining the Origin of Asylum Seekers

*Silvia Morgades**

1. Introduction

The object of this chapter is to deal with the procedure for asylum in Spain and determining the origin of asylum seekers during this procedure, especially when they have no documentation accrediting their origin, or when they cannot provide any other proof for their statements regarding the state of which they are nationals. In principle, language analysis is not used by the authorities to establish the origin of asylum seekers in Spain. However, based on an overall analysis of the procedures followed, and on the roles played by the various actors in the procedure, it appears that language analysis techniques have occasionally been used on an informal basis. In Spain, determining the origin of asylum seekers who cannot prove their identity and nationality is part of the assessment of the credibility. As regards this issue, it is fully pertinent to say that the assessment of credibility is 'often the single most important step in determining whether people seeking protection as refugees can be returned to countries where they say they are in danger of serious human right violations'.[1] This chapter considers the reasons why language analysis is not used in Spain, which techniques are used to determine the origin of the applicants, how the credibility of the asylum seekers in terms of this issue is assessed, and will also try to answer the question of whether the introduction of language analysis is necessary or advisable in the Spanish asylum procedure.

The Chapter will be divided into four parts. First, there is a brief overview of the situation of asylum on the ground in Spain. Second, the main aspects of the new Spanish Asylum Law, which has been in force since 20 November 2009, will be outlined. Third, the procedure for asylum in Spain will be studied. And fourth, an analysis will be undertaken on how the origin of asylum seekers is currently assessed, the shortcomings of the system, and the opportunities in the future for the implementation of language analysis techniques. In order to prepare this part, I have interviewed three groups of individuals involved in the process: staff at the Asylum and Refugee Office, which is the body of the Spanish Ministry of the Interior responsible for processing cases; lawyers at the CEAR (the Spanish Refugee Aid Committee), which is one of the main NGOs providing legal

---

* The author wishes to thank to the staff at the Oficina de Asilo y Refugio (OAR), Anna Figueras (Comissió Catalana d'Ajuda al Refugiat- CEAR), M. Carme Junyent and Marisa Iglesias for their comments and discussion.
1 Michael Kagan, Is Truth in the Eye of the Beholder? Objective Credibility Assessment in Refugee Status Determination, *Georgetown Immigration Law Journal*, vol. 17, 2003, 367.

advice services to asylum seekers; an interpreter involved in asylum procedures; and a linguist specialising in African languages. Finally, some conclusions will be suggested.

2. The Situation of Asylum on the Ground in Spain

The number of applications for asylum presented in Spain in recent years is low in comparison with other states in Southern Europe, such as Italy and Greece. The number of applications for asylum is around 5,000 per year, except for some years (such as 2007, when a significant number of applications from Iraqis were received). In recent years the trend has been downward, as shown by the most recent figure available, from last year, when only 3,000 applications for asylum were received.[2]

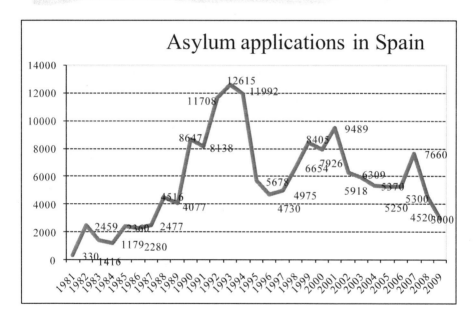

This suggests that the number of applications for asylum is proportional to the number of people arriving without an entry permit, and in the case of Spain, those arriving by sea, but the figures show that this is not the case. Calculations based on UNHCR figures suggest that 7,285 people arrived in Spain illegally last year (despite a figure of 32,000 in 2006), and this is only slightly lower than the number of people arriving in Italy (8.700)

---

2 Graph producing using data from the UNHCR, *Statistical Yearbook from 2001 to 2008* at www.unhcr.org and *Asylum Levels and Trends in Industrialized Countries 2009: Statistical Overview of Asylum Applications Lodged in Europe and Selected Non-European Countries*, 23 March 2010 http://www.unhcr.org/4ba7341a9.html [accessed 28.6.2010].

or Greece (10.165) illegally.[3] Notwithstanding this fact, Spain received only 3.000 applications for asylum whereas Italy received 17.600 applications, and Greece 15.930.[4]

Although it is difficult to ascertain the reasons behind this low number of applications, it is possible that the following may be contributory factors:

a. The transport networks involved; these mainly bring immigrants to Spain from countries where there is no fear of persecution or serious human rights violations.
b. Social and family networks
c. Historical background: colonial links, language and religion.[5]
d. The relatively recent nature of the tradition of asylum in Spain, which was a country of emigrants until some way into the twentieth century, and did not become a country of asylum until practically the point when it joined the European Community in 1986.
e. The Spanish asylum system, which has a procedure for the admissibility of applications for asylum - both those presented at the frontier and those on Spanish territory, which meant (at least until last year, when it was reformed) that many of the applications for asylum were deemed inadmissible.[6]
f. The fact that the number of people recognised as refugees or granted subsidiary protection is also very low.

The number of people protected is also quite low in Spain: only 179 individuals were recognised as refugees (151 in 2008), 162 were granted *subsidiary protection* (in the sense of the European Union Asylum Policy), and 8 received a residence permit for humanitarian reasons in 2009 (126 received a residence permit for humanitarian reasons in 2008, when the distinction with the *subsidiary protection* had not yet been made).[7]

---

3   UNHCR, *Asylum and Migration. Key facts and figures*, http://www.unhcr.org/pages/4a1d406060. html [accessed 28.6.2010]
4   UNHCR, *Asylum Levels and Trends in Industrialized Countries 2009: Statistical Overview of Asylum Applications Lodged in Europe and Selected Non-European Countries*, 23 March 2010   http://www.unhcr.org/4ba7341a9.html [accessed 28.6.2010], Table 1.
5   The a, b and c factors are those generally considered as having a role in the choice made by asylum seekers for a destination country. Nevertheless, studies show that they have a limited role because of a variety of reasons (some of them arbitrary) that asylum seekers may take into account. Michael Collyer, The Dublin Regulation, Influences on Asylum Destinations and the Exception of Algerians in UK, *JRS*, 17-4, 2004, p. 383-395.
6   Maryellen Fullerton, Inadmissible in Iberia: The Fate of Asylum Seekers in Spain and Portugal, *IJRL*, vol. 17-4, 2005, p. 659-687.
7   Ministerio del Interior (Government of Spain), Asilo en cifras 2008, Madrid, Ministerio del Interior, Secretaria General Técnica, 2009; and id., Asilo en cifras 2009, Madrid, Ministerio del Interior, Secretaria General Técnica, 2010. Available at http://www.mir.es/MIR/PublicacionesArchivo/publicaciones/catalogo/Asilo.html [accessed 28.6.2010] Most asylum seekers in Spain are from Africa, and come mainly from sub-Saharan Africa (Nigeria; Côte d'Ivoire; Guinea, RD Congo; Cameroon and Somalia); although depending on the year, there may also be a very large number of applicants from Colombia.

3.   The 2009 Spanish Asylum Law

The asylum procedure in Spain is regulated by Law 12/2009, which governs the right to asylum and subsidiary protection, and came into force on 20 November last year.[8] Previously, asylum in Spain was regulated by a 1984 Law (the first to be formulated under the terms of article 13 of the Spanish Constitution of 1978),[9] which was amended in 1994, basically in order to include a frontier procedure and a procedure for the admissibility of applications for asylum.

The Asylum Law of 2009 was adopted in order to transpose some of the Directives of the European Union making up the EU Asylum Policy framework until the Stockholm Programme:[10] European Council Directive 2003/9/EC of 27 January 2003, laying down minimum standards for the reception of asylum seekers; Directive 2004/83 on the qualification for recognition of refugee status; and Directive 2005/85 on minimum procedural standards.[11] The transposition of these directives was late (over 4 and a half years after the deadline for the reception directive had expired; 3 years after the deadline for the requirements directive; and almost two years after the deadline for the procedures directive), and took place after the European Union Court of Justice had ruled against Spain due to its failure to transpose the *qualification* directive.[12]

The main features of the new Law in terms of the transposition of the *qualification* Directive are as follows:

A. Among the main positive aspects are:
1.   The formal inclusion in law of the right to subsidiary protection, and the regulation of its legal statute according to the *qualification* Directive. In the conditions for granting

---

8   *Ley 12/2009, de 30 de octubre, reguladora del derecho de asilo y de la protección subsidiaria, Boletín Oficial del Estado (BOE)*, No. 263, 31 October 2009, p. 90860-90884.
9   Article 13 of the Spanish Constitution states that 'the law shall lay down the terms under which citizens from other countries and stateless persons may enjoy the right to asylum in Spain'.
10   *The Stockholm Programme: An open and secure Europe serving and protecting the citizen*, Doc. 17024/09. Council of the European Union. Brussels, 2 December 2009. The Stockholm Programme is the third five-year period for the implementation of the EU objective concerning the establishment of an Area of Freedom, Security and Justice. The first was the Tampere Programme (1999-2004) and the second was the The Hague Programme (2004-2009). Both have guided the adoption of the main legal instruments on asylum and immigration at EU level. On the development of this political objective of the EU, Pablo Antonio Fernández Sánchez, *Derecho comunitario de la inmigración*, Barcelona: Atelier, 2007; Alejandro del Valle Gálvez, Inmigración, extranjería y fronteras en la unión europea. Cinco problemas conceptuales, in J.J. Forner Delaygua et al., *Fronteras Exteriores de la U.E. e inmigración a España: Relaciones internacionales y derecho*, Valencia: Tirant lo Blanch, 2007, p. 43-80.
11   Council Directive 2003/9/EC of 27 January 2003 laying down minimum standards for the reception of asylum seekers (OJ L 31, 6.2.2003); Council Directive 2004/83/EC of 29 April 2004 on minimum standards for the qualification and status of third-country nationals and stateless people as refugees or as people who otherwise would need international protection and the content of the protection granted (OJ L 304, 30.9.2004); Council Directive 2005/85/EC of 1 December 2005 on minimum standards on procedures in Member States for granting and withdrawing refugee status (OJ L 326, 13.12.2005).
12   Ruling of the EUCJ of 9 July 2009, *Commission v Spain*, C-272/08.

subsidiary protection status, the requirement for *personal* risk in which the applicant claims 'serious threats to life or the integrity of civilians caused by indiscriminate violence in situations of international or internal conflict' (article 10 of the Spanish Asylum Law 12/2009) has been abolished.[13] The regulation of subsidiary protection in Spain, despite replacing the vague provision for 'humanitarian protection' which consisted of an authorisation of residency in Spain (*Disposición transitoria* number two of Law 12/2009), nonetheless does not exhaust all the possibilities by which the Spanish authorities can grant protection to individuals who do not meet the requirements for recognition as refugees, and who therefore cannot obtain asylum. According to the Spanish Immigration Law (amended most recently in December 2009) the Spanish authorities can authorise entry to Spain or to grant permission for temporary residency *for humanitarian reasons* for the grounds stipulated in the regulations.[14]

2. The definition of a *social group*, which also goes beyond the minimum standards of the *qualification* Directive because it includes age, gender and sexual identity as characteristics for identifying a social group in the sense of the refugee definition of the Geneva Convention. The Spanish Asylum Law 12/2009 states that 'depending on the circumstances prevailing in the country of origin, the concept of a specific social group covers a group based on a shared characteristic of sexual orientation *or sexual identity, and/or age*, without these aspects in themselves giving rise to the application of this article (...). *Likewise, and depending on the circumstances prevailing in the country of origin, individuals fleeing their country of origin due to well-founded fears of suffering persecution on the grounds of their gender and/or age are also included, without these aspects in themselves giving rise to the application of this article*' (article 7.1.e).[15]

3. Finally, a positive aspect of the Asylum Law 12/2009 is that it specifically provides a legal basis for the preparation of annual resettlement programmes in co-operation with the UNHCR and other International Organisations. However, the commitment

---

13 In contrast to article 15 of Directive 2004/83 which establishes that *serious harm* consists (among other situations) of 'serious and *individual* threat to a civilian's life or person by reason of indiscriminate violence in situations of international or internal conflict' (emphasis added). This abolition of the requirement of personal risk is consistent with the precedents concerning the relative nature of the personal nature of risk of the European Court of Human Rights (ECHR). The jurisprudence of the ECHR in this regard started with the rulings of 26 July 2005, *N v. Finland*, no. 38885/02, §162-165; and of 12 April 2005, *Shamayev and others v. Georgia and Russia*, no. 36378/02, §364-368. This jurisprudence was subsequently consolidated with other rulings including: ECHR ruling of 11 January 2007, *Salah Sheekh v. The Netherlands*, no. 1948/04, §147-148; ECHR ruling of 17 July 2008, *NA v. The United Kingdom*, no. 25904/07, §114-117; ECHR ruling of 28 February 2008, *Saadi v. Italy*, no. 37201/06, §140-143; ECHR ruling of 18 February 2010, *Baysakov and others v. Ukraine*, no. 54131/08, §49-50. It is also consistent with the European Union Court of Justice's ruling of 17 February 2009, *Meki Elgafaji*, C-465/07 (§43-44) which includes the evidence of the jurisprudence of the European Court of Human Rights in the European Union.

14 Articles 25 and 31 of *Ley Orgánica 4/2000, de 11 de enero, sobre derechos y libertades de los extranjeros en España y su integración social*, BOE No. 10, 12 January 2000, amended by *Ley Orgánica 8/2000, de 22 de diciembre*, BOE No. 307, 23 December 2000; *Ley Orgánica 11/2003, de 20 de noviembre*, BOE N° 279, 21 November 2003; and *Ley Orgánica 2/2009, de 11 de Diciembre*, BOE No. 299, 12 December 2009.

15 The aspects that go beyond article 10.1.d) of the Directive are in italics.

made by the Spanish government has been relatively modest, as the proposals in the programme scheduled for approval this year only cover the resettlement of twenty-five people.

B. The main negative aspects are:

1. The reduction in the scope for personal application of asylum regulations. According to article 1, the purpose of the Law is to 'establish the terms under which *nationals of non-EU countries* and stateless people can enjoy international protection in Spain' (emphasis added). The Law also specifically excludes European Union nationals from the right to asylum as a form of protection given to refugees (article 2); and from the right to apply for international protection (article 16) which according to the Law consists of the right of asylum and to subsidiary protection (article 1). EU citizens are not formally unable to obtain refugee status according to the definition of refugee status included in article 3 (which is consistent with the definition included in the Geneva Convention), but in practice the definition of the objective of the law makes it difficult to activate the right to apply for recognition of refugee status in Spain as a right that is different from the right to apply for international protection (asylum or subsidiary protection). This reduction is not imposed by the European directives, which because they are minimum standards, do not require member states to exclude the possibility of EU citizens obtaining asylum.[16] This means that the Protocol has a *serious internal impact* on asylum for nationals of European Union member states, in that it only obliges states to consider applications presented by EU nationals as inadmissible if the state of which the person is a national has not derogated from its obligations under the European Convention on Human Rights (article 15 European Convention), and is not the subject of EU proceedings which have declared or may declare the existence a serious and persistent violation of the human rights recognised in the European Union Treaty (article 6-7 EU Treaty).[17]

2. The basis for denial of refugee status and subsidiary protection, and especially the grounds for exclusion which consists of a well-founded justification for considering that the individual has committed a serious crime before being granted a residency permit as a refugee. In Spain, 'serious crimes' are those carrying a prison sentence of over five years, while the UNHCR interprets these grounds as covering more serious crimes and offences, and considers that the seriousness of the crime must be considered when taking into account the seriousness of the persecution which the applicant faces if he/she returns to the country of origin.[18] The Asylum Law states that *serious*

---

16 Ángel Sánchez Legido, Entre la obsesión por la seguridad y la lucha contra la inmigración irregular: A propósito de la nueva Ley de asilo, *Revista Electrónica de Estudios Internacionales*, No. 18, p. 6-7 (32 p.) http://www.reei.org/reei18/indice.htm [accessed 14.6.2010].

17 *Ibídem.*

18 Articles 13 and 33 of the Spanish *Código Penal* (Criminal Code) [available at http://noticias.juridicas.com/base_datos/Penal/lo10-1995.l1t3.html#a33, accessed 31.7.2010]; UNHCR, *Handbook on Procedures and Criteria for Determining Refugee Status under the 1951 Convention and the 1967 Protocol relating to the Status of refugees*, HCR/IP/4/Eng/REV.1, Geneva, January 1992, §151-161. On this is-
→

crimes that are grounds for exclusion from refugee status must affect 'life, freedom, sexual emancipation or fr4eedom, the integrity of people or assets, providing that they have been committed using force against objects, or violence and intimidation against people, and in cases of organised crime (…)'.[19]

3. Another aspect that may be considered negative in the new Spanish regulation, despite not being in breach of the 1951 Geneva Convention, is that the grounds on which a state could make an exception to the principle of *non-refoulement* in article 33 of the Geneva Convention constitute grounds for denying asylum. In principle, they are grounds for only denying territorial protection, and not for denying refugee status, but in practice it would be difficult to ensure the careful application of this distinction.[20]

4. The reduction of the opportunity to present an application for asylum at a Spanish embassy or consular office abroad. According to the previous Spanish rules on Asylum (in force before 2009), embassies and consular offices were places for presenting an application for asylum, as well as border posts and other official.[21] The new Law now only stipulates that Spanish ambassadors will be able to facilitate the transfer of the applicant to Spain to make the presentation of the application possible if 'his/her physical integrity is in danger'.[22]

4. Features of the Asylum Procedure in Spain

Under the terms of the new Law 12/2009, the asylum procedure in Spain is as follows:[23]

1. There is a single procedure for examining applications for the recognition of refugee status, asylum, and the right to subsidiary protection. This means that the refugee and asylum procedure and the procedure for granting the right to subsidiary protection are guaranteed the same rights, despite this not being a requirement of the *procedural standards* Directive. The rights and guarantees of the asylum procedure in Spain include:

   a. The applicants' right to be informed in a language that they can understand;[24]

---

sue, Ángel Sánchez Legido, Entre la obsesión por la seguridad y la lucha contra la inmigración irregular: A propósito de la nueva Ley de asilo, *loc. cit.*, p. 14-15.

19 Article 8.2.b of the *Ley 12/2009, de 30 de octubre, reguladora del derecho de asilo y de la protección subsidiaria.*

20 The Spanish Asylum Law stipulates that 'the right of asylum will be denied to: a) individuals who for well-founded reasons constitute a threat to the security of Spain; b) individuals who having been found guilty of a serious crime, constitute a threat to the community'. Article 9 of the *Ley 12/2009, de 30 de octubre, reguladora del derecho de asilo y de la protección subsidiaria.*

21 Article 4 of the *Real Decreto 203/1995, de 10 de febrero, por el que se aprueba el Reglamento de aplicación de la Ley 5/1984, de 26 de marzo, reguladora del derecho de asilo y de la condición de refugiado, modificada por la Ley 9/1994, de 19 de mayo,* BOE, No. 52, 2 March 1995, p. 7237-7246.

22 Article 38 of the *Ley 12/2009, de 30 de octubre, reguladora del derecho de asilo y de la protección subsidiaria.*

23 Vide the diagram in the Annex. Source: Translation with some variations made by the author from an original diagram made by the *Comisión Española de Ayuda al Refugiado,* published in *La situación de las personas refugiadas en España. Informe 2010,* Madrid: Enitema, 2010, p. 333.

SÍLVIA MORGADES

b. The application must be presented at a personal interview, in which the individuals responsible for carrying out the interview must help the applicants make the application, inform them of everything and 'co-operate' with them in order to establish the relevant facts regarding their application;[25]

c. The right to free legal aid, starting with the presentation of the application, and throughout the entire processing of the procedure. This aid is also compulsory in the procedure at the frontier.[26]

2. Applications for asylum and refugee status are presented by means of a single 'Application for international protection' which is made in person at an interview with a civil servant, with an interpreter and a lawyer in attendance. These interviews have been recorded in recent years. The applications can be presented in the following places: at frontier posts for entry into Spain, in Detention Centres for Foreigners (for foreigners awaiting the execution of a deportation order); at the Asylum and Refugee Office in Madrid; at Foreigner Offices; at some police stations; and at Spanish Diplomatic Missions and Consular Offices abroad. On the application form, applicants are informed of their rights and obligations, their family and socio-professional situation is ascertained, and applicants are asked for their personal documentation, an account of their travels, details on their membership of groups, political parties and other organisations, and finally, they are asked to give the reasons on which their application is based and the documentation they are providing to support these arguments. With the application form, asylum seekers receive an information leaflet on international protection in Spain, which is available in eleven languages, and a form to request 'family extension' if they are accompanied by their partner and/or children.

3. In Spain, there is initially a distinction between the procedure applicable to (a) applications made at the frontier, in Detention Centres for Foreigners, and by stowaways; and (b) applications presented within Spanish territory. In both procedures, there is an initial admissibility phase for applications for asylum, called 'admission for processing' which is resolved within various deadlines (4 days in the frontier procedure and one month in procedure within Spanish territory). However, they are based on the same grounds, which are more or less those in Directive 2005/85 on procedures (application of the Dublin system, first country of asylum, safe third country, repeated application) plus the grounds that the applicant is an EU citizen.

4. In the frontier procedure, applications for asylum can be declared inadmissible, or the application for asylum can be directly rejected. Among the grounds for rejection of asylum at the frontier are ulterior issues which were included in the previous regulations as grounds for inadmissibility (the applications being based on 'facts, details or arguments that are manifestly false or improbable', 'unfounded', or that 'grounds for the

---

24 Article 17.3 of the *Ley 12/2009, de 30 de octubre, reguladora del derecho de asilo y de la protección subsidiaria.*

25 Article 17.4-6 of the *Ley 12/2009, de 30 de octubre, reguladora del derecho de asilo y de la protección subsidiari.*

26 Article 16.2 of the *Ley 12/2009, de 30 de octubre, reguladora del derecho de asilo y de la protección subsidiaria.*

165

recognition of refugee status' are not given). According to the Spanish Asylum Law, asylum can be denied at the frontier on the following grounds:

a. That the only issues that arise are not related to the examination of the requirements for recognition of refugee status or the granting of subsidiary protection.

b. That the applicant comes from a country of origin that is considered secure.

c. That the applicant meets the requirements for exclusion from recognition of refugee status or the granting of subsidiary protection, or refusal of asylum or subsidiary protection.

d. When the applicant has presented 'inconsistent, contradictory, improbable, or insufficient arguments that contradict sufficiently established information about their country of origin, or their normal residence if they are stateless, to the extent that this clearly shows that their application is not justified in terms of a well-grounded fear of persecution or suffering serious harm'.[27]

This will possibly lead to fewer applications for asylum being declared inadmissible at the frontier, but on the other hand, there will be a percentage of applications in which asylum is denied at the frontier. It is early to assess the changes introduced by the new law, and to establish whether the changes promote an increased admissibility of applications, or the refusal of asylum at the frontier.

5. Applications declared admissible are processed either by the fast-track procedure, or by the ordinary procedure. In the procedure beginning inside Spanish territory, many of the applications that were previously declared inadmissible are now deemed admissible, and processed by the fast-track procedure, as the grounds for inadmissibility due to substantive causes no longer apply. There are no major differences between the fast-track procedure and the ordinary procedure, apart from the time involved: there is no therefore reduction in the guarantees for the asylum seeker.

6. The *Asylum and Refugee Office* (OAR), which is accountable to the Ministry of the Interior, and which has fourteen examiners specialising in different areas, is responsible for the investigation in the procedure. The OAR completes the process by making a proposal for a decision, which is passed on to the *Interministerial Asylum and Refugee Committee* (CIAR), which includes representatives from the Ministries of Justice, Social Affairs, Foreign Affairs and Equality. The CIAR makes a proposal to the Minister of the Interior, who decides whether to grant or deny asylum. The admissibility or inadmissibility of applications for asylum is also determined by the Minister of the Interior, after proposals from the OAR. Denial of asylum at the frontier is determined by the Minister of the Interior with no involvement from the CIAR (unlike the denial of asylum on Spanish territory, in which the CIAR is involved). The UNHCR is informed of all applications for asylum and can intervene, provide assistance and present reports on all the cases.[28]

---

27 Article 21.2 of the Ley 12/2009, de 30 de octubre, reguladora del derecho de asilo y de la protección subsidiaria.

28 Articles 34-35 of the Ley 12/2009, de 30 de octubre, reguladora del derecho de asilo y de la protección subsidiaria.

7. The final decisions that can be taken are: recognition of refugee status with asylum granted; granting of subsidiary protection; denial of asylum; or authorisation of temporary residency on humanitarian grounds (this only occurs in very exceptional cases).

8. Appeals to the executive authority in the frontier procedure are suspensory, as is judicial remedy in all the procedures in which the individual's deportation is applied for (at the frontier or on Spanish territory), until a judge's ruling on this suspension.[29]

5. Determining the Origin of Asylum Seekers: The Role of Language in Spanish Asylum Procedures

In Spain, determining the origin of asylum seekers who present their applications without providing any documentation proving their identity and nationality, and who cannot prove their country or area of origin by other means, is part of the general assessment of the credibility of the applicant's account[30]. As well as the evidence provided, this credibility is assessed based on the contents of their account, and the way in which the applicants express themselves. In this regard, it should be taken into account that 'refugee status determination involves formidable cultural, linguistic, legal and emotional challenges (including staff stress and 'burnout') which can affect UNHCR offices just as government agencies'.[31] Meanwhile, according to the legislation, it is incumbent on the asylum seeker to 'prove his/her identity'.[32]

There are three factors that play an important role in the assessment of the credibility of the applicant's country of origin in the Spanish procedures: nationality tests; information on the country of origin; and the interpreter.

1. Nationality Tests

In Spain, nationality tests are generally carried out for people who say that they come from a poorly structured country of origin, from where it is considered plausible that a person could arrive without any documentation, or with unreliable documentation that has enabled them to travel. They are carried out also for people coming from a region or country for which there is a UNHCR call that warns of the danger to people who come

---

29 Article 22 and 29 of the *Ley 12/2009, de 30 de octubre, reguladora del derecho de asilo y de la protección subsidiaria.*

30 With regard to 'credibility', the UNHCR has said that 'Credibility is established where the applicant has presented a claim which is coherent and plausible, not contradicting generally known facts, and therefore is, on balance, capable of being believed', Office of the UNHCR, *Note on Burden and Standard of Proof in Refugee Claims,* 16 December 1998, p. 3, http://www.unhcr.org/refworld/docid/3ae6b3338.html [accessed 13 July 2010].

31 Michael Kagan, The Beleaguered Gatekeeper: Protection Challenges Posed by UNHCR Refugee Status Determination, *International Journal of Refugee Law,* vol. 18-1, 2006, p. 21.

32 Article 9 of the *Ley 12/2009, de 30 de octubre, reguladora del derecho de asilo y de la protección subsidiaria.* Nevertheless, the 1951 Refugee Convention and authors consider that the burden is shared and that 'the state must bear some of the responsibility not only for evaluating the facts but also for ascertaining them', James A. Sweeney, Credibility, Proof and Refugee Law, *IJRL,* vol. 21-4, 2009, p. 724.

from these areas, or the worsening of situations of conflict that mean that people should not return there. Nationality tests can be carried out both in applications presented at the frontier and in applications presented on Spanish territory.

There are currently eight nationality tests, which are updated for the following countries and regions: Afghanistan; Côte d'Ivoire; Palestine; Nigeria; Sudan; Sri Lanka; Eritrea; and Somalia. There is also a test for Chinese Falun Gong members. The tests are produced by the documentation service of the Asylum and Refugee Office, in co-operation with examiners, who suggest content that helps to establish the credibility of the applicants.

These tests, which are completed through an interpreter and in the presence of a lawyer, are four or five pages long, and contain questions requiring some degree of knowledge of the country concerned (geographical landmarks, football teams, radio programmes, name of the country's capital city, basic concepts in the country's culture [e.g. the concept of *ivorité* in the Côte d'Ivoire test]); or on a specific region or area (names of universities, hotels, cuisine, neighbourhoods, dances, songs and traditions, colour of the taxis). The tests also include images, sometimes captured using Google Earth and blank maps that the applicants have to identify.

According to Spanish jurisprudence, applicants may be subjected to a questionnaire in order to determine their nationality. If the questionnaire is not answered or answered with a great deal of errors and vague answers, this is a determining factor in establishing that the applicants do not possess the nationality that they say they possess, or in rejecting the truthfulness or likelihood of their account, based on an unproved nationality about which serious doubts exist.[33] Failure to answer the questionnaire correctly is an even more significant determining factor in establishing the lack of the applicant's credibility if the UNHCR has issued a report advising against admissibility or granting asylum.[34] Notwithstanding the above, tribunals require that some formal requirements are met, such as:

a. If the applicant refuses to answer the questionnaire, the text must be signed by both the applicant and the interpreter;[35] and

b. The ruling on the denial of asylum or inadmissibility states the 'basic issues' about the country that the applicant does not know.[36]

---

33 Ruling of the *Audiencia Nacional* (Contentious–Administrative High Court Section 3) 27 February 2007, JUR\2007\132453; Ruling of the *Tribunal Supremo* (Contentious–Administrative Supreme Court Section 5) 6 November 2006, RJ\2006\7132 [All of the rulings cited have been obtained from the Westlaw.es data base of Spanish jurisprudence and norms (Thompson Reuters Aranzadi)].

34 Ruling of the *Tribunal Supremo* (Contentious–Administrative Supreme Court Section 5) 31 January 2006, RJ\2006\506.

35 Ruling of the *Tribunal Supremo* (Contentious–Administrative Supreme Court Section 1) 22 November 2002, RJ\2003\21.

36 Ruling of the *Tribunal Supremo* (Contentious–Administrative Supreme Court Section 5) 23 March 2006, RJ\2006\1600.

2. Information on the Country of Origin (or the country the applicant says he/she comes from)

Spain uses information on the country of origin prepared by a variety of sources, such as the *InterGovernmental Consultations* (ICG.ch); and the *European Country of Origin Information Network* (ECOI.net). The *Common EU Guidelines for processing Country of Origin Information* adopted in April 2008, as part of the ARGO Project, are taken into account for the preparation of the relevant information in each case.[37] Furthermore, interviews carried out with staff at the Spanish Asylum and Refugee Office suggest that Spanish authorities place importance on cooperation through the *General Director's Immigration Services Conference* (GDISC.org) and the shared information portal on the country of origin of the *European Asylum Support Office* (EASO).[38] With regard to the latter, discussions regarding the scope of possible access are still ongoing, in terms of whether they will only be accessible by governments of EU member states, or should be accessible to everyone in order to preserve 'equality of arms'.

3. The Interpreter

Finally, one of the key factors in assessing the asylum seeker's credibility with regard to their origin is the interpreter's role in all the phases of the procedure, and especially in the presentation of the application, and in the interview with the examiner, if there is one. In Spain, the interpretation services at the Asylum and Refugee Office in Madrid are currently provided by three interpreters employed by the Office and other temporary interpreters, but in other places where an application for asylum may be presented, interpretation services are provided by *Seprotec*, a private company that won the public tender convened to that end. The thoroughness of work, knowledge and professionalism of the interpreters at the Asylum and Refugee Office are beyond any doubt, but the training of the interpreters who provide their services through the company *Seprotec* is not always good enough, according to the information provided by lawyers and NGOs responsible for legal aid for asylum seekers. This means that the services received by asylum seekers differ depending on the place where they present their applications for asylum, both within Spanish territory and at the frontier.

In order to ensure that all the nuances in the accounts of asylum seekers are taken into consideration, the interpreter must be able to translate the content at the same linguistic level as the applicant, with all its inconsistencies, contradictions and details. For this reason, the interpreter must have sufficient experience and training, and possess a high level of fluency in the language used by the applicant. The interpreter's idiomatic register must be high enough to be able to interpret the applicant's explanations in the register used by

---

37 *Common EU Guidelines for processing Country of Origin Information* (COI), April 2008, ARGO project JLS/2005/ARGO/GC/03 http://www.unhcr.org/refworld/docid/48493f7f2.html [accessed 13 July 2010].

38 The *Regulation (EU) N° 439/2010 of the European Parliament and of the Council establishing a European Asylum Support Office*, OJEU, 25.9.2010, No. L 132/11-28 was signed on 19 May 2010.

the latter, whether this is higher or lower, according to his or her education, culture, etc. In Spain, one of the problems that need solving in order to improve the asylum procedure is therefore that of the training and recruitment of all the interpreters involved in applications for asylum.

As mentioned above, according to government sources, language analysis is not used to establish the origin of asylum seekers in Spain. Even if this is true, undertaking an overall analysis of the procedures followed and an assessment of the roles played by the various actors in the procedure (lawyer, interpreter, interviewer) it appears that language analysis techniques have occasionally been used on an informal basis, usually to confirm the legal assistant's or the examiner's impression when the person concerned was not a national of the country they said they came from. This occurs when the interpreter (having intervened in the presentation of the application or not), based on his/her experience, informally analyses the discourse of the asylum seekers in order to consider whether it is consistent with the supposed origin of the applicant. Usually this happens when the interviewer, the lawyer or the legal assistant have strong doubts about the reasonableness of the facts alleged, or whether they are manifestly inconsistent with basic information about the country of origin and they ask the interpreter. In order to intervene in criminal procedures, linguists are also asked to assist the Spanish authorities.

Finally, to complete the assessment of the credibility of asylum seekers in terms of their country of origin, the jurisprudence shows that in Spain, the asylum seeker's failure to mention or circumstantially justify the reasons for which he or she has no proof of origin in the application (or in the appeals presented against the decisions refusing asylum) acts against him or her. This is used:

a. In cases in which proof of individual persecution has not been put forward or presented, and the need for protection is based on the impossibility of returning to the country of origin due to the general situation of insecurity there. For example, in the case of the Democratic Republic of Congo;[39] and

b. In cases in which the government considers that the 'application is a prototype application' like those that 'were very common between the years 1998/2001, when many applicants claimed they were Congolese, and were closely related to Rwandans'[40].

However, the fact that the applicant speaks a minority language and can communicate with an interpreter in this language works in favour of the asylum seeker's credibility in terms of their origin. In the 2006 case ruled upon by the Spanish Supreme Court, the government considered improbable the account of an individual who had entered Spain with a Syrian passport (that he himself said was false) and who said that he was a Turkish national who suffered from persecution by the Turkish government due to being a Kurd

---

39 Ruling of the *Tribunal Supremo* (Contentious–Administrative Supreme Court Section 5) 27 February 2009, RJ\2009\1561; or in the case of Somalia, Ruling of the *Audiencia Nacional* (Contentious–Administrative High Court Section 4) 7 October 2009 JUR\2009\436442.

40 In this case, the fact that the passport must have been used on the journey, and the lack of an explanation for why they no longer had this passport was also taken into consideration [Ruling of the *Tribunal Supremo* (Contentious–Administrative Supreme Court Section 8) 26 May 2006 JUR\2006\170776.]

and that members of his family had participated in guerrilla actions by the PKK. Attempts were made to present the application for asylum with Turkish and Arabic interpreters, but it was only possible by using a Kurmanji Kurdish interpreter. The government considered that the applicant was able to speak Arabic, and had failed to comply with his obligation to co-operate as required by the asylum regulations. However, the Supreme Court, in a second judicial review of the rejection of the application, ruled that 'the fact that an applicant for asylum who says he is Kurdish insists on only speaking Kurdish, far from diminishing the credibility of his arguments, only increases the probability of his alleged ethnicity, as if he says he uses this language, if this is confirmed, it would be the best possible proof of the veracity of his account, without this fact necessarily being contradicted by the fact that he says he does not speak Arabic or refuses to speak in that language'. The Supreme Court also took into account the applicant's illiteracy and ruled that 'it can reasonably be inferred that if a person speaks and expresses themselves in a localised and minority language such as Kurdish, this is because he or she belongs to this group, or at least this is probable'.[41]

6. Conclusions

The asylum procedure in Spain has improved in terms of transparency, clarity and some guarantees due to the new Asylum Law of 2009, such as a reduction in the grounds for inadmissibility of applications for asylum presented on Spanish territory. Despite it being too soon for firm conclusions on this aspect to be drawn, it appears that many of the applications that were previously deemed inadmissible are now deemed admissible, and processed using the fast-track procedure. However, with applications presented at the frontier, it may be that many applications that used to be declared inadmissible now receive a ruling denying asylum, as the possibility of refusal of asylum at the frontier has been introduced. In any event, it is necessary to wait for figures for at least one year after the Law's implementation to ascertain the results arising from the changes made. There are also positive aspects, such as the inclusion of stays of execution pending appeal in judicial reviews, in which preventive measures against deportations are requested.

As well as the advantages and disadvantages of the new Asylum Law, I would also like to consider the possibility of the language analysis technique being used in Spain. In my opinion, there is considerable lack of resources for applications for asylum in Spain to be processed and decided upon as they should be, which is reflected in the few people working in the Asylum and Refugee Office, or in the shortcomings of the interpreters in some of the places where applications for asylum are presented, such as at the frontier. I therefore believe that it is more urgent to allocate resources to more basic issues, instead of establishing a language analysis system. In any event, some type of coordinated initiative in these areas through the *European Asylum Support Office* (EASO) may be of interest to Spain.

---

41 Ruling of the *Tribunal Supremo* (Contentious–Administrative Supreme Court Section 5) 27 January 2006, RJ\2006\335.

Lastly, as a final consideration, even without using language analysis in the asylum procedures, the authorities have sometimes used language as a method for keeping *prima facie* refugees or people deserving protection on Spanish territory. In Barcelona, for instance, in the summer of 2001, around fifty people in the country illegally claimed to be nationals of Sierra Leone. In order not to expel true nationals of this country, where they would have been victims of indiscriminate violence, the Spanish authorities decided not to expel those able to speak *krio,* the language spoken in the main cities of the country.[42] Nevertheless, over 30 thirty languages are spoken in Sierra Leone, and it is possible that some people coming from this country, especially monolingual women, do not speak *krio*, and instead speaks *kpelle* or *mende*. The use of language techniques has risks and in some cases women may be one of the main groups prejudiced.

Bibliography and References

Collyer, Michael (2004) The Dublin Regulation, Influences on Asylum Destinations and the Exception of Algerians in UK, *JRS*, 17-4, p. 375-400.

Comisión Española de Ayuda al Refugiado (CEAR) (2010) *La situación de las personas refugiadas en España. Informe 2010*, Madrid: Enitema.

Council of the European Union (2009) *The Stockholm Programme: An open and secure Europe serving and protecting the citizen*, Doc. 17024/09. Brussels, 2 December.

Fernández Sánchez, Pablo Antonio (2007) *Derecho comunitario de la inmigración*, Barcelona: Atelier.

Fullerton, Maryellen (2005) Inadmissible in Iberia: The Fate of Asylum Seekers in Spain and Portugal, *IJRL*, vol. 17-4, p. 659-687.

Kagan, Michael (2003) Is Truth in the Eye of the Beholder? Objective Credibility Assessment in Refugee Status Determination, *Georgetown Immigration Law Journal*, vol. 17, p. 367-415.

Kagan, Michael (2006) The Beleaguered Gatekeeper: Protection Challenges Posed by UNHCR Refugee Status Determination, *International Journal of Refugee Law*, vol. 18-1, p. 1-29.

Ministerio del Interior (Government of Spain) (2009) *Asilo en cifras 2008*, Madrid, Ministerio del Interior, Secretaria General Técnica. Available at http://www.mir.es/ MIR/PublicacionesArchivo/publicaciones/catalogo/Asilo.html [accessed 28-6-2010].

Ministerio del Interior (Government of Spain) (2010) *Asilo en cifras 2009*, Madrid, Ministerio del Interior, Secretaria General Técnica. Available at http://www.mir.es/MIR/PublicacionesArchivo/publicaciones/catalogo/Asilo.html [accessed 28.6.2010]

Sánchez Legido, Ángel (2010) Entre la obsesión por la seguridad y la lucha contra la inmigración irregular: A propósito de la nueva Ley de asilo, *Revista Electrónica de*

---

42 On this episode, without mentioning the question of language, see Jaume V. Aroca, La crisis de los sin papeles en Barcelona, *La Vanguardia*, 19 August 2001, www.lavanguardia.es.

Estudios Internacionales, No. 18, (32 p.) http://www.reei.org/reei18/indice.htm [accessed 14.6.2010]

Sweeney, James A. (2009) Credibility, Proof and Refugee Law, *IJRL*, vol. 21-4, p. 700-726.

UNHCR, *Asylum and Migration. Key facts and figures*, http://www.unhcr.org/pages/ 4a1d406060.html [accessed 28.6.2010].

UNHCR (2010) *Asylum Levels and Trends in Industrialized Countries 2009: Statistical Overview of Asylum Applications Lodged in Europe and Selected Non-European Countries*, 23 March, http://www.unhcr.org/4ba7341a9.html [accessed 28.6.2010].

UNHCR (1992) *Handbook on Procedures and Criteria for Determining Refugee Status under the 1951 Convention and the 1967 Protocol relating to the Status of refugees*, HCR/IP/ 4/Eng/REV.1, Geneva, January.

UNHCR (1998) *Note on Burden and Standard of Proof in Refugee Claims*, 16 December, http://www.unhcr.org/refworld/docid/3ae6b3338.html [accessed 13 July 2010].

UNHCR (2010) *Statistical Yearbook* from 2001 to 2008 at www.unhcr.org and *Asylum Levels and Trends in Industrialized Countries 2009: Statistical Overview of Asylum Applications Lodged in Europe and Selected Non-European Countries*, 23 March, http://www. unhcr.org/4ba7341a9.html [accessed 28.6.2010].

Valle Gálvez, Alejandro del (2007) Inmigración, extranjería y fronteras en la unión europea. Cinco problemas conceptuales, in J.J. Forner Delaygua et al., *Fronteras Exteriores de la U.E. e inmigración a España: Relaciones internacionales y derecho*, Valencia: Tirant lo Blanch, p. 43-80.

Common EU Guidelines for processing Country of Origin Information (COI), April 2008, ARGO project JLS/2005/ARGO/GC/03 http://www.unhcr.org/refworld/ docid/48493f7f2.html [accessed 13 July 2010]

Council Directive 2003/9/EC of 27 January 2003 laying down minimum standards for the reception of asylum seekers, OJEU 6.2.2003, L 31/18-25.

Council Directive 2004/83/EC of 29 April 2004 on minimum standards for the qualification and status of third-country nationals and stateless people as refugees or as people who otherwise would need international protection and the content of the protection granted, OJEU 30.9.2004, L 304/12-23.

Council Directive 2005/85/EC of 1 December 2005 on minimum standards on procedures in Member States for granting and withdrawing refugee status, OJEU 13.12.2005, L 326/13-34.

Ley 12/2009, de 30 de octubre, reguladora del derecho de asilo y de la protección subsidiaria, Boletín Oficial del Estado No. 263, 31 October 2009, 90860-90884.

Ley Orgánica 4/2000, de 11 de enero, sobre derechos y libertades de los extranjeros en España y su integración social, BOE No. 10, 12 January 2000, amended by *Ley Orgánica 8/2000, de 22 de diciembre*, BOE No. 307, 23 December 2000; *Ley Orgánica 11/2003, de 20 de noviembre*, BOE Nº 279, 21 November 2003; and *Ley Orgánica 2/2009, de 11 de Diciembre*, BOE No. 299, 12 December 2009.

Real Decreto 203/1995, de 10 de febrero, por el que se aprueba el Reglamento de aplicación de la Ley 5/1984, de 26 de marzo, reguladora del derecho de asilo y de la condición de refugiado, modificada por la Ley 9/1994, de 19 de mayo, BOE No. 52, 2 March 1995, 7237-7246.

Regulation (EU) N° 439/2010 of the European Parliament and of the Council establishing a European Asylum Support Office, OJEU 25.9.2010, N° L 132/11-28.

European Union Court of Justice (EUCJ), Ruling of 17 February 2009, *Meki Elgafaji*, C-465/07

EUCJ Ruling of 9 July 2009, *Commission v Spain*, C-272/08.

European Court of Human Rights (ECHR) Ruling of 26 July 2005, *N v. Finland*, no. 38885/02.

ECHR Ruling of 12 April 2005, *Shamayev and others v. Georgia and Russia*, no. 36378/02.

ECHR Ruling of 11 January 2007, *Salah Sheekh v. The Netherlands*, no. 1948/04.

ECHR Ruling of 17 July 2008, *NA v. The United Kingdom*, no. 25904/07.

ECHR Ruling of 28 February 2008, *Saadi v. Italy*, no. 37201/06.

ECHR Ruling of 18 February 2010, *Baysakov and others v. Ukraine*, no. 54131/08.

Audiencia Nacional (Contentious–Administrative High Court Section 3) Ruling of 27 February 2007, JUR\2007\132453 [*Westlaw.es*]

Audiencia Nacional (Contentious–Administrative High Court Section 4) 7 Ruling of October 2009 JUR\2009\436442 [*Westlaw.es*]

Tribunal Supremo (Contentious–Administrative Supreme Court Section 1) Ruling of 22 November 2002, RJ\2003\21 [*Westlaw.es*]

Tribunal Supremo (Contentious–Administrative Supreme Court Section 5) Ruling of 27 January 2006, RJ\2006\335 [*Westlaw.es*]

Tribunal Supremo (Contentious–Administrative Supreme Court Section 5) Ruling of 31 January 2006, RJ\2006\506 [*Westlaw.es*]

Tribunal Supremo (Contentious–Administrative Supreme Court Section 5) Ruling of 23 March 2006, RJ\2006\1600 [*Westlaw.es*]

Tribunal Supremo (Contentious–Administrative Supreme Court Section 8) Ruling of 26 May 2006 JUR\2006\170776 [*Westlaw.es*]

Tribunal Supremo (Contentious–Administrative Supreme Court Section 5) Ruling of 6 November 2006, RJ\2006\7132 [*Westlaw.es*]

Tribunal Supremo (Contentious–Administrative Supreme Court Section 5) Ruling of 27 February 2009, RJ\2009\1561 [*Westlaw.es*]

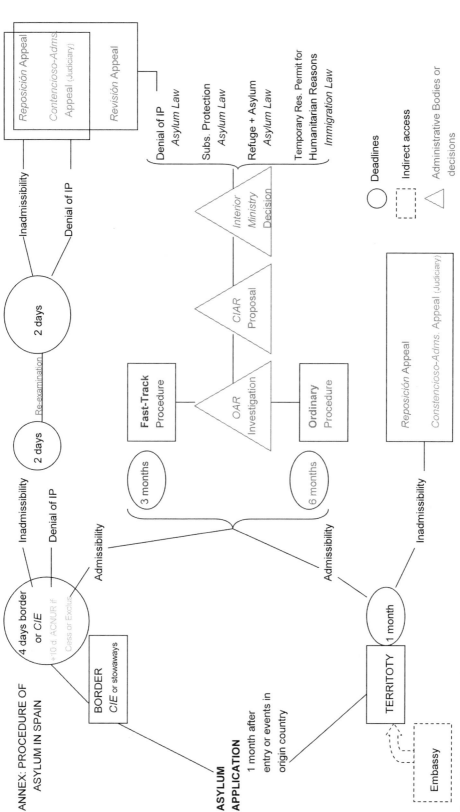

ANNEX: PROCEDURE OF ASYLUM IN SPAIN

ASYLUM APPLICATION

1 month after entry or events in origin country

BORDER
CIE or stowaways

TERRITOTY

Embassy

4 days border or CIE
+10 d ACNUR if Cess or Exclus

Inadmissibility

Denial of IP

Admissibility

1 month

Inadmissibility

Admissibility

3 months

6 months

Fast-Track Procedure

Ordinary Procedure

OAR Investigation

CIAR Proposal

Interior Ministry Decision

Reposición Appeal

Constencioso-Adms. Appeal (Judiciary)

2 days

2 days

Re-examination

Inadmissibility

Denial of IP

Reposición Appeal

Contencioso-Adms Appeal (Judiciary)

Revisión Appeal

Denial of IP
Asylum Law

Subs. Protection
Asylum Law

Refuge + Asylum
Asylum Law

Temporary Res. Permit for Humanitarian Reasons
Immigration Law

Deadlines

Indirect access

Administrative Bodies or decisions

Source: Translation with some variations made by the author from an original diagram made by the *Comisión Española de Ayuda al Refugiado*, published in *La situación de las personas refugiadas en España. Informe 2010*, Madrid: Entema, 2010, p. 333.

The Use of Language Analysis in the Belgian Asylum Procedure

Dirk Vanheule

1. Introduction

Language analysis is a relatively unknown practice in Belgian asylum procedures, both in terms of numbers of cases in which use has been made of this analysis and in terms of legal discussions on the issues involved.[1] Notwithstanding the anonymity of this practice, its use has raised questions that often touch upon fundamental issues of asylum and procedural law. This paper will, after a brief description of the decision-making process in asylum matters, set out the existing practice of language analysis in Belgium, both in the administrative and judicial phase of the asylum procedure. It will then focus on some of the legal questions that may arise out of this practice.

2. The Belgian Asylum Procedure

The granting of asylum in Belgium is regulated by the federal Aliens Act.[2] Refugees and persons in need of subsidiary protection are a category of aliens who automatically obtain residence status upon the recognition of their status.[3] To this end a recognition procedure has been set up. On the occasion of the transposition of the Qualification and Procedures Directives in 2006, the asylum procedure has been remodelled.[4] In the present day single procedure refugee and subsidiary protection status are examined consecutively. The procedure consists of an administrative and a judicial phase.

---

1   The author thanks Aldona Van Haesevelde at the Office of the Commissioner General for Refugees and Stateless Persons for the information and insights she provided in the LADO-practice in Belgium.
2   Act of 15 December 1980 regarding the Access, Residence, Settlement and Removal of Aliens, MB 31 December 1980 (hereafter: Aliens Act).
3   See Articles 49 (for refugees) and 49/2 (for beneficiaries of subsidiary protection).
4   On the procedure see S. Bodart, *La protection internationale des réfugiés en Belgique*, Brussels, Bruylant, 2008; M. Foblets, D. Vanheule and S. Bouckaert, De nieuwe asielwetgeving: het Belgische asielrecht kleurt Europeser, *Rechtskundig Weekblad* 2006-07, p. 942-957; Office of the Commissioner General for Refugees and Stateless Persons, *The Asylum Procedure in Belgium*, Brussels, 2008, http://www.cgvs.be/nl/binaries/PDF%20-%20The%20asylum%20procedure%20in%20Belgium _tcm127-42131.pdf; K. Pollet, The New Asylum Procedure in Belgium and its Compliance with the Asylum Procedures Directive: A Legal Analysis, in K. Zwaan (ed.), *The Procedures Directive: Central Themes, Problem Issues, and Implementation in Selected Member States*, Nijmegen, Wolf Legal Publishers, 2008, p. 57-73; D. Vanheule, The Qualification Directive: A Milestone in Belgian Asylum Law, in K. Zwaan (ed.), *The Qualification Directive : Central Themes, Problem Issues, and Implementation in Selected Member States*, Nijmegen, Wolf Legal Publishers, 2007, p.71-77.

In the administrative phase the Aliens Office,[5] a department of the ministry of the Interior, registers asylum claims, establishes the identity and travel route of the claimants and determines the responsibility of Belgium under the Dublin-rules.[6] The applications, for which Belgium bears responsibility, are then passed on to the Commissioner General for Refugees and Stateless Persons (CGRSP)[7] for an examination on the merits.

The CGRSP heads an independent agency for the determination of refugee and subsidiary protection status. This is done either in a normal or in an accelerated procedure (manifestly unfounded, fraudulent and claims unrelated to asylum). The CGRSP determines, consecutively, if the claimant is a refugee under Article 1 of the Refugee Convention or, when failing, a beneficiary of subsidiary protection status. The recognition rate of the CGRSP has increased in the last decennium from 10% to nearly 25%. In 2009 the CGRSP took 8.883 decisions. In 1.889 cases (21%) refugee status was awarded, with Iraq, Guinee, Russia and China being the main countries of origin. Subsidiary protection was obtained in 418 cases (4,7%); these claimants came predominantly form Iraq, Afghanistan, Somalia and Sudan.

An appeal against the decisions of the CGRSP is open to the Aliens Litigation Council (ALC).[8] This appeal stays the execution of the rejection of the asylum claim. The ALC is a judicial tribunal that hears appeals in all immigration cases. When hearing appeals in asylum cases, the ALC is said to hold full jurisdiction.[9] The Council can either grant or refuse refugee status or it can send the case back for reconsideration to the CGRSP. The procedure before the ALC is not based on a full oral re-hearing of the claimant. Nor does the ALC hold proper authority of examination or fact finding.

Finally, all judgments by the ALC may be appealed to the Council of State,[10] the supreme administrative court, sitting as a *juge de cassation* only. The Council of State must first give leave of appeal, which ordinarily is only done if the appeal does not appear to be ineffective or when a judgment appears necessary for the uniformity of case law. In the event of an annulment, the case is redirected to the ALC for reconsideration.

The number of asylum claims introduced in Belgium, a country of 10,4 million inhabitants, has fluctuated over the years, with peaks in 1993 and 2000. Whereas the number of new applications was relatively stable in the period 2003-2008 (between 1.000 and 1.300 claims per month), this number has nearly doubled again in 2010 (in September: 1.905 applications).

---

5   Dienst Vreemdelingenzaken, Office des étrangers.
6   The Aliens Office may also reject a repeated identical asylum application or refuse claimants access to the procedure for serious reasons of public order or national security.
7   Commissaris-generaal voor de vluchtelingen en de staatlozen, Commissaire général aux réfugiés et aux apatrides.
8   Conseil du contentieux des étrangers (CCE), Raad voor vreemdelingenbetwistingen (RVV).
9   In other than asylum cases, the ALC hears the appeals by way of judicial review. Such applications for annulment and/or stay of execution may be brought on the basis of violation of legal provisions. When successful, the case is being returned to the minister or Aliens Office.
10 Raad van State, Conseil d'Etat.

1981	2.449	2000	42.720
1985	5.387	2001	24.549
1991	15.444	2002	18.805
1992	17.657	2003	16.940
1993	26.421	2004	15.357
1994	14.568	2005	15.957
1995	11.655	2006	11.587
1996	12.401	2007	11.115
1997	11.602	2008	12.252
1998	21.967	2009	17.186
1999	35.778	2010[11]	13.760

Table 1. Number of asylum applications in Belgium (source: CGRSP)

3.   The Use of Language Analysis

3.1   The Use of Language Analysis in the Administrative Phase before the Commissioner General for Refugees and Stateless Persons

3.1.1 *The Place of Language Analysis in the Procedure*

Central in the status determination process before the CGRSP are one or more interviews of the claimant by a case officer. The case officers work in geographically described units that specialize in the situation in the countries of origin of a particular region. Interviews are conducted in the presence of an interpreter, appointed by the CGRSP, and of the claimant's counsel. Information obtained through the interview(s) and material documentation produced by the claimant, are then analyzed to see whether the claimant meets the criteria of refugee and subsidiary protection status. The case officer can call in the assistance of CEDOCA, the CGRSP's centre for documentation and research. This centre gathers country of origin information against which the claimants' accounts can be checked. It also organizes language analysis when requested upon by a case officer. To that end CEDOCA has a linguistic officer on the team.

There are no provisions on language analysis to be found in Belgian asylum legislation. Therefore CEDOCA has developed its own internal guidelines in connection to language analysis. An informative note on this instrument is publicly available upon request.[12]

Language analysis is seen as an instrument to determine and verify the region of origin of an individual. The central starting point is that the analysis will provide information about the region of origin of the individual and his or her migratory route. It is explicitly acknowledged that language analysis can never be an analysis of nationality, since linguistic and state borders do not coincide.[13]

---

11 From 1 January till 30 September 2010.
12 CGRSP-CEDOCA, *Informatieve nota inzake het instrument taalanalyse*, Brussels, s.d., on file with the author.
13 CGRSP-CEDOCA, *Informatieve nota inzake het instrument taalanalyse*, supra note 12.

The use of language analysis is rather exceptional, also given the limited budget that has been made available for language analysis. In 2009 approximately 20 analyses were performed, mainly on Bajuni (Somalia) and Baghdadi Arabic. Moreover, the awareness that language analyses are not a form of exact science may also have an influence on this limited use. Language analyses are only carried out upon request of a case officer who already has serious concerns about the credibility of the claimant and, more particularly, about his or her exact whereabouts in the past. They are usually carried out in the final stages of the administrative status determination process. The participation of the claimant is on a voluntary basis; the refusal to participate will have a negative impact on the determination of the (already weak) asylum claim.[14] The claimant will nevertheless be given an opportunity, in a further interview, to state the arguments for his refusal.

3.1.2 The Practice

The language analysis is carried out by means of a recorded conversation between the claimant and an interpreter, in the presence of an officer of the CGRSP who is preferably not the case officer. This conversation is conducted separately from and after the interview(s) by the case officer that is used to determine the status.

At least 45 minutes of conversation are deemed necessary. In order to achieve this length of conversation, the claimant will be asked to answer open questions about his linguistic situation, living conditions, (duration of the) migration route, knowledge about the country, region and city of origin, and a variety of issues like the administration there, family and kinship, economy, food, dress code, living conditions, religion, transport, daily life and nature. The internal instructions on language analysis state that the conversation should focus on these living conditions and remain distant from the reasons invoked in the asylum application.

The actual analysis is done by external analysts.[15] They are native speakers who have had academic schooling or have a degree of higher education, but are not necessarily linguists. The analysts are required to have broad socio-cultural knowledge of the language and cannot work as interpreter for one of the asylum authorities. Prior to their engagement in language analysis they are screened and tested on their skills.

The recordings of the conversation are sent to the analyst who comes approximately from the same region as the claimant and masters the same language or language variety. The analyst then reports back to the linguist officer at the CGRSP who may, depending on the analyst's academic background and experience, assist them in the analysis. A written report is submitted and added to the case file.

The analysis in the report relates to four linguistic elements: phonology, lexicon, syntaxis and particularisms (proverbs, interjections, non-verbal elements, etc.). In the conclusion the analyst indicates if he can confirm or exclude that the claimant originates from the region indicated by him and whether he belongs to the indicated language

---

14 The CGRSP bases its policy on the claimant's obligations in producing evidence as described in the UNHCR Handbook on Procedures and Criteria for Determining Refugee Status under the 1951 Convention and the 1967 Protocol relating to the Status of Refugees, Geneva, 1992, at para. 205.

15 In the past, language analysis has also been referred to the Dutch Immigration and Naturalization Service and to the Swiss Federal Office of Migration's LINGUA unit.

and cultural community. This conclusion can be 'certain', 'probable' or 'presumable'. In the event of exclusion from a region, the analyst may also indicate from which other region the claimant certainly, probably or presumably originates. If the analyst cannot come to any conclusion, he should indicate the reasons thereof.

The CGRSP's linguistic officer will then formalize the analysis into an advice, repeating the conclusion and briefly motivating that conclusion with findings from the analysis. The CGRSP's internal guidelines emphasize that the LADO–results can and may not be used as sole argument for the determination of a claim. The analysis has the value of an additional element in the final decision.

3.2   The Use of Language Analysis in the Judicial Phase before the Aliens Litigation Council

The judicial appeal to the ALC after a refusal of recognition of refugee status is a predominantly written procedure on the basis of information already on file. The claimant and the CGRSP will exchange their written observations, but without the ALC fully rehearing the claimant. The council will confirm the CGRSP's decision, reform it or, when necessary, return the case to the CGRSP for further examination.

Submission of new elements is subject to the condition that they demonstrate the well-founded nature of the asylum claim and could not have been presented before. In theory this would allow for language analysis being introduced for the first time at the appeal level. So far, no cases have been reported of such event occurring.

More likely, discussions on language analysis before the ALC will relate to the conclusions of the language analysis done on demand by the CGRSP. Their outcome and methodology could be an element of debate, with even the possibility of the introduction of a counter expert opinion. So far, however, there has been very little debate about language analysis in the ALC's case law. This is probably due to the limited use of language analysis and the additional evidentiary role it plays, confirming the already existing contradictions in a case file after the interview(s) on the merits of the claim.

In a case where the claimant had been caught on a number of inconsistencies and inexplicable gaps in her account, the ALC held that her sole statement that she came from Kazakhstan and lived there until she left for Chechnya, could not override the language analysis. The analyst had concluded with certainty that the claimant came from Ingushetia, based on the fact that she spoke Ingushian and Russian with an Ingushian accent. The Council added '*that the claimant does not succeed in giving an acceptable explanation for this absurdity, thus justifying the strong doubts about her genuine origin*'. [translation].[16]

The ALC, sitting in Grand Chamber, had the opportunity to rule on the relationship between language analysis and establishment of nationality and citizenship in a case involving a Somali asylum claimant. She claimed to be a Somali citizen coming from Mogadishu. The language analyst had established that she spoke a form of Somali which was usual for Northern Somali and Ethiopia. However, it had not been possible

---

16 ALC n° 41.257, 31 March 2010, http://www.rvv-cce.be. Similarly with regard to the absence of a declaration for the inexplicable lack of knowledge of the language of a region: ALC n° 36.360, 21 December 2009.

for him to come to an exact localisation of the language. Although the refusal of refugee and subsidiary protection status had not been based on the results of the language analysis, the Council disapproved of the use of language analysis in order to assess the claimant's origin from Mogadishu and her Somali nationality:

'To the degree that this has happened, it follows from the 'annex to the language analysis' joint to the language analysis itself, that a language analysis '*is explicitly not an enquiry on nationality and identity*'. With regard to knowledge of the country it follows from this annex that the (absence of) knowledge on the country demonstrated in the course of the language analysis, is only considered as an additional element when formulating the results of the language analysis and is not supportive of an enquiry on nationality. The Council cannot involve the language analysis in that sense in its assessment if the claimant has plausibly demonstrated her said nationality.' [original emphasis; translation][17]

From this decision it follows that language analysis and the substantial issues raised in that context are seen to have a limited scope. They can only relate to the examination of the linguistic background of an asylum claimant, without giving evidence as to his or her nationality or identity. Substantial information obtained in course of the language analysis cannot be used to contradict otherwise plausible declarations by the claimant.

4. Some of the Legal Issues Involved in Language Analysis in the Belgian Asylum Procedure

Even though there is little reported case law on language analysis in Belgium, this does not imply that its use is free of legal issues. A first, general, issue relates to the purpose of language analysis. The other two issues derive from the first and raise questions about the burden of proof and about due process in asylum procedures.

The general issue concerns the purpose of language analysis. As described above, language analysis in the Belgian practice is usually introduced at the end of the asylum determination process, after the claimant has had one or more interviews and doubts persist about the claimant's origin. This doubt can be the result of lack of written evidence about the origin, like a passport or other identity documents. If the declarations of the claimant are otherwise coherent and should lead to recognition of refugee or subsidiary protection status, the language analysis can be seen as giving an objective confirmation that the claimant's linguistic background is coherent (or not) with his declarations as to his origin. If serious doubts already persist about the (credibility of the) claimant's declarations and, henceforth, the well-founded nature of his claim, language analysis that confirms these contradictions with regard to a person's origin, can reinforce these doubts to a degree that the claim can be refused. In both instances, language analysis will be used to make the decision more objective and independent of an evaluation of the facts on file. Through a seemingly neutral process of language analysis,

---

17 ALC n° 45.395, 24 June 2010, http://www.rvv-cce.be.

the linguistic background is checked and compared with the data on file to come to a final decision that is felt to be otherwise more difficultly to motivate.

This brings about two sets of questions, on the burden of proof and due process respectively.

Traditionally, the *burden of proof* in asylum cases is seen as a shared one.[18] The claimant must present his case and the State must examine the well-founded nature or substantial grounds, taking into consideration all elements known about the claimant and the situation in the country of origin. One can ask the question if there is an obligation for the State to proceed at a language analysis and if the claimant can be forced into one? Although in the Belgian practice, participation in language analysis is on a voluntary basis, it has become obvious that refusal to do so will have a negative impact as this can be seen as a refusal to bring forward evidence. As such, the discretion of using language analysis lies with the CGRSP, with the claimant being obliged to participate at the risk of loosing his credibility. This may be difficult to reconcile with the other important notion of evidence in asylum cases, namely the benefit of the doubt:

> 'Even such independent research [by the examiner] may not, however, always be successful and there may also be statements that are not susceptible of proof. In such cases, if the applicant's account appears credible, he should, unless there are good reasons to the contrary, be given the benefit of the doubt.'[19]

One could question if the reluctance of participating in language analysis is a sufficiently good reason to be refused the benefit of the doubt. If and when the declarations of the claimant are coherent, the benefit of the doubt should be given. To what extent can a language analysis rebut these coherent declarations? It appears to me that in such cases only an analysis that excludes with absolute certainty the person from having the linguistic background that one would certainly expect from a person originating from the region, can matter and provided that other evidence on file corroborates this finding. Doubts about the linguistic origins, translated in findings that the claimant 'probably' or 'presumably' has (or not) a specific linguistic background, cannot contradict otherwise fully coherent declarations. The reason for this limited evidentiary role has to be found in the inherent difficulties in language analysis that cannot guarantee 100 % certainty about the findings. Moreover, language analysis will determine language socialization, rather than establishing origin.

If, on the other hand, the claimant's declarations and evidence already presented during the interviews show important incoherencies or gaps, language analysis can have a reinforcing effect to this negative evaluation. As the ALC has stated, language analysis should thereby not replace the other analysis and cannot be determining to establish a claimant's nationality or citizenship. Also the CGRSP has emphasized that

---

18 See UNHCR Handbook, supra note 14, at para. 196: 'Thus, while the burden of proof in principle rests on the applicant, the duty to ascertain and evaluate all the relevant facts is shared between the applicant and the examiner. Indeed, in some cases, it may be for the examiner to use all the means at his disposal to produce the necessary evidence in support of the application.'

19 See UNHCR Handbook, supra note 14, at para. 196.

'the result of language analysis can and may not be used as the only argument in the assessment of an asylum application. The value of language analysis is in all cases only that of an additional element in the final decision'. [translation][20]

The introduction and acceptance of language analysis in the asylum process also raises the issue of the possibility of counter expert opinions. This should be possible. The counter expert opinion can be seen at two levels. At the substantial level the counter expert can come on the basis of the same recordings to another finding. This would be the result of differences of opinion on matters like, for instance, phonology and syntaxis. The counter expert opinion could also relate to the process being used: are sufficient questions asked, what where the hearing conditions, were those questions pertinent to examine the linguistic background, etc.

This latter type of counter expert opinion brings us to the second set of questions, related *to procedural due process, i.e.* the obligation for the government to guarantee fair procedures when administering the law. Under Belgian administrative law this requires administrations to respect certain principles of good administration: motivation of the decisions, hearing of the parties, proportional and careful decision making. Especially the latter imposes a duty upon the government, when calling upon third parties for expert opinions, to guarantee that certain guarantees are met. The basic idea is that when a third party, in this case a language analyst, is consulted, this person has the proper knowledge that is lacking within the administrative service, to answer a particular and usually more technical issue. With regard to language analysis, this may raise a number of methodological questions about the expertise of the analyst and the analysis. The answers to the following relevant questions are to be found in other disciplines than law:

- What are the qualifications needed to be a language analyst (only for trained linguists)?
- Does the language analysis process, using external analysts under the supervision of a linguist, meet scientifically accepted norms?
- Does the process itself (duration of the conversation, type of questions, settings, presence of a case officer, criteria used, …) contribute to a useful analysis?

Some of the procedural issues will have an impact on the evidentiary value of the language analysis as well. From the above cited ALC decision of 24 June 2010 it has already become clear that language analysis cannot be conclusive in the determination of nationality and identity.[21] Similarly, one can argue that the use of other substantial information obtained in the course of the language analysis conversation (for instance on family situation, problems experienced, travel route, etc.) cannot be used for the status determination from a due process perspective. The interpreter conducting the conversation is, for one, not a trained case officer, so the questions asked by him may be incomplete. Furthermore and contrary to a normal asylum interview, the conversation is not translated and hence the claimant's counsel has no opportunity to ask for further questions or to add clarifications at that time. It is therefore highly questionable if the

---

20 CGRPS, *Jaarverslag. Veertiende en vijftiende jaarverslag. Werkingsjaren 2001 en 2002*, Brussels 2003, p. 37, http://www.cgra.be/nl/binaries/Jaarverslag%202001-2002_tcm127-17625.pdf.
21 ALC n° 45.395, 24 June 2010, http://www.rvv-cce.be.

use of substantial elements (other than the language related ones) obtained from such a language analysis can play a determining role in the asylum process.

5.   Conclusion

Language analysis has played a modest part in the Belgian asylum practice until now. It has not been the subject of heated legal debate and litigation.[22] The limited scope of the praxis seems to demonstrate in itself the relative weight given to language analysis by the CGRPS. Both the examining authority (CGRSP) and the supervising court (ACL) have emphasized that the outcome of such analysis can only be an additional element in the determination process. In that sense, they respond to the legal concerns that may be raised about the use of such analysis as determinant factor in the assessment of asylum claims. Notwithstanding this limited role of language analysis, its actual use may still give rise to a number of legal questions in terms of due process that have been left unanswered so far. An interdisciplinary approach of these questions, when it comes to the evaluation of the methodology and protocols to be used, is needed thereto.

---

22 For an ethnographical study on language and communication in the Belgian asylum procedure, see K. Maryns, *The Asylum Speaker: Language in the Belgian Asylum Procedure*, Manchester: St. Jerome Publishing 2006.

The Use of Language Analysis in the Italian Asylum Procedure

Claudia Pretto

1. The Absence of the Use of Language Analysis to Determinate the Asylum Seeker's Origin

In the Italian legal system the right to asylum is circumscribed by different laws but none of these laws refer to linguistic analysis to identify asylum seekers' origin:
- Law 722 of 1954 giving application to Geneva Convention;[1]
- Article 10(3) of the Italian Constitution;[2]
- Legislative decrees 251 of 2007 and 25 and 159 of 2008, giving application to the Qualification ad Procedures Directives;
- Article 19 of the Legislative Decree 286 of 1998 that forbid the Italian system to send a person back to a country where she or he could be either victim of a form of persecution not covered by Geneva Convention or of any other inhuman treatment and human rights violation.[3]

Considering article 24 of Italian Constitution, *language* should not be considered as an instrument to identify the asylum seeker but as one of the main instruments to guarantee the right to defence.[4]

---

1 The Italian legal system is a dualistic one, which means that with the exception of European regulation all the European and international laws must be adopted trough domestic law. In fact in the Italian legal system the relations between the Italian system and arrangements of international law are set according to the principle of separation of legal systems, according to the dualistic conception coming from Verdross. This means that standards produced in the international order do not affect the validity of the internal rules nor are they immediately effective in national law, namely international standards into national law shall not take effect if not for self-determination of the State.

2 Article 10 comma 3 Italian Constitution: 'A foreigner who is denied in his country the effective exercise of democratic liberties guaranteed by the Italian Constitution has the right to asylum in the Republic as laid down by law.'

3 Article 19 section 1 of Aliens Decree of July 25th, no. 286, *Official Gazzette of Italian Republic*, General Supplement, 18 August 1998, no 191. http://www.giustizia.it/cassazione/leggi/dlgs286_98.html
Prohibition of expulsion and refoulement:
'1. In no case can be disposed the expulsion or the refoulement to a State in which the alien may be persecuted for reasons of race, sex, language, nationality, religion, political opinion, personal or social conditions, or might risk being returned to another State where not protected from persecution. (…).'

4 Article 24 of the Italian Constitution: 'Everyone can take legal action to protect their legitimate rights and interests.'
The defence is inviolable at every stage and level of the proceedings.
Are guaranteed to the poor, through appropriate institutions, the means to act and defense in each jurisdiction.

→

The general guidelines given by the Minister of the Interior have never referred to linguistic analysis as a reliable instrument to identify asylum seekers.[5]

Language, however, remains one of the most important pieces of evidence to understand the asylum seeker's claim and to guarantee his/her rights. The right to a translation is part of the right to defence, as the Italian Constitutional Court underlined in a case concerning the right to a mandatory translator in charge of the State during a criminal procedure.[6]

Italy gives application to the Directive 85/2005/EC through the Legislative Decrees 25/2008 and 159/2008.[7] In the Italian asylum procedure the only reference to language is in article 10 of the Legislative Decree 25/2008.[8] It prescribes the obligation to guarantee, during the entire asylum procedure, the access to a complete translation either in the asylum seeker's own language or in a language that the asylum seeker may know, in order to be aware of his/her entitlements and to be able to understand the result of his/her request.[9]

The law determines the conditions and means for the redress of miscarriages of justice.'

5   See Ministero dell'Interno, Commissione Nazionale per il Diritto d'Asilo, Linee guida per la valutazione delle richieste di riconoscimento dello status di rifugiato, edited by S. Sonnino; M. Denozza 2005. See also Handbook on the criteria and determination of refugee status, United Nations High Commissioner for Refugees, under the 1951 Convention and 1967 Protocol Relating to the Status of Refugees Geneva, September 1979.

6   Italian Constitutional Court, decision number 254 of 2007: article. 6, no. 3, letter e of ECHR, that entered into the Italian legal system with Law no. 848 of 1955, and article 14, of ICCPR, that entered into the Italian legal system with Law no. 881 of 1977, prescribes the defendant's right to be a conscious part of the trial. To be conscious also applies when he/she is not able to understand the language to chose a translator. The right to translation is prescribed by article 24 of the Italian Constitution and it guarantees a due process of law as prescribed by article 111 of the Italian Constitution. As said in its decision no. 10 of 1993 and no. 341 of 1999, the Italian Constitutional Court underlined that the right to a translator is not just a judge's discretion, but it a fundamental right that must also be respected for non-citizens.

7   On 28 January 2008 by Legislative Decree 25/2008 the Italian Parliament gives application to the Procedure Directive (PD); for a complete analysis of the PD implementation in the Italian legal system before Legislative Decree 159/2008, see: L. Olivetti, Implementation of procedure directive in Italy, in K. Zwaan (ed.), The Procedures Directive: Central Themes, Problem Issues and Implementation in Selected Member States, Nijmegen: Wolf Legal Publishers 2008, p. 161. Legislative Decree 3 October 2008, no. 159 amends Legislative Decree 28 January 2008, no. 25, implementing Directive 2005/85/EC on minimum standards on procedures in Member States for granting and withdrawing refugee status

8   For a complete analysis of the Italian asylum procedure see also M. Benvenuti: http://www.unhcr.org/4ba9d99d9.pdf.

9   Legislative Decree 25/2008, Art. 10.
    Asylum seeker's guarantees
    1. At the time of application the competent police office gives information on his rights and duties during the procedure and the time and means at its disposal to accompany the application of all relevant information concerned, to that end delivers to the applicant the brochure referred to in paragraph 2.
    2. The National Commission shall then, in the manner defined in the regulation to be adopted in accordance with Article 38, publish an information booklet with:
    a) the steps in the recognition of international protection;
    b) the main rights and duties of the applicant during his stay in Italy;
    c) health services and acceptance and how to receive them;

→

2.   Recruitment of Translators/Interpreters in Italian Legal Procedure

For the purpose of this analysis, it is important to assess the role of translators/interpreters in civil proceedings and in criminal procedures. Translators and interpreters in the Italian legal system do not have an official Council or an official code, they just are foreign persons or people with a Degree in Translation-Interpretation or in Foreign Languages.[10] If they want to work at Court as translators/interpreters in legal procedures, they decide to register themselves on a list of experts at the local district Court.

The absence of mandatory experts on legal translation and the absence of an official code on translation and legal translation cause a clear difficulty in finding expert translators in a specific language during civil and criminal proceedings.

Translators and interpreters are considered in the same way as all the other *consultants* during civil and criminal procedures. However, in the Italian practice medical and scientific consultants as well as translators/interpreters are paid by the State, but with a lower salary than those employed for the same activity in the private sector.

When in civil or criminal procedure, the law prescribes the right to a translator/ interpreter. Either the lawyer or the judge asks the Court office for one of the translators/interpreters registered on the list (they are not obliged to have attended any specific legal course, and they only have to demonstrate the capacity to translate and to speak the language required).[11]

The law prescribes only that the translator speaks a language that the defendant is supposed to know. In criminal and civil procedures translation for foreign people is compulsory in order to respect the due process of law and the right of defence. However, the translator could also not be a 'legal expert' and in some cases he/she speaks a language similar but not identical to the asylum seeker's one.

---

d) the address and telephone number of the UNHCR and the main protection organizations seeking international protection.

3. To the applicant is guaranteed at all stages of the procedure, the possibility to contact the UNHCR or other organization or a trusted authority on asylum.

4. The applicant is promptly informed of the decision. All communications regarding the procedure for recognition of international protection are given to the applicant in the first language indicated by him, or, if this is not possible, in English, French, Spanish or Arabic, according to the preference indicated by the person concerned. At all stages of the procedure concerning the presentation and examination of the application, the applicant is ensured, if necessary, the assistance of an interpreter of his/her language or other language which he/she understands.

5. In case of appeal of the denial in front of a court, the foreigner is assured the same guarantees as referred to in this article.

10 See A. Longhi, L'interprete nel processo penale italiano: perito, consulente tecnico o professionista virtuale? In 'intralinea', http://www.intralinea.it/volumes/eng.

11 The right to have a translator must be supported by proof that the person is not able to understand the Italian language. See: Cass. pen. Sez. I Sent., 12-11-2009, n. 6587: 'For the purposes of entitlement to an interpreter under Article. 143 c.p.p. is necessary not just the simple allegation concerning the status of alien, but it also requires the evidence about the lack of knowledge of the Italian language. The lack of translation of documents or the failure to appoint an interpreter, however, determines only a general nullity of intermediate speed, a nobody, which then must be raised, not to be corrected automatically before the completion of the act which would require that presence or, if this is not feasible, immediately after.'

In contrast, in Italian administrative procedures, as in all the procedures connected to migration and asylum law, there may be no translation into the original language of the foreigner, because the translation is done at the local police office, and for logistical reasons a translator in that specific language may not be available. In many cases foreigners do not immediately understand the meaning of the notified document and end up signing documents without exactly knowing the content. During the asylum hearing at the administrative police (in Italian *questure*), where the asylum seekers have to present their asylum request, the presence of translators or interpreters is not compulsory. Indeed, the police may only provide asylum seekers with an leaflet explaining their rights and duties.[12] The asylum procedure goes on just with a written format translation into one of the official language of the EU. For this reason, in many cases, during the appeal, many asylum seekers declare that they were not able to understand the translator during the first audition before the police headquarters and the competent asylum Commission.[13]

3.   The Use of Language in the Asylum Procedure in the First Phase

The asylum request must be submitted to the frontier police or at the police headquarters close to the place where the applicant intends to reside or where the *Prefetto* decides that the irregular asylum seeker has to live (in case of undocumented asylum seekers).[14]

The police headquarter is the first authority meeting the asylum seeker and collecting his/her own personal story/asylum request. Hence, all the information he/she provides will become part of the asylum request. If the asylum seeker arrives at the police headquarter and there are no translators/interpreters in the asylum seeker's specific language, the police may not be able to write down all of the asylum seeker's story, thus altering evidence.

The absence of translators – because of structural and logistic problems – in a specific language could be considered as a gap in the Italian domestic asylum procedure: in fact without a good translation and understanding, the police and, as a consequence, the

---

12 It is important to analyse that right to translation of aliens is not prescribes into Legislative Decree 286 of 1998, but it comes up from the main criminal law jurisprudence, the Supreme Court underlined that the right to translation of the main documents during the appeal is a guarantee necessary to respect alien's right to defence, see among all Cass. Sez. III, 8.9.1999 n. 1527 (c.c. 26.4.1999), Braka, in *Archivio della Proc. Pen.* 1999, 598; cfr. Cass. Sez. V 22.6.1995, n. 1310, Alagra: . *'Even the order of remand as the decree establishing the court, in fact, is an act in front of which the suspect foreigner who did not understand the Italian language would be prejudiced his right to participate in the proceedings against him in the person free because, not understanding what it wrote, not in a position to evaluate or which are considered the evidence against him (and then defend themselves with reference to themselves) or whether or not the conditions for the applicant to proceed ' order for annulment under Article. 292 paragraph 2, criminal procedure code'.*

13 In administrative procedure the absence of translation is not a cause of invalidity of the act but just an irregularity that could be solved with a second regular act. See: T.A.R. Lombardia Milano Sez. III Sent., 12 November 2009, n. 5033, *'The absence of measure translation is not simply a case of illegality, but only a mere irregularity, which allows the preservation of the right of defence of the person, restoring its right to appeal, where it is shown that the failure has prevented the prompt commencement of judicial'.*

14 See art. 7 co 1 legislative decree n 25/2008 after modified by legislative decree n 159/2008: *'The prefect responsible establishing a place of residence or geographical area where the applicants are free to move'.*

Minister of the Interior, have difficulties in identifying the asylum seekers and waste a lot of time in checking the Schengen System II and the Eurodac System. In many cases, a bad initial translation can alter the asylum request. Asylum seekers' requests at police headquarters will be verbalized by police officers using a form, the so-called *format C3*, in which there are personal data and a few questions about the causes that motivated the applicant to flee his/her country to seek protection.

It is advisable for the asylum seeker then, at the moment of the asylum request, to bring a written memorial, in his/her native language and/or a translation. If there is no possibility to translate the personal story, it will arrive at the competent commission in the native language. For the editing of this memorial the applicant may ask help from the municipality or from those associations dealing with the protection of asylum seekers.

The applicant has to show documentation that attests what he/she is declaring, if available (news items, photos, official documents like police reports or medical reports, etc.).

The request cannot be rejected by the police, but the asylum seeker's attempt to explain his story could be hampered by the intervention of a translator/interpreter in the administrative procedure. During administrative expulsion proceedings, even if Article 13, no. 7 of Legislative Decree 25.7.1998, no. 286 attests the use of translation in the alien's vernacular, too often the police declares that for logistical and organizational problems it is impossible to find a translator in the foreigner's original language, for this reason the expulsion translation can be just in English or French. The same happens in case of asylum seekers' denials of international protection, thereby violating, because of the logistical absence of translators, Article 10 of the Legislative Decree 25/2008. In migration law administrative proceedings the principle established by the Italian Council of State section IV, case number 2345, emerges: '*the language of the alien applicant must be known and understood by them and, therefore, the language of the foreign national shall not be construed in a technical sense, with reference to the official languages of different countries, but in relation to the specific lexical and syntactic contexts that are embedded with so much variety, in communities throughout the world and in some populations and sometimes in groups using exclusive*'. This principle should become a mandatory rule and it should not remain without concrete consequential implementation in order to respect the due process of law.

The concrete problem in the Italian asylum procedure is that if the asylum seeker is not able to explain that he/she is an asylum seeker at the local administrative police office, he/she is still 'just an irregular person': in other terms, under Law 94/2009, he/she is committing a crime. In fact Law 94/2009 prescribes that all persons without documents are committing a crime if they are not able to demonstrate that they seek international protection.[15]

In the latter case he/she would be put in a C.A.R.A (detention center for asylum seekers; these centers are inside the center for identification and expulsion in a separated area). Sometimes the asylum seeker receives, before being able to explain that he/she

---

15 For a complete analysis of article 10bis of legislative Decree 286/98 as modified by Law 94/2009 see among others: L. Masera, 'Terra bruciata' attorno al clandestino: tra misure penali simboliche e negazione reale dei diritti, in O. Mazza and F. Vigano (eds), *Il pacchetto sicurezza 2009*, Giapichelli 2009, p. 27.

wants to ask for asylum, an administrative expulsion order and is then sent to the center for identification and expulsion. In this case, only after days or weeks, thanks to translator/interpreter, NGOs activities in the center or the lawyer, the would-be refugee is able to ask for asylum and put in motion a procedure that could take weeks.[16]

The administrative police or the authority in the center for administrative detention will give out a document that certifies the request and the verbalizing appointment date at the competent local Refugee status commission. This document is not translated into the asylum seeker's native language and there are no translations into EU languages.

4.   The Hearing at the Competent Asylum Commissions

The audition is not mandatory, but the applicant must present him/herself if summoned. The Territorial Commission may decide even without the interview if there are enough elements to concede the International Protection, so there would be no audition.[17] The competent authority that evaluates the international protection request is the Territorial Commission for the International protection recognition.[18]

At the commission there are no adjudicators who have the duty to translate. Only in the case in which the asylum seeker asks for a translator/interpreter and language assistance, the local Commission finds translators-interpreters on the Court list or on a private company's list. The Minister of Interior has signed agreements to assure translators/interpreters' service at the Refugee Commission, but at present there are no translators/interpreters for all native languages.

In fact the Italian law just prescribes the right to receive a little leaflet but does not contemplate any explicit right to a translator/interpreter during the audition.

In many cases the competent commissions receive only a short paper by the Questura, the so-called format C3, and a short story not translated. The absence of a complete detailed file on the asylum seeker causes the delay of a commission's decision.

During my PhD studies in the last 3 years (2007-2010) I collected and monitored almost 100 asylum cases all over Italy. During this empirical research I have been able to observe that it could happen that during the audition before the Commission an

---

16 In that case the Italian legal system in which the absence of a translator altered the evidence and caused the delay of the request, could also violate Dublin Regulation 343/2003/EC. Even if the asylum seeker is on the Italian territory for a long time, only from the moment at which he asks for asylum Italy considers his/her presence on the Italian territory. Italy violates the Dublin regulation, in fact the European Court of Human Rights has repeatedly expressed its concern about this, see among others the decision of 18.11.2008 by which the Court, following a request by emergency measure, ordered the Italian authorities to suspend the transfer of an Afghan citizen in Greece (European Court of Human Rights Appl. No 55240/08, *Mirzai v. Italy*).

17 As underlined in the UNHCR studies, Improving asylum procedures comparative analysis and recommendations, p 77: 'Without the services of an interpreter or a translator for the submission of the subsequent application, an applicant who does not know the language of the Member State may be unable to make further representations or may be unable to fully substantiate the subsequent application. This is particularly significant in those Member States which may omit the personal interview, and which insist that any documentary evidence submitted is in or translated into the language of the Member State.'

18 Art 3 of Legislative Decree n 251/2007.

Afghani Pastun translator is the only one available for assisting an Afghani Hazara asylum seeker, or an Iranian translator for an Afghani Hazara asylum seeker. After the hearing, the Hazara asylum seekers told their co-nationals at the local center for asylum seekers that they were not able to understand the translator/interpreter and that they were not sure that the verbal report would contain their whole personal story.[19]

This is proof of the importance of language and translation as high-quality interpretation that can be done only by a good translator/interpreter. The absence of understanding can falsify the evidence and cause 'false asylum seekers' or violate genuine ones and their rights in asylum procedures.[20]

For example when a francophone translator of Cameroon has to translate and interpret an English asylum seeker from Cameroon, there could be cultural differences between the two persons.

The UNHCR and the National Commission on asylum procedure suggest to make asylum seekers as comfortable as possible, by creating an atmosphere which respects asylum seekers' possible psychological troubles.

In order to analyze the language used by asylum seekers, the National Commission gives some advice but there are no specific language analyses drafted by linguistic experts. Translators and interpreters in many cases affect the translations with their own interpretation, but in that case, from the national Commission's point of view the authority has to stop the interview and to change translators. Indeed, in the Italian procedure the translation must be limited to the information provided by the asylum seeker and during the interviews by police officers, commissions' members or interpreters/translators, any kind of subjective analysis must be avoided. Then the members of the commissions could ask some legal help or cultural-linguistic analysis from the UNHCR legal office or from the Italian embassy in the original country. The same is done during the claim by the judge, but with specific linguistic consultants.

5.   The Absence of a Translation of the Commission's Denial

The Territorial Commission is entrusted with the recognition of the refugee status, the subsidiary protection, the humanitarian protection or the rejection of the application (if it has been presented to another state as well), not recognizing any type of protection.[21]

For serious humanitarian reasons the Commission may ask the *Questura* to issue a permission for humanitarian protection (this is different from permits of stay for huma-

---

19 During this research on the 'Italian asylum procedure in a multi-level system of human rights protection' I interviewed asylum seekers, lawyers and adjudicators all over Italy.

20 On the application of Procedure Directive in the Italian legal system see: G. Schiavone and D. Consoli, Verso una migliore tutela dello straniero che chiede asilo? Analisi delle principali novità in materia d'asilo introdotte a seguito del recepimento della direttiva 2005/85/CE con il d.lgs.25/2008 e il d.lgs.159/2008, *Diritto, immigrazione e cittadinanza*, 2008, p. 88-119.

21 For a complete analysis on the Italian asylum system see i.a.: P. Bonetti, Il diritto d'asilo in Italia dopo l'attuazione della direttiva comunitaria sulle qualifiche e sugli status di rifugiato e di protezione sussidiaria, in *Diritto, immigrazione e cittadinanza*, 2008, 1, pp.13-53. P. Bonetti, Il diritto d'asilo. Profili generali e costituzionali del diritto d'asilo nell'ordinamento italiano, in B. Nascimbene, *Diritto degli stranieri*, Padova, 2004, p.1135-1157. See also M. Benvenuti, *Il diritto d'asilo nell'ordinamento costituzionale. Un' introduzione*, Padova 2007, p. 1-39, 86-98.

nitarian reasons issued until January 2008, equal to subsidiary protection). The decision, provided only in the Italian language, is passed on to the person directly or through a legal adviser if the asylum seeker has nominated a lawyer.

The denial of the Commission may be handed over by the local *Questura* where the asylum seeker has his/her residence (declaring a residence is mandatory, the absence of residence can cause considerable violation of asylum seekers' rights!). In the Italian law there is no mandatory duty to translate the Commission's denial. Therefore, many asylum seekers are not able to understand what the *Questura* notify them if they have no lawyer or no NGO assistance. Lawyer assistance during the administrative procedure at the *Questura* or Commission audition is not compulsory and there is no free legal assistance during administrative procedures for foreigners, including asylum seekers. Indeed, the lawyers who assist asylum seekers during these phases of the procedure are not paid by the State, they work voluntarily or they ask money from asylum seekers.

As a matter of fact, in many cases the absence of translation of the denial into the asylum seekers' native language violates article 13 ECHR, article 39 Procedures Directive and article 47 of the European Charter on Human Rights.[22]

6. Conclusions

In the Italian asylum procedure, *language* is not considered an instrument to identify genuine asylum seekers; rather it is only a mechanism to provide the applicant with the opportunity to be conscious of his/her rights and duties and to understand his/her claim. Once the asylum seeker asks for asylum at the administrative headquarters or at the frontier, the main objective would be to guarantee the possibility to understand his/her rights. Nonetheless, in many cases, concrete logistical problems violate these rights. The absence of a specific regulation for translators/interpreters' recruitment in administrative procedures could limit asylum seekers' access to a complete understanding and could violate their right to due process of law. Indeed, Italian law simply provides that the asylum seeker will receive a little leaflet in different languages, but not a specific translation into his/her language. Considering the asylum procedure as a sort of trial where the asylum seeker has to prove his/her claim, the right to be conscious seems to be violated more often than in the course of civil or criminal proceedings. This concrete absence of guarantees, even if translations during the entire asylum procedure are prescribed by article 10 of the Legislative Decree 25/2008, contrasts with the idea that asylum seekers' rights should be protected more than in case of a defendant in a criminal procedure. In fact the asylum seeker seems, in some cases, to have less guarantees than a defendant in the Italian legal system because the violation of the guarantees are not immediately put in front of a judge and are not prescribed by laws as in Italian criminal procedure.[23]

---

22 In fact not to be able to understand the meaning of the notified documented violates the right to have access to an effective remedy as prescribed by article 39 of the Procedures Directive and Article 13 ECHR.

23 This contrasts with UNHCR suggestions on the more generous standard of proof and with the flexibility which the decision-makers must take into account in assessing asylum or refugee status,

→

Duties and rights in the asylum procedure are explained through a dossier translated in the main languages that the asylum seeker is assumed to know. Often the absence of a translator/interpreter causes the impossibility to have a good understanding between the authority and the asylum seeker. This can alter the evidence of the asylum request from the outset since at the administrative police office the asylum seeker tells his personal story and then this is sent to the competent commission. The impossibility to understand the asylum seeker's request, for example because of the absence of a translator, transforms the asylum seeker into an illegal migrant. As a matter of fact, the authorities cannot distinguish immediately, without translators, an *asylum seeker* from an irregular economic migrant. The recent Law 94/2009 prescribes that all illegal migrants should receive an expulsion order under article 10bis of the Aliens Law, Legislative Decree 286/98. In that case, if in the administrative procedure there would be a mandatory duty to ask for a translator or an interpreter, there would be the possibility to understand immediately that that foreign person is asking for asylum or he/she is an asylum seeker.

The criminalization of irregular people and the absence of a mandatory right to translators/interpreters in the Italian law could be considered as a big gap in the system of legal guarantees, which could cause refoulement and human rights violations. Nowadays, once asylum seekers enter the Italian territory, they face the problem of explaining themselves to authorities. Furthermore, the bilateral agreement Lybia-Italy, together with the current policy of criminalization of migrants, has caused a massive decrease of asylum seekers in Italy in 2009 as compared to 2008.

The European Procedure Directive prescribes that an asylum seeker must have effective access to procedures, the opportunity to cooperate and properly communicate with the competent authorities so as to present the relevant facts of his/her case and sufficient procedural guarantees to pursue his/her case throughout all stages of the procedure. The absence of translation and interpretation could be regarded as an obstacle to the asylum procedure access. During the overall asylum procedure there should be special attention to language analysis of the asylum seeker, to avoid the possible asylum seekers' fear and story-changing in case of translators/interpreters of opposite cultural or political groups coming from the same country of origin.

The absence of good translation causes possible gaps in the asylum procedure and violates article 6 (3) ECHR and, as a consequence, art. 3 ECHR in the asylum procedure.[24] Indeed, credibility and evidence stem from the asylum seekers' account, and the lack of good translations or interpretations could affect the credibility itself.

---

see on this point: UNHCR Training Module 'Interviewing Applicants for Refugee Status', Geneva 1995.

24 Concerning the right to interpreters and translators as prescribed by article 6 (3) ECHR in criminal procedures, see Brecht Vandenberghe, *The European Convention on Human Rights: The right to the free assistance of an interpreter*, (2003), p. 53-59: 'For anyone who cannot speak or understand the language used in court, the right to receive the free assistance of an interpreter, without subsequently having claimed back from him payment of the cost thereby incurred.'

1. Article 6 ECHR: 'In the determination of his civil rights and obligations or of any criminal charge against him, everyone is entitled to a fair and public hearing within a reasonable time by an independent and impartial tribunal established by law. Judgment shall be pronounced publicly but the press and public may be excluded from all or part of the trial in the interests of morals, public order or national security in a democratic society, where the interests of juveniles or the protection

$\longrightarrow$

If a suspect wants to be able to effectively exercise his rights, he must in any case be able to obtain information on his legal position in a language that he understands. Likewise, an asylum seeker should enjoy the same guarantees during the asylum procedure. For these reasons both in criminal procedures and in asylum procedures interpreters and translators have a crucial role in safeguarding a fair trial and fair access to the exercise of the right to asylum.

In many cases the absence of a good translator is a problem for women and unaccompanied minors as these people are vulnerable. Without good assistance they may not be able to explain their well-founded fear of persecution. Hence, this absence of translator assistance affects the reliability of their request.

If an asylum seeker were so fortunate as to ask for asylum in a place where the local system of protection organizes a good legal and translation service he/she would be facilitated at the commission audition. The commission itself with a good translator/interpreter and language analysis service would be facilitated to understand if the asylum seeker's request is well-founded. Domestic legislators must consider the role of language analysis as well as translation and interpretation to protect the asylum seekers from misunderstandings and violations. The Italian legislator should invest in multicultural and independent consultants in order to protect asylum seekers' rights and follow international and European law on human rights protection.

Language, meant as the right to be informed, should be a specific guarantee in the European Common Asylum System in order to respect article 6 (3) ECHR. The mandatory presence of an interpreter/translator from the first step in the asylum procedure until the end of the process could also help adjudicators to understand, as well as possible, the validity of an asylum seeker's request, thus guaranteeing a stronger protection of fundamental human rights in asylum procedures.

Language analysis in the Italian legal system could be considered to contrast with the Supreme Court position that refers directly to paragraph 196 of the UNHCR Handbook: '*While it is a general principle of law to the applicant evidence in support of his statements, the assessment and evaluation of all relevant facts will be responsible jointly to the applicant and the examiner, in some cases ... examiner's task is to use all means at his disposal to gather the necessary evidence to support the claim, finally, that if such independent research is not successful, or*

---

of the private life of the parties so require, or to the extent strictly necessary in the opinion of the court in special circumstances where publicity would prejudice the interests of justice.

2. Everyone charged with a criminal offence shall be presumed innocent until proved guilty according to law.

3. Everyone charged with a criminal offence has the following minimum rights:

(a) to be informed promptly, in a language which he understands and in detail, of the nature and cause of the accusation against him;

(b) to have adequate time and facilities for the preparation of his defence;

(c) to defend himself in person or through legal assistance of his own choosing or, if he has not sufficient means to pay for legal assistance, to be given it free when the interests of justice so require;

(d) to examine or have examined witnesses against him and to obtain the attendance and examination of witnesses on his behalf under the same conditions as witnesses against him;

(e) to have the free assistance of an interpreter if he cannot understand or speak the language used in court.'

whether certain statements are not susceptible of proof in such cases, if the account of the applicant is credible, they have to give the benefit of the doubt, unless valid reasons not to (…).'[25]

Language Analysis for the Determination of Origin (LADO) may not be infallible to identify the asylum seeker's identity, in case of different influences it could be difficult to understand the real asylum seeker's origin and the result given by the linguistic analysis could be in contrast with some others aspects. The open question then is: what about the respect of the principle of the benefit of doubt?[26] If linguistic analysis would be introduced into the Italian asylum procedure and the question about its legitimacy would be posed in the Italian Supreme Court, the Italian Supreme Court would analyze if linguistic analysis for the determination of an asylum seeker's origin in respect to article 24 of the Italian Constitution, article 6 (3) ECHR, is used to respect asylum seeker's rights and the principle of the benefit of doubt, it would underline possible contrasts with these principles.

25 Italian Supreme Court, United Chambers, decision no. 27310 of 21.10.2008 see: http://www.cortedicassazione.it/Notizie/GiurisprudenzaCivile/SezioniUnite/SezioniUnite.asp.
26 A. Reath, Language analysis in the context of the asylum process: Procedures, validity, and consequences, *Language Assessment Quarterly*, p. 1-4, 209–233, 2004.

The Use of Language Analysis in the Danish Asylum Procedure

Jens Vedsted-Hansen

1.   The Procedure for Examining Asylum Applications

1.1   Admissibility Decisions vs. Substantive Examination

The asylum procedure under the Danish Aliens Act[1] is organised on the basis of a clear distinction between admissibility issues and the substantive examination of asylum applications. The procedural safeguards differs significantly between the two types of decision-making, in that there are quite extended safeguards in the substantive examination procedure,[2] while safeguards in the sense of appeal rights are almost absent in the procedure deciding on the issue of admissibility to the territory and the examination procedure in Denmark.[3]

When an alien claims to be in need of international protection either as a Convention refugee or under the supplementary provision on 'protection status',[4] the initial stage of the procedure is concerned exclusively with the application of the Dublin II Regulation[5] and the national 'safe third country' rule in Danish law.[6] These decisions are made at the administrative level, in the first instance by the Danish Immigration Service whose decisions may be appealed to the Ministry of Refugee, Immigration and Integration Affairs. Notably, such appeal carries no suspensive effect.[7] Thus, the prospective asylum applicant may in principle be transferred or retransferred to another Dublin State or deported to a third country presumed to be safe immediately after the first instance decision according to which the applicant – and, indeed, the application – is inadmissible in Denmark.

If neither the Dublin II Regulation nor the Danish 'safe third country' rule leads to a decision on inadmissibility, the application is admitted into the substantive examination procedure, and the asylum applicant is allowed to remain in Denmark during the

---

1   Aliens Consolidation Act No. 1061 of 18 August 2010.
2   See, in particular, Aliens Act sections 53-56 on the appeals procedure before the Refugee Appeals Board, described below in section 1.2.
3   Cf. Aliens Act sections 48 a – 48 d.
4   Cf. Aliens Act section 7 (1) and (2). Section 7 (1) incorporates the Refugee Convention definition , while section 7 (2) incorporates the prohibition of refoulement under the European Convention on Human Rights and other human rights treaties.
5   Council Regulation No. 343/2003 of 18 February 2003 (OJ 2003 L 50). Due to the Danish EU reservation, Denmark has concluded an agreement extending the provisions of the Dublin II Regulation to apply under international law between the EU and Denmark, cf. Council Decision 2006/188 of 21 February 2006 (OJ 2006 L 66).
6   Cf. Aliens Act section 48 a (1).
7   Aliens Act section 48 d.

examination of the application. The substantive examination is then carried out by the Danish Immigration Service as the first instance, in accordance with the general rules on administrative procedures. Despite its organisational status as a directorate under the Ministry of Refugee, Immigration and Integration Affairs, the Immigration Service is officially considered to be an independent body in terms of the substantive examination and decision-making on asylum applications. The political implications of this allegedly independent status of the Immigration Service are quite obvious, inasmuch as the implied incompetence on the part of the Ministry allows the Minister to decline approaches from any political actors, organisations or the media concerning individual cases or even the general criteria for the recognition of asylum applicants. Nonetheless, this organisational setup represents a remarkable exception from the general hierarchical principles of Danish administrative law, and it would further seem to be at variance with the Minister's express authorisation to issue rules to the Immigration Service.[8]

1.2. Appeals Procedure

The examination of asylum applications provides an example of the various kinds of administrative appeals boards that have been established in Denmark, as an alternative to reviewing administrative decisions in a specialised court system. There are mainly three features characterising such special administrative appeals boards. First, appeals boards normally imply increased *procedural safeguards* for the applicants or appellants, as compared to those of ordinary administrative review. Second, partly with a view to obtaining these procedural safeguards, some appeals boards have been set up as *quasi-judicial* bodies allowing for procedures that are to some extent equivalent to those in ordinary court review. Third, the special appeals boards will normally be able to include various kinds of *expertise* that will often not be available in ordinary administrative review proceedings.

The Refugee Appeals Board is a rather clear example of these general features of administrative appeals boards. Due to its procedural safeguards, the Refugee Appeals Board is normally described as a *quasi-judicial* body. When reviewing individual asylum cases the Refugee Appeals Board is normally composed of the chairman or an alternate chairman, and two other members among whom one shall be nominated by the Minister for Refugee, Immigration and Integration Affairs, while the other shall be nominated by the Council of the Bar and Law Society.[9] Given that the chairman and the alternate chairmen shall be judges in the ordinary courts, the Refugee Appeals Board is secured a high degree of independence. This is primarily so in the functional dimension of independence, and it is expressly stipulated that the Board members are independent and may not seek or receive instructions from the appointing or nominating authority or organisation.[10] In contrast, the personal independence is questionable as regards those members who are being nominated by the Minister for Refugee, Immigration and Integration Affairs, as these members cannot continue sitting on the Board if they no

---

8 Aliens Act section 46 (4).
9 Aliens Act section 53 (2), (3) and (6).
10 Aliens Act section 53 (1).

longer hold posts within the central department of that Ministry.[11] Given the hierarchical organisation of ministries, these members are subject to the Minister's and her leading officials' discretionary decisions on their organisational and functional career. Due to that subordination, the personal independence of these Board members must be considered quite significantly modified.

It is beyond doubt that the review mechanism of the Refugee Appeals Board provides procedural safeguards beyond the average of traditional administrative review in Denmark. However, the Refugee Appeals Board cannot be considered equivalent to an ordinary judicial instance, neither as regards the personal independence and impartiality of the totality of its membership, nor in terms of procedural safeguards and transparency of the examination proceedings in individual appeals cases. Therefore, the strictly limited access to review in ordinary courts – in reality, the nearby absence of such judicial review – is a significant aspect of the Danish asylum procedure.[12]

2. Principles of Evidence in the Examination of Asylum Cases

Two general features of the Refugee Appeals Board and its approach to examining asylum cases should be mentioned as particularly relevant to the issue of application of language analysis in asylum decisions. First, and probably most importantly, it is a firmly established principle of Danish law that the courts are not bound by any formal rules in their assessment of evidence. This principle is often reflected in the Refugee Appeals Board's manner of examining asylum applications, as well as in the way in which the Board gives reasons in its written decisions. The principle of free assessment of evidence is also likely to have quite significant bearing on the way in which the Refugee Appeals Board deals with the results of language tests.

Given the organisational position of the Board as an appeals body, the principles guiding the examination of asylum cases at this second instance level are most likely to influence the approach taken to similar evidentiary issues at the first instance examination carried out by the Danish Immigration Service. In that connection it has to be kept in mind that language analysis will, as the most usual course of proceedings, be initiated by the Immigration Service during the first instance examination of asylum applications. The decision to request such an analysis will, however, normally be influenced by the way in which the Refugee Appeals Board can be expected to apply the results. Thereby the Refugee Appeals Board's application of the results of language analysis could be said to have primarily indirect influence on the approach to language tests in the first instance proceedings of the Danish Immigration Service. The usage of language analysis in the practices of the Immigration Service will not be further described for the simple reason that the Immigration Service does not publish its case law within the area of asylum applications.

---

11 Aliens Act section 53 (2) and (4).
12 Aliens Act section 56 (8). See, for a critical account, Jens Vedsted-Hansen, The Borderline Between Questions of Fact and Questions of Law, in Gregor Noll (ed.), *Proof, Evidentiary Assessment and Credibility in Asylum Procedures*, The Hague 2005, p. 57-65.

Second, as a partly related feature of the Danish asylum procedure, there is no tradition for issuing general guidelines concerning the examination of asylum applications, neither as ministerial guidelines to the Danish Immigration Service[13] nor as internal guidelines within the Refugee Appeals Board. As regards the latter, there is actually a Coordination Committee among whose tasks it is to consider issues of general impact to the activities of the Board, including the issue of possible criteria that may influence the decisions on particular types of cases.[14] Nonetheless, the Coordination Committee rarely adopts such general criteria, let alone guidelines that might be perceived as to some degree binding upon the Board members in their examination of individual cases.

It should probably be seen as a result of these general features that no general guidelines or criteria appear to have been adopted by the Coordination Committee concerning the application of language analysis in asylum cases before the Refugee Appeals Board. The Board has, on the other hand, paid some attention to the existence of more general issues pertaining to such analyses, in that the Board sent representatives to a EURASIL meeting in October 2003 on the determination of the nationality and identity of asylum applicants in connection with the first instance examination of cases. One of the workshops at this meeting dealt with exchange of experience concerning the application of language analysis and age determination of asylum applicants.[15] Nonetheless, this exchange does not seem to have resulted in any formal initiatives among the members of the Refugee Appeals Board.

3. Language Analysis in Appeals Cases

3.1 Application of Language Analysis

A survey of asylum decisions published by the Refugee Appeals Board during the past few years (2003-2010) discloses regular, yet not very frequent usage of language analysis as a basis for the examination of appeals cases. The general tendency seems to be that the asylum authorities most frequently initiate language tests in cases concerning certain national or ethnic groups of applicants. These groups are apparently often determined by some more or less clear combination of the number of successful asylum applications submitted by persons belonging to the group in question, and the particular linguistic characteristics of the various groups defined by their nationality, ethnicity or both features. Thus, the logic underlying the application of language analysis would seem to be rather simple, insofar as these tests are often initiated in order to prevent suspected abuse of the asylum system by applicants who might attempt to misrepresent themselves as belonging to a group of potentially successful applicants by way of fraudulently alleging the nationality, or perhaps only the ethnicity, of that group. Such a risk is likely to be bigger in cases where the linguistic characteristics are similar or the differences at least

---

13 See above section 1.1.
14 Cf. the Refugee Appeals Board's rules of procedure, Ministerial Order No. 1089 of 25 November 2009, section 17 (1).
15 Cf. the Refugee Appeals Board's *Annual Report 2003*, p. 43.

insignificant, thereby making the probability of successful outcome of the misrepresentation appear high in the first place.

An apt illustration of this tendency is the prevalence of language tests in recent years in decisions concerning asylum applicants claiming to be Burmese nationals who belong to the ethnic Rohingya group. In such cases the results of language analysis are often, yet indeed not always, accepted by the Refugee Appeals Board as decisive evidence of the nationality when there is doubt as to whether the applicant is a Bangladeshi or a Burmese national. In case of accepting the alleged Burmese nationality, the Board has very often drawn the conclusion that the applicant should then be considered in need of international protection. Alternatively, if the applicant is held to be from Bangladesh, the result will normally be refusal of the asylum application. Thus, establishing the identity and nationality of the applicant generally implies a strong presumption in favour or disfavour of recognising the need for international protection and granting asylum. Due to the relatively high prevalence of application of language analysis in cases concerning allegedly Burmese nationals, and their apparent reflection of representative features of the Refugee Appeals Board's approach to the results of such analyses, this case law shall be described in some detail in the following.

Examples of the aforementioned tendency are two decisions from 2004 in which the male applicants were considered nationals of Bangladesh, despite their claims to Burmese nationality. They had both alleged to be ethnic Rohingyas from Burma, exposed to harassment by the Burmese military authorities. The Refugee Appeals Board, however, did not consider the claimed nationality sufficiently established, and held both of these applicants to be of Bangladeshi nationality instead. One of the applicants had arrived legally with a Bangladesh passport containing a visa for Denmark, and the Board's assessment of nationality was supported by the results of a language test. In this connection it was considered decisive that the applicant had demonstrated very poor knowledge of Rohingya words, and that he had been unable to answer questions of central importance to Rohingyas, in particular relating to the language.[16] In another partly similar case the Board reached the same conclusion, albeit only by a majority of the members who attached weight to the results of a language test demonstrating that the applicant appeared to originate from southern Bangladesh in that he was using terms not applied by Rohingyas, but rather by persons originating from Bangladesh.[17]

Other means of evidence may support the results of the language analysis carried out. For example, in a decision from 2005 the Refugee Appeals Board set aside the applicant's alleged Burmese nationality, not only because the language and nationality tests had demonstrated his lack of knowledge of that country, but also due to his inconsistent explanations as well as the fact the Burmese family registered by UNHCR under the relevant name had five children and repatriated to Burma in 2003, according to information contained in a 'family book' kept by UNHCR. The applicant was therefore held to be a Bangladeshi national, and his asylum application was refused.[18]

16 Refugee Appeals Board decision BR13/72 of August 2004, reported in *Annual Report 2004*, p. 147-48.

17 Refugee Appeals Board decision BR13/73 of August 2004, reported in *Annual Report 2004*, p. 148.

18 Refugee Appeals Board decision Burma/2005/1 of July 2005, published on the Board's website www.fln.dk (accessed 16 April 2010).

Another example of combining language analysis with other means of evidence concerned an applicant who claimed to be an ethnic Rohingya from Burma. Due to the unstable situation in Burma, he and his mother and brother allegedly left the country for Bangladesh in 1994 when the applicant was around 16 years of age. In the appeals case, the decision was expressly made contingent on his nationality, in that the representative of the Danish Immigration Service accepted the granting of asylum should the applicant be a Burmese national. The majority of the Refugee Appeals Board members, however, held him to be Bangladeshi, due to a number of factors, and therefore refused the application for asylum. One of these factors was the language analysis according to which the applicant was speaking Arakan-Bangla at the level of mother tongue, as spoken in the Chittagong area. Among the other factors that supported the majority finding were the technical evidence disclosing that the applicant's identity card had been forged, inconsistent explanations, and the fact that the applicant had entered Denmark with a Bangladesh passport indicating his Bangladeshi nationality and his origin in Chittagong. Notably, the fact that the applicant had answered a number of questions about Burma and the Rohingya correctly was not considered decisive by the Board majority, inasmuch as the applicant was held to originate from the border area and persons belonging to the Rohingya were living on both sides of the border.[19]

Similar combined assessment of the results of language analysis and other means of evidence, sometimes including the asylum applicant's general lack of credibility, have been the basis of setting aside the alleged Burmese nationality also in more recent decisions by the Refugee Appeals Board.[20] In that kind of situations it is sometimes made explicit by the Board that only limited weight has been attached to the results of a language test, so that it is being made clear that the decision is based on the totality of the evidence before the Board.[21]

Particular factors pertaining to the mental state of health of the asylum applicant may reduce the relative impact of language analysis. This can be illustrated by the Refugee Appeals Board decision concerning an applicant allegedly originating from Serbia-Montenegro. Here the Board expressly stated that the results of the language test could not have any decisive weight, given the applicant's mental situation. His Serbia-Montenegro nationality was therefore accepted by the Board, despite the language test suggesting his linguistic background to be Albania.[22]

Among the other alleged countries of origin that have been subject to language analysis are Bhutan,[23] Sudan (Darfur),[24] Nigeria,[25] Russia (Chechnya),[26] Georgia,[27] and

---

19 Refugee Appeals Board decision BR14/92 of January 2005, reported in *Annual Report 2005*, p. 201.

20 Refugee Appeals Board decision Bangla/2006/4 of October 2006, reported in *Annual Report 2006*, p. 147-148. Refugee Appeals Board decision Bangladesh/2007/1, reported in *Annual Report 2007*, p. 196-197.

21 Refugee Appeals Board decision Burma/2010/2 of March 2010, published on the Board's website www.fln.dk (accessed 8 October 2010).

22 Refugee Appeals Board decision BR14/21 of December 2005, reported in *Annual Report 2005*, p. 73.

23 Refugee Appeals Board decision BR12/149 of June 2003, reported in *Annual Report 2003*, p. 192.

24 Refugee Appeals Board decision BR14/58 of May 2005, reported in *Annual Report 2005*, p. 149. Refugee Appeals Board decision Sudan/2007/1 of May 2007, reported in *Annual Report 2007*, p. 141.

Somalia (Northern Somalia or Mogadishu).[28] In general, the approach taken by the Refugee Appeals Board in these cases appears to be in line with the aforementioned decisions, as modified by certain factors specific to the individual cases.

3.2 Language Analysis Outweighed by Other Means of Evidence

As mentioned above, the results of language analysis are not always accepted as decisive evidence of the correct nationality of the applicant. Illustrative examples of this can also be found in the case law of the Refugee Appeals Board concerning allegedly Burmese asylum applicants.

One such example is a decision from 2003 in which the Refugee Appeals Board granted asylum to a male applicant from Burma who was held to be a refugee in accordance with the Refugee Convention definition. The applicant alleged to be a Rohingya of the Muslim faith who had been a member of an illegal Islamic organisation, and had been arrested and abused by the Burmese military. The majority of the members of the Refugee Appeals Board accepted the identity information provided by the applicant, holding that it had been essentially consistent and credible. Thus, the Board's majority did not attach decisive weight to the fact that the applicant had entered Denmark on a formally genuine Bangladesh passport, nor to the result of a language test which was not considered unequivocal. Under these circumstances it was therefore not considered relevant to initiate further investigations into the identity of the applicant.[29]

Two Refugee Appeals Board decisions from 2004 can be seen as following the same approach to the results of language analysis. The first of these asylum applicants had given consistent explanations and produced an identity document corresponding to his alleged Burmese nationality. Given that he was originating from a border area and had been living in Bangladesh during around 13 years from the age of 17, the results of the language test did not provide sufficient basis for setting aside his claim to originate from the Arakan region in Burma.[30] According to the language test carried out in the second case, the applicant was speaking Arakan-Bengali in the way it is spoken in south-eastern Bangladesh, and his knowledge about Burma was only general, at certain points even incorrect. However, given that the applicant had alleged Burmese nationality throughout the Danish authorities' examination of his case, and that his explanation could not be set aside on the basis of inconsistencies or lack of probability, the Refugee Appeals Board held the applicant's identity sufficiently established and considered him

---

25 Refugee Appeals Board decision Nigeria/2007/5 of March 2007, published on the Board's website www.fln.dk (accessed 8 October 2010).

26 Refugee Appeals Board decision BR13/13 of November 2004, reported in *Annual Report 2004*, pp. 56-58. Refugee Appeals Board decision Rus/2005/10 of October 2005, published on the Board's website www.fln.dk (accessed 16 April 2010).

27 Refugee Appeals Board decision Georgien/2007/2 of October 2007, reported in *Annual Report 2007*, p. 201-202.

28 Refugee Appeals Board decisions Somalia/2006/10, Somalia/2006/4, and Somalia/2006/5 of October, March and April 2006, reported in *Annual Report 2006*, p. 179-181.

29 Refugee Appeals Board decision BR12/155 of February 2003, reported in *Annual Report 2003*, p. 196.

30 Refugee Appeals Board decision BR13/74 of May 2004, reported in *Annual Report 2004*, p. 148-149.

to be an ethnic Rohingya originating from Burma. The results of the language test, the fact that the applicant had applied for a visa at the Danish embassy in Bangladesh using a Bangladeshi national identity, were held insufficient to reach a different conclusion.[31] Both of these applicants were consequently considered Convention refugees and granted asylum.

In a similar manner, the Refugee Appeals Board has been willing to accept other means of evidence as outweighing the results of language analysis in more recent decisions. In these cases significant weight was attached to the general consistency and credibility of the information provided by the asylum applicants, as well as to the correct answers they had given to the additional questions that had been asked in order to verify their nationality and identity. These applicants were therefore accepted as ethnic Rohingyas from Burma, and they were granted asylum in accordance with the Refugee Convention definition.[32] Notably, the Board pointed out that two of the applicants were originating from the border area of Burma and Bangladesh. Similarly, in a case concerning a Somali woman, the Board did not consider the results of the language analysis, suggesting her linguistic background to be Northern Somalia, inconsistent with her to alleged origin in the Mogadishu area, because of her usage of more southern terms and her mother's family origins in Northern Somalia.[33]

A particular method of verifying or negating the results of language analysis might be the additional translation of the tests carried out. For example, in a case concerning an asylum applicant allegedly originating from Bhutan, the majority of members of the Refugee Appeals Board accepted this nationality as they, upon such additional translation, did not find sufficient basis to set aside his explanation in that regard. He was consequently granted asylum in accordance with the Refugee Convention definition.[34]

3.3 Concrete Assessments of the Totality of Evidence – Linguistic and Procedural Inferences

The above survey of presumably representative Danish asylum decisions of the past few years illustrates the manner in which the Refugee Appeals Board and – as a likely indirect consequence of the Board's case law – the Danish Immigration Service utilise language analyses in order to help identify asylum applicants' national origin in cases concerning certain national or ethnic groups of applicants. The general feature of these cases seems to be that establishing the applicant's identity and nationality often implies a strong presumption in favour or disfavour of recognising the need for international protection and granting the applicant asylum. Since that kind of presumption may imply an incentive to misrepresent personal data in order to obtain asylum on the basis of fraudu-

---

31 Refugee Appeals Board decision Burma/2004/4 of August 2004, published on the Board's website www.fln.dk (accessed 16 April 2010).

32 Refugee Appeals Board decisions Burma/2008/1 and Burma/2008/2 of June 2008, reported in *Annual Report 2008*, p. 49-50. Refugee Appeals Board decision Burma/2009/1 of March 2009, published on the Board's website www.fln.dk (accessed 16 April 2010).

33 Refugee Appeals Board decision Somalia/2006/4 of March 2006, reported in *Annual Report 2006*, p. 180.

34 Refugee Appeals Board decision BR12/149 of June 2003, reported in *Annual Report 2003*, p. 192.

lent ethnic or national affiliation, there is a corresponding incentive on the part of the asylum authorities to detect and prevent such fraud by the usage of language analysis.

The summarised cases illustrate, however, the need for caution inasmuch as language tests may suggest the national origin, but not necessarily the formal nationality and country of origin of the asylum applicant. Language analysis appears to be only one means of evidence among others, and it only demonstrates or indicates a factual condition from which certain inferences can be made, yet often contingent on other elements of evidence that have to be taken into account. The Refugee Appeals Board has demonstrated its general willingness to do so, as illustrated by the fact that the Board often attaches weight to additional factors in support of the results of the language analysis, or to evidentiary factors contrary to the results of language analysis.

Due to the need for caution, as well as the complexity of the usage of the results of language analysis in asylum decisions, as reflected in the case law described above, it is quite remarkable that the Refugee Appeals Board apparently has developed no explicit criteria for the examination of cases in which language tests have been carried out, neither as general internal guidelines or criteria adopted by the Coordination Committee nor by way of elaborated general reasoning in selected decisions that raise issues of principle. This is well in line with the principles of evidence in Danish law, described above in section 2, as well as with the tradition of pragmatic decision-making on a case-by-case basis that is also firmly established by the Refugee Appeals Board over the past quarter of a decade. These factors may be part of the explanation of certain variations, if not inconsistencies, that might seem to appear in some of the cases studied here. At the same time, however, such variations are extremely difficult to assess and explain, due to the general complexity inherent in evidentiary issues in the examination of asylum applications. This would in itself seem to favour the elaboration of at least some kind of principled approach to the usage of language analysis as a means of evidence.

Part Five: LADO as Evidence

Gregor Noll shows how in a particular case the courts in Sweden dealt with the evidence obtained in a LADO analysis. *Karin Zwaan* describes how LADO is approached by the Dutch courts. LADO has received relatively much attention in the Dutch courts, as a result of the fact that both the government and asylum seekers have put forth LADO-reports on a larger scale than is usual in other countries. Zwaan concludes that language analysis is a difficult topic for judges to handle, especially since linguists often seem to disagree, and definitive conclusions – required by the legal system – may easily be disputed. *Blanche Tax* (UNHCR, Belgium) confirms the current interest of the United Nations High Commissioner for Refugees in LADO, and takes a close look at where LADO fits in with the current debate about the EU Procedures Directive.

The 2007 Rejection of Anonymous Language Analysis by the Swedish Migration Court of Appeal: A Precedent?

Gregor Noll

This is a case brief of the judgment rendered by the Migration Court of Appeal (*Migrationsöverdomstolen*) on 7 June 2007 in the case UM 583-06. The Migration Court of Appeal is the third and final instance in the Swedish asylum system. Its judgments command informal precedent authority. The present case is the only reported court case to date addressing the evidentiary value of language analysis.

The applicants (a mother and her daughter) claimed to originate from Burma, and more specifically from the area adjacent to the border to Bangladesh. They feared persecution on account of their Rohingya ethnicity upon return to Burma. The applicants did not submit documentary evidence of their Burmese origin.

The first instance Migration Board (*Migrationsverket*) ordered a language analysis. It took the form of a telephone conversation between the analyst and the applicant, in the course of which the applicant's local and regional knowledge was tested.[1] As emerged from the representations made by the Migration Board in the second-instance proceedings in the Migration Court (*Migrationsdomstolen*), this language analysis led the Board to believe that the applicants were citizens of Bangladesh rather than Burmese, and therefore not in need of protection.

The applicants appealed. The Stockholm Migration Court rejected the appeal.

The Migration Court found it to be probable that the applicants originated from Bangladesh, basing itself mainly on arguments related to language and local knowledge. It found it improbable that a 32-year old person who had moved to another language area would completely forget its original dialect (Arakanbengali). Also, the Court noted that the applicant could not speak any Burmese, and was unable to name any of the larger cities in her home region.

The applicant appealed to the Migration Court of Appeal (*Migrationsöverdomstolen*), which granted leave to hear the case.

In proceedings at the Migration Court of Appeal, the applicants asserted that the judgment of the Migration Court was based to an excessive degree on the language analysis carried out at first instance. From their point of view, this analysis cannot possess a high evidentiary value, as the analyst is anonymous. The applicants argued that anonymity impedes any assessment of his or hers competence. It also bars a proper assessment of questions and answers on local knowledge. Additionally, the applicants gave explanations relating to the mother's linguistic characteristics and to her lack of lo-

---

1   There are two types of analysis in Swedish practice. One is based on a recording (stated to last about 10 minutes), another, termed 'direct analysis' (direktanalys) based on a telephone conversation between analyst and applicant, in the course of which the applicant's local knowledge might be tested as well. In the present case, the latter type was used.

cal knowledge and of the Burmese language. The applicants also stressed that the Migration Board itself no longer cooperates with the language analysis business which carried out her analysis as it does not identify its analysts, and that a Board report conceded that at least one in ten language analysis reports is wrong.

Moreover, the applicants drew the attention of the Court to the fact that Court interpreters were required by law to undergo authorization by the Swedish Chamber of Commerce, in the course of which the knowledge of the interpreter is tested. Giving a language test evidentiary value would presuppose that the analyst be subjected to the same demands.

The Migration Board informed the Court that its current contract with its sole provider of language analysis services (Verified AB) stipulates that the identity of an analyst is to be made known to the Board if this information is needed as evidence in court proceedings or otherwise in order to affirm the correctness and/or quality of the language analysis. In the case under appeal, however, language analysis was provided by another company and the analyst is anonymous. However, it has been made known to the Board that the person in question has a higher education degree from Sweden and grew up both in Burma and in Bangladesh. Arakanbengali is his mother tongue and he has a good command of Burmese.

The Migration Court of Appeal held that it is for the applicant to render probable his statements on nationality or country of origin. It believes that the language analysis in question had a more than negligible impact on the assessment of the applicants' origin. The Court pronounced itself on its evidentiary value as follows:

> It is the view of the Migration Court of Appeal that a language analysis of the kind at issue in the present case can only possess a marginal evidentiary value, as it has been carried out in a manner that does not fulfil reasonable demands on legal certainty. No quality control has been possible, because it was impossible to identify neither the analyst nor the qualifications and capabilities of that person for that assignment.[2]

The Migration Court of Appeal found however, that an assessment of all elements of the case and 'mainly disregarding from the result of the language analysis' ('*med bortseende i huvudsak från resultatet av språkanalysen*') resulted in that the applicants had not made probable that they originated from Burma. It therefore rejected the claim.

Author's comment

It is perfectly reasonable that the Migration Court of Appeal expresses great scepticism with regard to language analysis by anonymous analysts. Nonetheless, the significance of this judgment is diminished by shortcomings in its evidentiary reasoning.

To my mind, it is obvious that the Migration Court of Appeal has relied on the content of the language analysis to a great degree. Most of the claims presented in the judgments and related to language, dialect and local knowledge stem from the language

---

2   Author's translation.

analysis report. If the evidentiary value of these is reduced to a minimum, the Migration Court of Appeal can only have relied on two other sets of evidence. One is the set of statements made by the applicant. As the Court of Appeal chose to reject the appeal, this set obviously had an insufficient evidentiary value. The other are the interviews on local knowledge conducted by the Migration Board in its own interviews (which contained questions on regional cities in Burma and Burmese national holidays). While the interviewed applicant performed badly, her counsel gave reasonable explanations (denial of education and the right to travel to Rohingya in Burma and the fact that Hindu holidays were of no relevance to her ethnic group).

In order to consider the statements of the applicant as incredible, the Court of Appeal must have attached great importance to certain elements in the second set, i.e. the applicant's lacking knowledge of city names and holidays. Given that the Court of Appeal failed to comment on the explanations by the applicants' counsel, there are only two alternatives. One alternative is that the judgment was badly drafted and omitted an essential doubt the Court entertained on counsel's explanation of the applicant's inability to answer satisfactorily. This doubt would have diminished the evidentiary value of the counsel's explanation greatly. In fact, it would do no less than to decide the case. I cannot believe that the Migration Court of Appeal would omit mention of such a decisive doubt from its judgment. The second alternative is that the Migration Court of Appeal tacitly relied on the language analysis it had all but rejected. Most likely, the language analysis will have affected the Court's assessment of the applicants' credibility, an assessment which it claims to run throughout the whole procedure.[3] As I do not believe in the first alternative, this is the only remaining explanation.

I see myself compelled to conclude that the Swedish Migration Court of Appeal simply did not practice what it preached in the paragraph quoted above. This judgment is a performative self-contradiction.

Yet it is not without interest, although it will leave us at loss if we try to extract precedent value from it. It tells us that any "objective" assessment of the applicant's origin by means of her language or her knowledge of what is "local" to her origin brings us straight back to the most subjective of all questions: what are the markers of truth, and how are we to read them? The Court did not wish to delegate this question to profit-seeking businesses employing anonymous "experts". In that, it did well. But it actually substituted the shadowy language experts with its own shadowy and inarticulate finding.

3　Elsewhere, Jennifer Beard and I have analysed the way the Migration Court of Appeal conceives of the asylum procedure: '[W]e may imagine RSD as consisting of two parallel procedures: one is explicit; it determines the refugee objectively on the basis of the evidence. It is shadowed by a second one, which is dedicated to the truthfulness of the refugee ... It is, however, the second, shadow procedure that is supervening the first, overt one, apparently due to the enigmatic rule of the "benefit of the doubt".' [Reference omitted]. Jennifer Beard and Gregor Noll, Parrhesia and Credibility. The Sovereign of Refugee Status Determination, 18 *Social and Legal Studies* 2009, p. 455–477, at p. 463.

Dutch Court Decisions and Language Analysis for the Determination of Origin

Karin Zwaan

1.   Introduction

Language analysis for the determination of origin (LADO) is used in a number of countries to investigate the veracity of claims made by asylum seekers and other immigrants with regard to their – proclaimed – origin.[1] Compared to other countries, in the Netherlands the instrument of LADO is used quite frequently. It is estimated that in the Netherlands every year between 1500-2000 language analysis are performed by the Immigration and Naturalisation Service[2], this is the authority that decides upon asylum applications (hereinafter INS). In 2009 there were 1600 reported cases of language analysis.[3] In comparison, there were 17.900 registered asylum claims.[4] In 2008 the Dutch Secretary of State also indicated that in around 10% of all asylum applications, a language analysis report is asked for.[5] In the first six months of 2010 there have been only 217 reported cases of language analysis, and in comparison, there were around 7.300 registered asylum applications.[6]

The Dutch LADO system is used in three different instances: firstly in asylum application cases, secondly in cases in which admitted refugees are suspected of having lied about their origin (and therefore the Immigration Service wants to withdraw their residence permit, or their acquired Dutch nationality). Thirdly, LADO may be used in cases in which the rejected asylum seeker or immigrant has to be sent back to his or her country of origin and the INS has to determine to which country these immigrants have to be returned.

2.   Language Analysis in the Dutch Asylum Procedure

Language analysis is an integrated part of the Dutch asylum procedure.[7] LADO is regarded by the INS as a reliable and scientifically valid tool to assess the credibility of an

---

1   See D. Eades and J. Arends, Using language analysis in the determination of national origin of asylum seekers, an introduction, *Speech, Language, and the Law* 2004, p. 179-199.
2   In Dutch: Immigratie- en Naturalisatiedienst, IND.
3   Information obtained from the Dutch Refugee Council.
4   Source www.ind.nl.
5   TK 2008-2009, Aanhangsel bij de Handelingen, Kamervraag 2605.
6   Source www.ind.nl, and information obtained from the Dutch Refugee Council.
7   For the institutional constellation of the Dutch language analysis see, J.D. ten Thije, Language politics at European border; The language analysis interview of asylum seekers in the Netherlands, in: Georges Lüdi, Kurt Seelmann, Beat Sitter-Liver (Eds.) *Sprachenvielfalt und Kulturfrieden Sprachmin-*
$\rightarrow$

asylum seeker's claimed origin. One should bear in mind however, that in the Nether-lands the instrument of LADO is only applied if there are already doubts as to the ori-gin of the asylum seeker. Within the INS a specialised unit, the Office for Country In-formation and Language Analysis (in Dutch: BLT)[8] carries out the language analysis.[9] To this end, an interview with the asylum seeker is recorded and analysed.[10] The re-cordings of the conversation will be analysed by the language analyst from BLT. The analyst will give its opinion on the area of socialization based on the speech spoken on the recordings and the expressed knowledge of the area of origin. The analyst will also give his opinion on the level of certainty of his conclusions. He thereto chooses be-tween the qualifications "definitely (not)" , "probably", "either.. or" , related to the claimed area of origin. It is also possible that the language analyst will come to the con-clusion that the asylum seeker cannot be related to an area of socialisation. Asylum seekers may react to the INS language analysis report by producing a so-called contra-expertise, a counter language analysis report by an independent expert. In most cases this is the only way to rebut the outcome of the language analysis.[11] The asylum seeker can buy or obtain a copy of the recorded language analysis interview to have this inter-view assessed by an independent expert.[12]

In the end, it is the judiciary that has to weigh these language analyses. That is why the present paper is largely dedicated to the description of Dutch court cases on LADO in asylum cases. I will go into seven elements of LADO which were under discussion in a number of court decisions and finally I will draw a conclusion.

3.   Which Elements of LADO are under Judicial Scrutiny?

Adjudicating and judging asylum claims is not an easy task. Judges, INS-decision mak-ers and lawyers are sometimes in need for objective or scientific information to help them with this. The use of LADO needs to be seen in this context. If someone seeking refugee status has no identity papers, it is sometimes possible for language analysis to of-fer evidence as to their origin. During the past years, at least seven topics were subject of cases with regard to LADO in asylum cases.[13]

a.   The substantiating of the INS language analysis.
b.   The relationship between already existing documents, including those stating a na-tionality, and language analysis.

---

derheit – Einsprachigkeit – Mehrsprachigkeit: Probleme und Chancen sprachlicher Vielfalt, Fribourg: Paulus-Verlag / Academic Press und Stuttgart: Kohlhammer Verlag 2007, p. 233, Figure 2.

8   In Dutch: Bureau Land en Taal, BLT.

9   The unit within BLT responsible for undertaking language analyses consists of four (general) lin-guists and around 45 freelance language analysts.

10   See INS/BLT September 2007, Vakbijlage Taalanalyse: a memo in which the language analysis by BLT is described.

11   For an exception – the language analysis was invalidated without a contra-expertise - see CoS 7 October 2010 2010000553/1/v2; District Court Zutphen 17 November 2010, AWB 09/22444.

12   The price of a copy is around 7 Euro.

13   These topics are mainly derived from Vluchtweb, and from an article by A. Pinxter, Het instru-ment taalanalyse in de Nederlandse asielprocedure, Asiel- & Migrantenrecht 2010, p. 72-80.

c. The importance of including knowledge on the country of origin (geographical end cultural) in the language analysis.

d. The use of anonymous language experts.

e. LADO to be asked for by the courts.

f. Recording materials used for LADO.

g. Procedural rules and LADO

In the following each of these elements will be briefly discussed.

3.1 Substantiating LADO

In Dutch asylum cases, according to the jurisprudence, the burden of proof rests primarily upon the asylum applicant. Article 31 (1) of the Dutch Aliens Act reads:

> 'An application for the issue of a residence permit for a fixed period as referred to in section 28 shall be rejected if the alien has not made a plausible case that his application is based on circumstances which, either in themselves or in connection with other facts, constitute a legal ground for the issue of the permit.'[14]

Most asylum applicants have no documents to substantiate their claim. The effect of a negative language analysis, should also be considered then in the context of the heightened standard of proof following from Article 31 (2)(f) of the Aliens Act.[15] In general, an asylum seeker is granted the benefit of the doubt if his statements given during the asylum procedure, are consistent and not improbable on a general level. Moreover, the information the

asylum seeker has provided should comply with the information known by the authorities on the country of origin. An important requirement of the asylum seeker's credibility, is that he has to substantiate his claim with relevant documents such as travel and identity documents. However, it is quite often difficult for an asylum seeker to live up to this requirement. If an asylum seeker is unable to substantiate his claim with documents, and he does not have a plausible reason for not being able to render the documents, Article 31 (2)(f) Aliens Act applies. This Article reads:

> 'The screening of an application shall take account, among other things, of the fact that: (f) in support of his application the alien is unable to produce a travel docu-

---

14 In Dutch: Artikel 31 lid 1 Vw: 'Een aanvraag tot het verlenen van een verblijfsvergunning voor bepaalde tijd als bedoeld in artikel 28 wordt afgewezen indien de vreemdeling niet aannemelijk heeft gemaakt dat zijn aanvraag is gegrond op omstandigheden die, hetzij op zich zelf, hetzij in verband met andere feiten, een rechtsgrond voor verlening vormen.'

15 The CoS indicates that the statements of the asylum seeker should have a positive persuasiveness, CoS 27 January 2003, 200206297/1. See also the Expert opinion of the Dutch Council for Refugee in the case of *Abduluahidi v. The Netherlands* (21741) by the Dutch Refugee Council, 25 March 2010, Vluchtweb.

ment, identity card or other papers necessary for assessment of his application, unless the alien can make a plausible case that he is not to blame for their absence;'[16]

The INS indicates that therefore, if they perform a language analysis, this is to be seen as a kind of concession to the asylum seeker.[17] Of course, the asylum seeker may refuse to cooperate, but this will eventually be detrimental to his case.

From European asylum law it follows, that LADO forms only one element to be weighed in the asylum determination procedure (see also the contribution of Tax in this book). But as LADO is only used in cases in which there are no documents and the INS sees reason to doubt the alleged origin of the asylum seeker, this implies that in many cases a 'negative' language analysis (whenever the analysis does not confirm the stated origin of the applicant) means his or her case is closed, without getting a status. In 2008, 43% of the INS language analysis reports concluded that the asylum seekers claimed origin, was not the origin that followed from LADO.[18] In figures this means that in 2008 approximately 1,500–1,750 asylum seekers were confronted with a language analysis of which approximately between 600-750 had a negative outcome for the asylum seeker.

It is well known that the way a person speaks holds clues as to their region of origin, and this information can be useful in many ways in various forensic contexts. Judges are trying to answer the question whether the language analysis was performed in a thorough and methodological way, so that its conclusions are valid. This matter merits serious consideration. Of course, the use of language analysis is about evidence.

If LADO is performed by the INS, the judge must , in principle, rely upon the language analysis, unless concrete evidence to doubt this language analysis is submitted.[19] By making use of INS language analysis reports the substantiating is given. The rules on the performance of a language analysis in the Dutch asylum procedure are laid down in two internal INS guidelines.[20] These internal guidelines describe among other things in which cases a language analysis should be performed and within which period of time. They also stipulate how the result of a language analysis should be interpreted, and under which conditions a contra expert opinion can be handed in.

But if there are serious doubts raised in the specific case with regard to the language analysis, and these doubt can in the majority of cases only come from a counter expertise, the Minister of Immigration and Asylum (formally responsible for taking the decision) cannot do away with these doubts by simply referring to the fact that the analysis was performed by the INS. The report of the language analysis does have to give in-

---

16 In Dutch: Artikel 31 lid 2 sub f Vw: '2.Bij het onderzoek naar de aanvraag wordt mede betrokken de omstandigheid dat: f. de vreemdeling ter staving van zijn aanvraag geen reis- of identiteitspapieren dan wel andere bescheiden kan overleggen die noodzakelijk zijn voor de beoordeling van zijn aanvraag, tenzij de vreemdeling aannemelijk kan maken dat het ontbreken van deze bescheiden niet aan hem is toe te rekenen;'
17 In Dutch the term used is: handreiking. See e.g. CoS 29 December 2009, 200907502/1; CoS 12 March 2010 200909252/1; CoS 12 April 2010, 201000766/1.
18 TK 2008-2009, Aanhangsel bij de Handelingen, Kamervraag 2605, answers to the questions asked by a Member of the Second Chamber, De Wit.
19 CoS 19 May 2009, 200806369/1.
20 IND-Werkinstructies 270A and 2005/23.

sight in how the conclusions have been drawn.[21] This element highlights that the main question with regard to LADO is that under what circumstances judgements about the asylum seekers' regional and social identity are accurate and reliable enough to form part of the basis of a decision whether an asylum seeker should be granted a status.[22] Here strong similarities with forensic linguistics exist.[23] The linguist Eades argues that in certain cases LADO reports would not be helpful, if e.g. there is inadequate research on the relationship between related language varieties; one language variety is spoken by more than one ethnic/regional group, including one or more which could not claim a well-founded fear of persecution; the language recordings are of poor quality; the asylum seeker was not interviewed in their own language and; the interpreter was not speaking the same dialect as the asylum seekers, who may well then engage in speech accommodation, shifting to incorporate some linguistic features of the interpreter's dialect.[24] Also the linguist Corcoran presents arguments against the use of language analysis in asylum cases whenever the case involves questions of dialect, sociolect, closely related languages or distinguishing between languages which are both used in the applicant's claimed speech community.[25]

Discussions with regard to the following languages/origins have emerged in the past years: the discussion around Sierra Leone with regard to Krio (Sierra Leone), Nigerian Pidgin English (Nigeria) and Liberian English (Liberia) and the use of Mandingo, Malinke and Susu (Sierra Leone); with regard to the Dinka (Sudan), Cabinda (Angola), Konyanka (Liberia and/or Guinee), Nuba-languages (Sudan) and Bajuni (Somalia).[26]

In Dutch case law reference is also made to the, in this book already often described, Guidelines for the Use of Language Analysis (see annex I). This is done also from the viewpoint of ascertaining the validity of LADO.[27] The Guidelines address various aspects of language analysis, like the qualifications of the analyst, the collection of reliable data, the degree of certainty of reaching conclusions, the issue of accommodation of speech and the issue of multilinguism.

---

21 CoS 18 February 2010, 200907334/1.

22 See also H. Fraser, The role of 'educated native speakers' in providing language analysis for the determination of origin of asylum seekers, *International Journal of Speech, Language and the Law* 2009, p. 113-138.

23 T. Cambier-Langeveld, The role of linguists and native speakers in language analysis for the determination of speaker origin, *International Journal of Speech, Language and the Law* 2010, p. 67-93.

24 D. Eades, Testing the Claims of Asylum Seekers: The Role of Language Analysis, *Language Assessment Quarterly* 2009, p. 30-40.

25 C. Corcoran, A critical examination of the use of language analysis interviews in asylum proceedings: a case study of West African seeking asylum in the Netherlands, *Speech, Language and the Law* 2004, p. 200.

26 See Vluchtweb. The following reports are mentioned there: Gerd Bauman, *Rapport Betrouwbaarheid Onderzoek Herkomstbepaling in Soedan*, 2002; S. Grootendorst, *Validiteit van door IND gehanteerde taalanalyse*, 2003; J. Arends, *Taalsituatie in het Engels in Liberia, Sierra Leone*, 2003; S. Ellis & D. Ngom, *Liberia and Konyanka*, 2003; A. Vydrine, *Sierra Leone, Mandingo, Malinke en Susu-talen*, 2003; Nuba Mountain Solidarity Abroad, *Nuba*, 2003; Refugee Documentation Centre Ireland, *Bajuni*, 2010.

27 CoS 20 September 2007, 200703094/1; District Court Middelburg 20 May 2010, AWB 09/29133.

3.2   Documents and LADO

Sometimes, the result of the language analysis can set aside nationality documents. In a number of cases, the Council of State held that although the Embassy of Sierra Leone (situated in Brussels) had given a so-called nationality declaration (indicating that the person has the nationality of Sierra Leone) this did not mean that they actually were from Sierra Leone, if the language analysis had indicated that they were not.[28]

But also, in incidental cases documents may set aside the outcome of the language analysis.[29] In a case, in which the asylum seeker got a so-called nationality statement of the embassy of Congo, according to the district court this statement outweighed the language analysis.[30] From LADO it was previously concluded that the asylum applicant was not from Congo. The Council of State however ruled in appeal that this nationality statement was not individualised enough (there was e.g. no photo on the statement or other identifying elements) to outweigh the BLT language analysis.[31]

3.3   Socialization and LADO

Language analysis by the INS/BLT is based on the assumption that if someone claims to have lived in, or originates from a certain area, it is expected that this person speaks at least one of the language varieties (accent, dialect) which is characteristic for that specific area.[32] Therefore the primary aim of a language analysis of BLT is to determine which language or languages someone actually speaks. Secondly, the language analysis of BLT includes an analysis of the knowledge of the asylum seeker of the claimed region of origin. Investigated is whether the information given by the asylum seeker about the place of origin is accurate and detailed. In most cases, country of origin knowledge, or the lack of it, is seen as subsidiary evidence. In the new format (introduced in 2009) used in the Netherlands for LADO by the INS, there seems to be less attention for socialization than in the old format.[33]

3.4   Anonymous Experts and LADO

The Council of State also ruled on the use of anonymous language experts. In general the Court seems to hold the opinion that making use of anonymous experts is not forbidden, as long as they work for a well known bureau, like the INS Bureau on Language Analyses (BLT) or De Taalstudio (De Taalstudio produces the vast majority of language analysis reports as well as contra-expertises in the Netherlands). The BLT as well as De Taalstudio can reveal the identity of the language expert upon request of the Court. The INS holds the opinion that anonymous experts cannot invalidate their lan-

---

28 CoS 23 November 2007, 200707103/1.
29 District Court Assen 23 July 2007, AWB 07/10851.
30 District Court Zwolle 8 January 2010, AWB 09/26881.
31 CoS 15 June 2010, 201001266/1/v3.
32 See INS/BLT September 2007, Vakbijlage Taalanalyse.
33 A. Pinxter, Het instrument taalanalyse in de Nederlandse asielprocedure, *Asiel- & Migrantenrecht* 2010, p. 72.

guage reports. The Council of State has judged otherwise. According to the Council also the experts of De Taalstudio may be anonymous.[34]

A problem here however was, that in the rules for reimbursement of the costs for performing a counter-expertise, it is included that the analysis may not be performed by an anonymous expert.[35] Due to the jurisprudence of the Council of State reimbursement of an anonymous expert is possible.[36]

3.5 LADO Reports Asked for by the Court

Sometimes the District courts ask for their 'own' LADO. This is only done in very exceptional cases, and also the Council of State allows the appointing of an independent language expert by a District court in very few instances. This is mainly the case when there is already a language analysis (by BLT) and there is also a counter-expertise that completely contravenes the BLT analysis. But it may also be done in cases in which there is no counter expert language analysis report, but the Court simply has concrete evidence to doubt the IND language analysis.[37] It must be the motivation of the decision that is at stake and not the evaluation of the proof.

3.6 Recording Materials Used for LADO

The contra language analysis must preferably make use of the same recording materials that the first analysis was based upon.[38] In previous decision by the District Courts, the use of additional recording materials by counter experts was not forbidden. Additional recording materials were sometimes asked for by the counter expert, because otherwise, to their opinion, they could not perform LADO. Also the European Court of Human Rights, in a case, ordered the Dutch authorities to take a submitted additional recording of speech into account.[39] From jurisprudence it does not become clear under what kind of conditions additional recording are or are not allowed.

3.7 In Search of Concrete Evidence: A Hired Gun?

In the Dutch asylum procedure the validity of the INS reports can only be countered by making use of a counter-expertise. This counter-expert, who gives evidence upon request of the asylum seekers, is asked to provide an independent opinion on the linguistic data that BLT has collected. The judge will assume that the INS report is reliable unless the contra-expert's report provides concrete evidence to doubt the validity and reliability of the language analysis. Such doubt will not arise easily. In general, only when the contra-expert comes to a conclusion, with the highest possible degree of cer-

---

34 CoS 16 April 2010, 200903085/1/v1; CoS 4 June 2010, 200904906/1/v1.
35 District Court Den Haag 21 October 2009, AWB 09/13691.
36 CoS 1 September 2010, 201000506/1/v1.
37 District Court Amsterdam 23 April 2007, AWB 03/17558: CoS 7 July 2009, 200809205/1.
38 CoS 3 October 2008, 200801429/1.
39 Appl.nr. 19333/09.

tainty, on the given origin of the asylum seeker by the asylum seeker, the judge will conclude that there is reason to doubt the reliability of the INS report. For the expert (be it from the INS or a e.g. De Taalstudio) it also seems to be essential to have the 'last say', also from the perspective of creating 'doubt'.[40]

From 2009 on, the Council of State seems to be demanding more and more that the contra-expert becomes a hired gun.[41] In some cases the Council of State as well as the district Courts argue that the report of the contra-expert is not convincing enough.[42] When the contra-expert argues that according to his professional opinion it sometimes is simply not possible to come to a conclusion that the person is definitely, or definitely not, related to the claimed area of origin, the Council of State holds the asylum seeker accountable.[43] Because of this supposition of the counter-expert, it follows that then there is no concrete evidence to doubt the outcome of the INS language analysis.

This situation is problematic when it comes to gathering objective evidence.

3.8   Procedural Rules on Evidence and LADO

In a number of cases with regard to language analysis the European Court of Human Rights have been issuing interim measures, forbidding the government to expel the alien during the time the Court is handling the case. The Court, for instance, has been asking the Dutch government whether in a certain case, information from the contra language analysis would have changed the outcome of the case. In the Dutch asylum procedure, sometimes the outcome of the contra language analysis is not taken into account because, according to the procedural rules, it was too late. This for instance may be the case when a contra-expertise is given during the appeal stage. A number of cases before the ECtHR concern Somali asylum seekers, whose claims were rejected, also on the basis that according to the INS language analysis they did not originate from South Somalia.[44] In the contra-expertise (that was not taken into account) this outcome was seriously contested. In their application before the ECtHR these Somali asylum seekers claim there is a breach of Article 3 European Convention on Human Rights and Fundamental Freedoms (ECHR) and of Article 13 ECHR.

The only way to cast doubt on the outcome of the language analysis (in most cases) is to have a counter expert opinion performed. As mentioned in the article by Cambier (that is contained in this book) we must take into account that in the Dutch asylum

---

40 District Court Haarlem 24 June 2009, AWB 08/29783; in this case there was a BLT language analysis; a contra-expertise by De Taalstudio; a reaction by BLT on the contra-expertise; a reaction by De Taalstudio on the reaction of BLT.

41 A hired gun is the somewhat vernacular expression, but still used, mainly by courts in the United States of America, to refer to an expert witness who does not appear to be impartial. See also the Article by T. Woods, *Impartial Expert or 'Hired Gun': Recent Developments at Home and Abroad*, published 19 February 2005, British Columbia, Canada.

42 CoS 18 December 2009, 200806254/1/v1; CoS 18 December 2009, 200801087/1/v1; CoS 2 July 2010, 200905055/1/v3; District Court Arnhem 16 October 2009, AWB 07/25358; District Court Groningen 25 January 2010, AWB 09/11659.

43 CoS 18 December 2009, 200806254/1/v1.

44 ECtHR 10 February 2010, appl.nr. 60860/09; ECtHR 19 November 2009, appl.nr. 60915/09; ECtHR 19 25 August 2009, appl.nr. 43618/09.

procedure the validity of the INS reports can only be countered by making use of a counter-expertise. The INS is only asked for language analysis if there are already doubts about the credibility of the asylum seeker. And a counter expertise is only asked for if there already is an IND language analysis, and only when the contra-expert comes to a radically different conclusion on the origin of the asylum seeker, with the highest possible degree of certainty, the judge will conclude that there can be reason to doubt the reliability of the INS report.

Also there is the problem of the costs. Who will be paying for the contra-expertise? There has been much ado about this during the last year in the Netherlands. It falls in the domain of the asylum seeker to substantiate his case, and thus also to present a contra-expertise.[45] In some cases, it is possible to get the costs for the counter expert opinion reimbursed, but only under increasingly strict conditions and to a certain maximum.[46] But if the money is there, this does not mean that there is a contra-expert available, or that the contra-expertise will be produced in time. Judicial, procedural, practical and financial impediments may stand in the way of submitting a counter expert opinion.

4.　　Conclusion

LADO is perceived to be a valuable tool for governments to assess asylum claims. Dutch case law rules that the INS may rely on their language analysis reports. It should be clear however, that from a judicial point of view, the reliability of language analysis can be undermined by, for instance, the absence of comprehensive descriptions of a certain language, the lack of objective linguistic assessment, the absence of validated methods for LADO, and also the arguing – among linguists themselves – on an independent standard. If the linguistic experts themselves are that far removed from consensus on almost all of the just mentioned issues, or keep on arguing about it, how can the judiciary ever make use of such a contested method as means of evidence in the asylum procedure? Also if LADO is about determining the probability of linguistic evidence, one should be aware that asylum cases are far removed from forensic application of linguistics.

45　CoS 30 September 2004, 200405508/1; CoS 18 December 2009, 200901087/1.
46　The costs may be paid for by the COA, a semi-governmental organisation. The maximum reimbursement is set at around 800 Euro.

The Use of Expert Evidence in Asylum Procedures by EU Member States – The Case for Harmonized Procedural Safeguards

*Blanche Tax**[*]

Introduction

Making decisions on asylum claims is a tremendously difficult job. It is difficult because of the possible grave consequences of a wrong decision – a senior official of a national asylum service told me once of having sleepless nights over the negative decision in the cases of two young men who ended up in an informal prison in their home country, most likely being subjected to torture. Adjudicating asylum claims is also difficult because it is not an exact science. As a decision-maker, you can spend hours or days researching information on the country of origin, reviewing other cases with similar elements, going over your interview notes and relevant guidelines and policy instructions and all evidence available and weighing those elements; but in the end it usually boils down to deciding what to believe in the absence of hard proof. From my own experience of having interviewed and having made eligibility decisions in many cases, I consider it a heavy responsibility which does not get easier with experience.

It is thus not surprising that asylum decision-makers look for all the help they can get. Specialized and detailed country-of-origin information, medico-legal reports by specialized medical doctors relating the psychological or medical state of an asylum-seeker who claims to have been tortured or subjected to other human rights abuses, documents or testimonies by persons who knew the asylum-seeker in his or her country of origin are all examples of elements which may help the decision-maker reach a decision on the credibility of the asylum claim. In recent years, there appears to be an increasing emphasis on and interest in the use of so-called 'objective' or 'scientific' evidence in asylum claims. In this article, I will refer to this form of evidence as expert evidence. While not wanting to define this form of evidence, different examples of expert evidence have in common their reliance on specific technical expertise, and their claim of providing objective or scientific information on a specific aspect of the credibility of an individual asylum claim. Some examples are the use of medical methods for assessing the age of an asylum applicant claiming to be a child, the use of medico-legal reports to document the medical and psychological consequences of claimed past torture or of other past experiences, and the use of language analysis for the determination of an asylum-seeker's origin (hereafter referred to as LADO). It can easily be understood that decision-makers consider such expert evidence as helpful in facilitating the process of reaching a decision on credibility. Relying on the advice of experts would appear to reduce the burden or responsibility resting on the shoulders of individual de-

* The views expressed here are the author's own and do not represent the position of UNHCR or the United Nations.

cision-makers, especially if the expert evidence claims to result from an objective scientific process. This is potentially of particular interest given there are often few tools to aid in the subjective process of assessing an asylum claimant's credibility.

Whereas expert evidence may have a place in asylum procedures depending on a number of factors, a more in-depth analysis is required of how and why it is used, how it impacts on the process of reaching a decision and the outcomes of that process. The use and reliability of e.g. medical methods used for determining age, or of linguistic methods for determining origin has been discussed in many fora,[1] with involvement of technical experts, practitioners and lawyers, and there does not seem to be consensus. Where different methods exist for reaching conclusions as e.g. in the case of age assessment, practitioners and experts have discussed which methods are most reliable and most appropriate, and again, there is no agreement. The fact that communities of experts do not agree on the reliability and appropriateness of methods, reliability of outcomes and on how to report outcomes, should be taken as a warning against relying too heavily on such methods. Indeed, there is an emerging body of case-law resulting from the different views on the use of expert evidence.

As a policy officer with a legal background, I lack expertise to contribute to debates on the reliability of methods and validity of outcomes of particular forms of expert evidence. I will instead make a number of remarks on another element of the use of expert evidence, including LADO, in asylum procedures. I am referring to the need for strict and clear procedural guarantees surrounding the use of such evidence in asylum procedures. In this article, I explore in a non-exhaustive way some of the procedural safeguards in the European legal framework for adjudicating asylum cases, and some of the gaps that can be identified. In addition, I review the need for a more harmonized approach to the use of expert evidence, including LADO, in the asylum procedure, and what legal and/or practical steps towards that end could be taken within the EU framework. I will not review or comment on national practices, national legislation or jurisprudence on the use of LADO or other expert evidence.

International Refugee Law and the European Union Legal Framework

European Union Member States have been cooperating for many years in this sector, and have sought agreement on joint rules governing most aspects of the asylum process, in an effort to make the granting of international protection more predictable and reduce divergences in outcomes of asylum cases. Predictable and consistent outcomes throughout the European Union in comparable cases could potentially reduce onward travel to and lodging of new asylum claims in other EU Member States by persons who had their claim rejected in a first EU Member State. Common rules on most aspects of the asylum process are now in force in the European Union e.g. to determine which State is responsible for determining a claim; on asylum seekers' entitlements and obligations as regards their reception in Member States; to regulate the asylum procedure it-

---

1 E.g. recently at the international conference organised by CORI (Country of Origin Research and Information) on 10, 11 June 2010 "Challenges and Commonaliteis in Providing Objective Evidence for Refugee Status Determination", see http://www.cori.org.uk/3.html

self; and to determine who qualifies for international protection. The EU asylum *acquis* which is to result in a 'Common European Asylum System' does not stand on its own, but builds on the international refugee protection regime. EU legislation states that the Common European Asylum System is to be based on a full and inclusive application of the Geneva Convention relating to the Status of Refugees.[2]

Whereas some common EU rules in the asylum field take the form of directly binding 'Regulations', most take the form of 'Directives', which require member states to achieve a particular result without dictating the means of achieving that result. Directives are usually transposed in national legislation. Two such Directives, the so-called Qualification Directive[3] and the Asylum Procedures Directive,[4] contain a number of relevant provisions on the use of evidence in the asylum procedure. I will review some of the procedural safeguards relevant in case of use of expert evidence, as contained in provisions of those Directives.

Procedural Elements and Safeguards relevant to Language Analysis

Responsible Authority

In Article 4(1), the Asylum Procedures Directive provides that Member States shall designate a 'determining authority' responsible for an appropriate examination of asylum applications. This article is relevant to the use of expert evidence in that it provides a guarantee against 'outsourcing' of the decision-making authority. In other words, the designated authority cannot delegate the responsibility to make a decision to a technical expert. This suggests that it would also not be appropriate to base a decision solely on the outcome of LADO or another form of expert evidence, as that would *de facto* shift the responsibility for decision-making from the designated authority to the expert.

Standard of Proof, Burden of Proof and Benefit of the Doubt

The same conclusion flows from the rules relating to the *standard of proof* (in the Qualification Directive, Article 4), which make clear that a report containing expert evidence can never be the sole basis for reaching a decision. The assessment of an application has to take into account, amongst others, all relevant facts, statements, documentation, the individual position and personal circumstances of the applicant. This implies that an expert report can only be one element to be weighed in the process of assessing all avail-

---

2   See: Council Directive 2004/83/EC of 29 April 2004 on minimum standards for the qualification and status of third country nationals or stateless persons as refugees or as persons who otherwise need international protection and the content of the protection granted Official Journal L 304, 30/09/2004, consideration 2, at http://eur-lex.europa.eu/LexUriServ/LexUriServ.do?uri= CELEX: 32004L0083:EN:HTML.

3   *Op. cit.*, footnote 2.

4   Council Directive 2005/85/EC of 1 December 2005 on minimum standards on procedures in Member States for granting and withdrawing refugee status, Official Journal L326/13, 13/12/2005, at http://eur-lex.europa.eu/LexUriServ/LexUriServ.do?uri= OJ:L:2005:326: 0013:0034:EN:PDF.

able evidence and concluding on the credibility of the claim as presented by the applicant.

Another relevant element as regards the credibility assessment is the grounds on which expert evidence is requested by the determining authority. While the *burden of proof* in principle rests on the applicant, the duty to ascertain and evaluate all the relevant facts is shared between the applicant and the examiner. UNHCR's Handbook on Procedures and Criteria for Determining Refugee Status under the 1951 Convention and the 1967 Protocol relating to the Status of Refugees,[5] which is an important reference for the interpretation of the 1951 Refugee Convention (the full and inclusive application of which should be ensured in the European asylum *acquis*, as indicated above) states that in some cases, it may be for the examiner to use all the means at his disposal to produce the necessary evidence in support of the application.[6] In many states, decision-makers only resort to the use of LADO in case of doubt regarding the asylum seeker's claimed origin. But what level of doubt justifies resorting to the use of LADO? Some States have applied or apply a policy of routine referral for LADO for asylum seekers of certain claimed origin, for instance to all asylum seekers claiming to be Afghan, or all claiming to be Somali. Is that needed or justified for individuals whose asylum claim is otherwise convincing to the caseworker?

The Qualification Directive states in article 4(4) that, when certain conditions are met, aspects of the claim which are not supported by documentary or other evidence shall not need confirmation. The principle of the 'benefit of the doubt' should be applied when the applicant's account appears credible, but where it is impossible to produce evidence.[7] This may be the case when the applicants' statements are generally not susceptible to proof. In such cases, there may be a tendency to over-rely on 'expert evidence' as the only form of 'proof' which can be obtained, but as indicated above, the outcome of e.g. LADO can never be the sole element on which a decision is based. When the outcome of an effort to obtain expert evidence is inconclusive, it is even more obvious that, when applicant's statements appear credible and in the absence of other evidence, the principle of the 'benefit of the doubt' should be applied.

Information & Legal Advice

The Asylum Procedures Directive indicates in Article 10 the need to inform an applicant about the procedure, his or her rights and obligations, in a language (s)he may 'reasonably be supposed to understand'. Being fully informed of all elements of the procedure, including any methods applied in an effort to obtain expert evidence, is a crucial procedural guarantee for applicants. The applicant should also be made aware of the consequences of non-cooperation with e.g. a LADO procedure. An applicant should be allowed to provide reasons for non-cooperation, and the asylum authorities should take those into account. For the provision of information on the procedure and the ap-

---

5   UNHCR, *Handbook on Procedures and Criteria for Determining Refugee Status under the 1951 Convention and the 1967 Protocol relating to the Status of Refugees*, Geneva, January 1992, at http://www.unhcr.org/refworld/pdfid/3ae6b3314.pdf.
6   UNHCR Handbook, *op. cit.*, para. 196.
7   UNHCR Handbook, *op. cit.*, para. 196.

plicant's rights and duties relating to the procedure to be relevant and effective, such information should be given in a language the applicant actually understands.

In addition, it is important for an applicant to have access to legal advice when subjected to a process for obtaining expert evidence. A lawyer or legal adviser can advise and support the applicant if the applicant considers that the outcome of a procedure to obtain expert evidence is wrong, by assisting him/her in challenging the outcome in court, or by seeking counter-expertise. The current legal framework does not guarantee access to legal advice. Proposed amendments to the Asylum Procedures Directive would strengthen applicants' access to legal advice, but Member States have not welcomed those proposals and negotiations are expected to be lengthy.

Equality of Arms

The EU asylum *acquis* does not codify the principle of 'equality of arms'. Whereas the proposed amendments to the Asylum Procedures Directive would strengthen in important ways the position of the applicant, equality of arms is not guaranteed. Methods to obtain expert evidence are often costly, and expertise may not be readily available. Equality of arms with regard to the use of expertise could take the form of a right under certain conditions to seek counter-expertise, funded at an appropriate level by the state.

The Case for Harmonization

At present, despite harmonization of asylum legislation, protection rates continue to vary significantly across the Member States of the European Union, including for groups of applicants of the same nationality. In 2009, protection rates in first instance decisions for e.g. Afghans in different EU Member states varied from 0% to 87%. For Somalis, the figure varied from 0% to 96%.[8] This lack of predictability in asylum outcomes has been referred to as the 'asylum lottery'.[9] Persons in need of protection may not be able to get it in the state where they are expected to apply for asylum, and for this reason may choose not to apply in the first EU Member State where they arrive. This results in persons trying to remain undetected until they reach a state where they believe to have a better chance of finding protection.

One can wonder if the non-harmonized use of expert evidence contributes to divergence in outcomes. Further research would be needed to determine, for instance, whether as a result of differences in policy or practice as regards to which cases to refer for LADO, in the methods used, in reporting and interpreting outcomes, and in access to counter-expertise, the outcome of the same case would be different in different

---

8   See UNHCR Statistics, *2009 Global Trends*, Table 12 - Asylum applications and refugee status determination by origin and country/territory of asylum, 2009, at http://www.unhcr.org/globaltrends/2009-Global-Tends-annex.zip.
    Please note that the 'protection rate' includes both refugee status and complementary forms of protection.

9   See e.g. European Council for Refugees and Exiles (ECRE), *Memorandum to the JHA Council Ending the asylum lottery – Guaranteeing refugee protection in Europe*, April 2008, at http://www.unhcr.org/refworld/pdfid/480c86872.pdf.

Member States. Other Member States do not use LADO at all, not taking language into account when determining origin, or relying on informal advice of interpreters without any training qualifying them to speak out on an asylum seeker's origin. Even though the outcome of expert evidence cannot be the sole element determining if a person is in need of protection, it still appears likely that differences in interpretation of results of procedures to obtain expert evidence (e.g. in case of LADO ranging from confirming with near certainty the asylum-seeker's claimed origin, to disputing with near certainty the claimed origin), or the fact that such procedures are not used at all, can result in opposite decisions on the need for international protection. A more harmonized approach to (the use of) expert evidence including LADO can likely contribute to more harmonized, predictable asylum outcomes across Europe, and thus to ensuring that persons in need of protection can actually obtain it.

Harmonization – Of What?

When considering harmonization of the use of expert evidence, there is a need for clarity on what exactly should be harmonized. One could consider further harmonization of procedural safeguards relating to the use of expert evidence in the asylum procedure. Whereas the proposed recast of the Asylum Procedures Directive would generally strengthen a number of important procedural safeguards, it does not include systematic procedural safeguards specifically relating to the use of expert evidence.[10] In light of the minimal appetite of Member States for further legislative harmonization, and negative reactions to some of the proposals, the prospect of future agreement on even more far-reaching amendments introducing further procedural safeguards, including specifically relating to expert evidence, is very remote.

In the absence of any significant chance for progress towards harmonization of legal standards, an alternative way forward could be cooperation among experts toward harmonization of technical aspects of specific forms of expert evidence (including LADO). Cooperation toward standard operating procedures, agreed minimum qualifications for experts, or standardized reporting, including agreement on methods for interpretation of results, encompassing for instance standardized margins of error, all as appropriate for the specific form of expert evidence, could be considered as a means to improve the fairness and effectiveness of this method.

Harmonization – How and by Whom?

In EU legislation, the European Commission has the exclusive right of initiative, and would thus need to initiate further legislative changes, if harmonization of procedural safeguards for use of expert evidence in asylum procedures were to be pursued further. However, as already indicated, for the time being any expectation of extensive further legislative change would appear unrealistic.

---

10 The recast Asylum Procedures Directive does however contain in proposed article 17 some limited guidance with regard to the use of medico-legal reports in asylum procedures, including an obligation to Member States to ensure the availability for impartial and qualified medical expertise for medical examinations in this context. See http://eur-lex.europa.eu/LexUriServ/LexUriServ.do?uri=COM:2009:0554:FIN:EN:PDF.

Another approach seems more likely to yield success, namely alignment of practice through practical cooperation. A new EU Agency, the European Asylum Support Office (EASO), is expected start functioning in 2010-11 in Valletta, Malta. This Office, established by Regulation[11], is mandated to coordinate practical cooperation among Member States on asylum. It can gather information on specific or good practices, relating to the asylum procedure and share this information among Member States. In the EU Action Plan on Unaccompanied Minors,[12] the EASO has been tasked with preparing technical documents on a specific form of expert evidence, age assessment, which should form the basis for the development of "best practice guidelines" by the European Commission. It is not specified what elements of age assessment should be covered by such guidelines, but it is assumed they can relate to all aspects, including technical matters and procedural safeguards. A similar approach could be envisioned for LADO, as well as for the use of medical reports to document effects of claimed torture, etc. It will however be important that all relevant stakeholders will be engaged in this process – technical experts and legal experts, both those employed by States and independent experts including academics or representatives of civil society with relevant expertise. The views of asylum-seekers or former asylum-seekers who have been subjected to the use of expert evidence should also be sought and taken into account.

The EASO should also explore other, creative forms of practical cooperation. It could facilitate the functioning of expert networks, and host virtual platforms – communities of practice - where experts could upload and exchange information, where case-law on the use of expert evidence can be made accessible and where questions can be asked and answered. One can think of networks of persons engaged in language analysis, of doctors responsible for drafting medico-legal reports which are used in the asylum procedure, of social workers, medical doctors and others engaged in medical and non-medical forms of age assessment. Exchange between such experts and expert lawyers should be encouraged. There could be cross-fertilization between the different networks on issues where there is overlap, such as on procedural safeguards. The EASO could also implement or provide financial support for comparative research on national practices and on the growing body of jurisprudence on the use of expert evidence. Development of training materials and the organization of expert meetings, exchange visits or joint trainings can also be taken up by the EASO. The possibilities are extensive, but much will depend on the direction and priorities the EASO management will choose.

Final Remarks

Not surprisingly, in view of the subject matter, this article raises as many questions as it answers. I have not touched on technical aspects, national practices or case-law on the use of expert evidence. The article is intended to offer a starting point to explore the

---

11 Regulation (EU) No 439/2010 of the European Parliament and of the Council of 19 May 2010 establishing a European Asylum Support Office, at http://eur-lex.europa.eu/LexUriServ/LexUriServ.do?uri=OJ:L:2010:132:0011:0028:EN:PDF.

12 Communication from the Commission to the European Parliament and the Council. Action Plan on Unaccompanied Minors (2010 – 2014), SEC(2010)534, at http://eur-lex.europa.eu/LexUriServ/LexUriServ.do?uri=COM:2010:0213:FIN:EN:PDF.

need for harmonized procedural safeguards for the use of expert evidence and the possibilities for harmonization through practical cooperation. In doing so, it considers only some of the procedural safeguards usually applied in refugee law, and does not make a comparison with other fields of law, such as criminal law. Comparative research between standards and burden of proof and the use of expert evidence in other field of law may bring refreshing insights.

Development of a set of strong, harmonized procedural safeguards would to a certain extent help to regulate the use of evidence in asylum procedures. A word of caution may however be appropriate here. The use of expert evidence risks being seen as absolving the asylum adjudicator of part of his/her responsibility, by creating a strong reliance on an external expert judgment on the credibility of a specific aspect of the asylum claim. But in the same way, relying on procedural safeguards to mitigate the risks in the use of expert evidence, may effectively serve to justify excessive reliance such evidence. Even if, from a procedural viewpoint, the use of expert evidence is flawless in an individual case, the outcome may still be problematic if the technical method is not reliable or the outcome not interpreted correctly. The adjudicator, and similarly a judge who would review a case, cannot hide behind procedural safeguards in order to take the expert evidence for granted. The adjudicator's responsibility carefully to weigh all aspects of the claim, and review the outcome of the use of expert evidence in light of all information and evidence available in the individual case, remains in all circumstances.

Whereas the use of expert evidence may be a relevant tool that can support the decision-making process if a number of conditions are met, making decisions on asylum applications will always remain a very difficult job. As decision-maker, one will hardly ever be completely sure about one's decision. An asylum adjudicator who cannot live with that reality should probably choose another profession. Decision-making in asylum cases will always demand careful and respectful assessment of the credibility of what people state, in the absence of comprehensive evidence. No method or no expertise can make that into an exact science.

Guidelines for the Use of Language Analysis
in Relation to Questions of National Origin in Refugee Cases

June 2004
Language and National Origin Group
[an international group of linguists whose names appear below]

Language analysis is used by a number of governments around the world as part of the process of determining whether asylum seekers' cases are genuine. Such analysis usually involves consideration of a recording of the asylum seeker's speech in order to judge their country of origin. Use of language analysis has been criticized on a number of grounds, and some uncertainty has arisen as to its validity. This paper responds to calls for qualified linguists to provide guidelines for use by governments and others in deciding whether and to what degree language analysis is reliable in particular cases.

We, the undersigned linguists, recognize that there is often a connection between the way that people speak and their national origin. We also recognize the difficulties faced by governments in deciding eligibility for refugee status of increasing numbers of asylum seekers who arrive without documents. The following guidelines are therefore intended to assist governments in assessing the general validity of language analysis in the determination of national origin, nationality or citizenship. We have attempted to avoid linguistic terminology. Where technical terms are required, they are explained (eg 'socialization' in Guideline 2, and 'code-switching' in Guideline 9c). The term 'language variety' which is used in several guidelines, refers generally to a language or a dialect.

GENERAL GUIDELINES

1) LINGUISTS ADVISE, GOVERNMENTS MAKE NATIONALITY DETERMINATIONS
Linguistic advice can be sought to assist governments in making determinations about national origin, nationality or citizenship. Linguists should not be asked to make such determinations directly. Rather, they should be asked to provide evidence which can be considered along with other evidence in the case.

2) SOCIALIZATION RATHER THAN ORIGIN
Language analysis can not be used reliably to *determine* national origin, nationality or citizenship. This is because national origin, nationality and citizenship are all political or bureaucratic characteristics, which have no necessary connection to language.

In some cases, language analysis CAN be used to draw reasonable conclusions about the country of socialization of the speaker. (This refers to the place(s) where the speaker has learned, implicitly and/or explicitly, how to be a member of a local society, or of local societies.) The way that people speak has a strong connection with how and where they were socialized: that is, the languages and dialects spoken in the communities in which people grow up and live have a great influence on how they speak.

1

It is true that the country of a person's socialization is often the country of their origin. Therefore linguisic conclusions about a speaker's country of socialization may, in conjunction with other (non-linguistic) evidence, be able to assist immigration officials in making a determination about national origin in some cases. However, linguistic expertise cannot directly determine national origin, nationality or citizenship, which are not inherently linked to language, in the way that socialization is.

3) LANGUAGE ANALYSIS MUST BE DONE BY QUALIFIED LINGUISTS

Judgements about the relationship between language and regional identity should be made only by qualified linguists with recognized and up-to-date expertise, both in linguistics and in the language in question, including how this language differs from neighboring language varieties. This expertise can be evidenced by holding of higher degrees in linguistics, peer reviewed publications, and membership of professional associations. Expertise is also evident from reports, which should use professional linguistic analysis, such as IPA (International Phonetic Association) transcription and other standard technical tools and terms, and which should provide broad coverage of background issues, citation of relevant academic publications, and appropriate caution with respect to conclusions reached.

4) LINGUIST'S DEGREE OF CERTAINTY

Linguists should have the right and responsibility to qualify the certainty of their assessments, even about the country of socialization. It should be noted that it is rarely possible to be 100% certain of conclusions based on linguistic evidence alone (as opposed to fingerprint or DNA evidence), so linguistic evidence should always be used in conjunction with other (non-linguistic) evidence. Further, linguists should not be asked to, and should not be willing to, express their certainty in quantitative terms (eg '95% certain that person X was socialized in country Y'), but rather in qualitative terms, such as 'based on the linguistic evidence, it is possible, likely, highly likely, highly unlikely' that person X was socialized in country Y'. This is because this kind of language analysis does not lend itself to quantitative statistics such as are often found in some others kinds of scientific evidence.

5) LANGUAGE ANALYSIS REQUIRES USEFUL AND RELIABLE DATA

Linguists should be allowed to decide what kind of data they need for their language analysis. If the linguist considers the data provided for analysis to be insufficiently useful or reliable, he or she should either request better data or state that a language analysis can not be carried out in this case. Some relevant examples include a recording of poor audio quality, a recording of insufficent duration, or an interview carried out with an interpreter who is not speaking the language of the interviewee.

To avoid such problems, it is preferable for linguists to collect the language sample(s) for analysis, or to advise on their collection.

6) LINGUISTS SHOULD PROVIDE SPECIFIC EVIDENCE OF PROFESSIONAL TRAINING AND EXPERTISE, WITH THE RIGHT TO REQUIRE THAT THIS INFORMATION REMAIN CONFIDENTIAL

Linguists should provide specific evidence of their professional training and expertise, for example in a curriculum vitae, so that a court may have the opportunity to assess these matters. But linguists should have the right to require that this information is kept confidential, and not revealed to either the asylum seeker, or the country from which they are fleeing.

7) THE EXPERTISE OF NATIVE SPEAKERS IS NOT THE SAME AS THE EXPERTISE OF LINGUISTS

There are a number of reasons why people without training and expertise in linguistic analysis should not be asked for such expertise, even if they are native speakers of the language, with expertise in translation and interpreting. Just as a person may be a highly accomplished tennis player without being able to analyze the particular muscle and joint movements involved, so too, skill in speaking a language is not the same as the ability to analyze a language and compare it to neighboring language varieties.

MORE SPECIFIC GUIDELINES

8) WHERE RELATED VARIETIES OF THE SPEAKER'S LANGUAGE ARE SPOKEN IN MORE THAN ONE COUNTRY

In many regions throughout the world, national borders are not the same as linguistic borders, and the same language, or closely related varieties of the same language, is/are spoken in more than one country (eg ethnic Armenians living in both Armenia and Azerbaijan speak what is known as 'Standard East-Armenian', and ethnic Hazaras living in both Afghanistan and Pakistan speak Hazargi Dari).

In such situations, while linguistic analysis may often be able to determine the *region* in which the speaker's socialization took place, it can not be used to determine in which *nation* the speaker's socialization took place. In such situations, an analyst should
(a) be able to specify in advance whether there exist linguistic features which can reliably distinguish regional varieties, and what they are,
(b) be able to devise reliable procedures, similar to linguistic field methods, for eliciting these features from the speaker without distortion or bias,
(c) be prepared to conclude, in the event that such features do not exist or do not occur in the data, that in this case linguistic evidence simply cannot help answer the question of language socialization.

9) LANGUAGE MIXING
It is unreasonable in many situations to expect a person to speak only one language variety in an interview or other recording, for the following reasons:

(a) Sociolinguistic research shows that multilingualism is the norm in many societies throughout the world.
(b) In many multilingual societies, it is common for two or more language varieties to be used on a daily basis within a single family. In such families, it is also common for

the speech of individuals in one language variety to show some influences from other varieties spoken in the family.

(c) Many bilingual or multilingual speakers use more than one language variety in a single interaction: this use of 'code switching' or 'style shifting' is very complex, and often subconscious.

(d) Further, there is variation in all language varieties, that is, more than one way of saying the same thing.

(e) It can often be hard for linguists to determine the difference between variation within a single language variety, and code-switching between related varieties. For example, when analyzing the speech of a person from Sierra Leone, it may be very difficult to know for some particular utterances whether they are in Krio, the creole language, or Sierra Leonean English. It is also important to note that while linguists distinguish these as separate varieties, their speakers often do not.

(f) Another factor which complicates this issue is that language varieties are always in the process of change, and one of the most influential sources of change is the vocabulary and pronunciation of related language varieties.

(g) A further complicating factor is that interviews may be done several years after an asylum seeker has left their home country, and their language variety/varieties may have undergone change in the interim.

(h) While linguists are devoting a great deal of research to language mixing, they have been unable to determine the extent to which an individual can consciously control the choice of language variety or of variables.

10) WHERE THE LANGUAGE OF THE INTERVIEW IS NOT THE SPEAKER'S FIRST LANGUAGE

In addition to the use of language to assess national origin, issues of professional concern to linguists also arise during the interview in relation to the assessment of the truthfulness of the applicant's story. We note that in some countries, such as Germany, an international lingua franca (eg English) is the language of asylum seeker interviews, used either for language analysis in the determination of national origin, and/or in the assessment of the applicant's truthfulness. These cases call for particular care.

An interviewee with limited proficiency in the language of the interview may – simply because of language difficulties – appear to be incoherent or inconsistent, thereby leading the interviewer to a mistaken conclusion concerning the truthfulness of the interviewee.

In many post-colonial countries there are a number of language varieties related to the former colonial language, such as English or Portuguese. These varieties may include pidgin and/or creole languages. There are frequently not clear-cut boundaries between these different varieties (see point 9 above). Asking a person to speak only English or only Krio (the creole language of Sierra Leone), for example, may well be a linguistically impossible demand.

11) WHERE THE DIALECT OF THE INTERVIEWER OR INTERPRETER IS DIFFERENT FROM THE DIALECT OF THE INTERVIEWEE
In some situations interviewees who are speakers of a local dialect are interviewed by an interpreter speaking the standard dialect of the language. In such situations it is common for people to accommodate to the interviewer's way of speaking, whether consciously or sub-consciously. This means that interviewees will attempt to speak the standard dialect, in which they may not necessarily have good proficiency. This accommodation, brought about by dialect or language difference, may make it difficult for interviewees to participate fully in the interview.

CONCLUSION:
For all of the reasons outlined in these guidelines we advise that language analysis should be used with considerable caution in addressing questions of national origin, nationality or citizenship.

FOR FURTHER INFORMATION: Diana Eades, <eades@hawaii.edu>

SIGNED BY:
Jacques Arends, Lecturer in Linguistics, Department of Linguistics, University of Amsterdam, The Netherlands.

Jan Blommaert, Professor of African Linguistics and Sociolinguistics, Ghent University, Belgium.

Chris Corcoran, PhD student, Department of Linguistics, University of Chicago, USA.

Suzanne Dikker, Research Assistant, De Taalstudio, The Netherlands.

Diana Eades, Associate Professor, Department of Second Language Studies, University of Hawai'i, USA.

Malcolm Awadajin Finney, Associate Professor, Department of Linguistics, California State University Long Beach, USA.

Helen Fraser, Senior Lecturer, School of Languages, Cultures and Linguistics, University of New England, Australia.

Kenneth Hyltenstam, Professor, Centre for Research on Bilingualism, Stockholm University, Sweden.

Marco Jacquemet, Assistant Professor, Communication Studies, University of San Francisco, USA.

Sheikh Umarr Kamarah, Assistant Professor, Department of Languages and Literature, Virginia State University, U.S.A.

Katrijn Maryns, Research Associate, National Science Foundation Flanders, Department of African Languages and Cultures, Ghent University, Belgium.

Tim McNamara, Professor, Department of Linguistics and Applied Linguistics, The University of Melbourne, Australia.

Fallou Ngom, Assistant Professor of French and Linguistics, Western Washington University, USA.

Peter L Patrick, Professor of Linguistics, Department of Language and Linguistics, University of Essex, UK.

Ingrid Piller, Senior Lecturer, Department of Linguistics, University of Sydney, Australia.

Vincent De Rooij, Assistant Professor, Department of Sociology and Anthropology, University of Amsterdam, The Netherlands.

Jeff Siegel, Associate Professor, School of Languages, Cultures and Linguistics, University of New England, Australia.

John Victor Singler, Professor of Linguistics, Department of Linguistics New York University, USA.

Maaike Verrips, Director, De Taalstudio, the Netherlands.

JUNE 2004.